BOARDS
THAT
LEAD

WHEN TO TAKE CHARGE, WHEN TO PARTNER, AND WHEN TO STAY OUT OF THE WAY

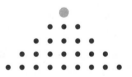

RAM CHARAN

DENNIS CAREY

MICHAEL USEEM

Harvard Business Review Press

Boston, Massachusetts

The web addresses referenced in this book were live and correct at the time of the
book's publication but may be subject to change.

Library of Congress Cataloging-in-Publication Data

Charan, Ram.
  Boards that lead : when to take charge, when to partner, and when to stay out of
the way / Ram Charan, Dennis Carey, Michael Useem.
     pages cm
  ISBN 978-1-4221-4405-3 (hardback)
  1. Boards of directors.   2. Corporate governance.   I. Carey, Dennis C.
II. Useem, Michael.   III. Title.
  HD2745.C44195 2013
  658.4'22—dc23

                                                                      2013023638

ISBN: 9781422144053
eISBN: 9781422144077

CONTENTS

A Call to Leadership

Here is the main point of all that follows: Chief executives must run the corporation, but directors must also lead the corporation on the most crucial issues. Monitoring is still important. Governance matters. But the time has come for boards to rebalance their responsibilities. Directors need to know when to take charge, when to partner, and when to stay out of the way.

Regulators, investors, and employees are all pressing boards to deliver on their responsibilities—and their company's results. That requires a handful of decisions that only the board can make: the decisions to select, retain, or dismiss the chief executive; to establish a climate of ethics and integrity; to set the goals and incentives for the executive team; and to pinpoint the company's central idea, risk appetite, and capital structure.

Why does board leadership matter? Because the fate of enterprises, employees, and shareholders so often hangs in the balance. For examples of where directors turned the tide in fortune's favor, we offer accounts of America's Ford Motor Company, Australia's BHP Billiton, Brazil's Grupo RBS, Britain's GlaxoSmithKline, India's Bharti Airtel,

China's Lenovo, and other enterprises. To see how boards have some-times failed both their businesses and their stakeholders, we also dissect companies that have faltered, including several that slid into the abyss.

A board's leadership can create value, and its absence can destroy value. Drawing on emergent practices at a number of firms, this book offers actionable advice on how directors can best make that leadership difference.

1.

From Ceremonial to Monitor to Leader

The authors of this book have occupied a front-row seat for seeing the gap between boards that are well run and led and are boons to the companies they serve, and those that are far less so. We have seen how public agencies and governance activists have sought to close that gap by insisting on tougher rules, check-the-box lists, and tighter regulations. We believe, however, that much of the variance stems instead from a very different source: the human dynamics, social architecture, and business leadership of the board itself.

We seek as a result to focus attention on building more engaged leadership in the boardroom, not just the executive suite. The manifesto that follows makes an uncomplicated argument to that end: *Governing boards should take more active leadership of the enterprise, not just monitor its management.* For the reasons behind doing so, the principles of how to do so, and the costs of not doing so, read on.

In bringing this argument to life, we make it pragmatic and we keep it short. And along the way, we expand the working concept of corporate governance from one of shareholder oversight to director leadership of the most vital company decisions. To do otherwise, we believe, is an opportunity lost, a responsibility abdicated.

We also believe that many of the thrusts of government regulators, activist investors, and governance raters have focused on the wrong issues. Rather than being concerned with whether the chief executive should be the same person as the board chair or whether directors should have staggered terms, we worry more about whether the board leader can help direct the board in setting strategy and gauging risk in concert with the CEO, and whether the directors' talent and collective chemistry make the board a substantive player at the table.

We identify a distinctive social architecture that is now required of companies if directors are to lead the enterprise along with executives, not just stand guard over it. This calls for a different kind of vigilance in the boardroom, a deeper kind of relationship between directors and executives, and a new kind of leadership from both.

The emergent model is a result of forces not of its own making. Increased regulation, shareholder pressures, and governance reforms over the past decade were intended to strengthen the board's oversight function. Yet as boards have become better monitors, they have also become better leaders, delving into a host of other areas that had been delegated to management in earlier times. We believe that directors can and will more actively lead in the years ahead, and on balance we anticipate that this should fortify company performance. But that is not a given. Poorly handled, this new board enablement can cause serious damage, resulting in fractured authority and dangerous meddling.

We seek a practical road map for knowing when to lead, when to partner, and when to stay out of the way. In developing it, we are less concerned with theories of corporate governance or ratings of good governance and more focused on the practical steps that directors and executives can take to make their collaborative leadership most effective.

A New Model of Collaborative Leadership

In a 2002 letter to Berkshire Hathaway shareholders, Warren Buffett famously lamented his multiple derelictions of duty as a director of some forty corporations over nearly two decades: "Too often I was silent when management made proposals that I judged to be counter to the interest of shareholders," Buffett wrote. "In those cases, collegiality trumped independence [and a] certain social atmosphere presides in boardrooms where it becomes impolitic to challenge the chief executive."[1]

A decade later, Amgen chairman Kevin Sharer painted an almost opposite picture of the relationship between board and corner office: "You're a lion tamer and they're the lions. Respect them, but if you let them eat you, they will. Working with the board is vital, complex, and beyond your prior experience—unlike anything you've done before. It is among the most complex human relationships, especially if you're the chairman, when you're their boss, and they're your boss. Get the relationship right, or it will hurt you."[2]

Allow for a little hyperbole on both sides—Warren Buffett was never *that* neglectful, and Kevin Sharer carried neither whip nor chair to keep his directors at bay. Still, the difference between the two observations illustrates a striking reconfiguration taking place in how boards operate and how company directors work with top management: the emergence, in an extraordinarily short time, of the potential for boards to be a vital leader and new force in corporate governance.

But note the qualifier—*potential*. This leadership capacity has yet to be fully exploited or even realized at many firms. Too often, directors remain one of the most valuable but least utilized of a company's assets. Smart, experienced, and dedicated men and women are ready to serve. They are sworn to protect and advance the enterprise, to ensure that it does what is best for customers and investors. Yet their wisdom and guidance are still too often closeted in the boardroom.

But the prevailing model is changing, and quickly. At company after company, boards and management have been embracing new practices that help define a more directive, more collaborative leadership of the firm. They are taking charge of CEO succession, executive compensation, goal choices, merger decisions, risk tolerance, and other functions that have traditionally been the province of management.

Based on our work, interviews, and research with executives and directors of multiple *Fortune* 500 firms ranging from Agilent Technologies and Boeing to Infosys and Pfizer, and their equivalent in other countries, *Boards That Lead* maps out what active leadership of both directors and executives should look like. We have drawn, for instance, on interviews with Procter & Gamble CEO A.G. Lafley on how his board shaped its $54 billion takeover of Gillette; with Apple board leader Edgar S. Woolard Jr. on how he secured his directors' agreement to bring Steve Jobs back to run the firm; with Ford board leader Irvine O. Hockaday Jr. on the directors' recruitment of a turnaround chief executive; and with Lenovo chair Liu Chuanzhi on how he transformed his board to globalize the business.[3]

What follows is our mapping of an emergent model of company leadership, one increasingly defined by the actions of both executives *and* directors. We draw the map by looking inside and around boardrooms, and in doing so, we witness moments of both great and disastrous leadership.

If you are already on a governing board or aspire one day to join one, our account can serve as a boardroom companion. If you invest in publicly traded companies, analyze them, rate them, regulate them, or consult with them, this book will reveal an emergent dynamic of the boardroom. And if you work with a board as a manager reporting to it or soon will be doing so, our account can inform your work with directors who are often ready to embrace a more proactive leadership role. Our book builds on the tangible experience of directors and executives in the boardroom to offer better navigation through it, and it closes with a set of director's checklists for leading both the boardroom and the company.

Though the emergent argument is largely rooted in the American corporate experience, the same logic, we believe, should certainly apply elsewhere. The rationale would extend as well to small and medium enterprises, nonprofit organizations, and even public agencies overseen by a board of some kind—regardless of national setting.[4]

This rising power of the new model outside the United States can be seen, for instance, at Barclays PLC, one of Britain's premier financial services institutions, when it was swept up in a scandal in 2012 over its improper setting of LIBOR (the London Interbank Offered Rate). The government forced the board to dismiss both its non-executive chair and its CEO, and the company came under criticism for directors who fell far short of their duties. When the Barclays board brought in Sir David Walker—a former government official, author of a report on governance in British banking, and chairman of Morgan Stanley International—as its new non-executive chair, he promptly declared that boardrooms "have been too reactive, passive and accepting of what's proposed by the executive." Disagreements in the boardroom are still seen by too many as "discourteous," warned the new Barclays chair, and he vowed that he would end that reflexive mind-set.[5]

We agree. That does not mean directors should wade into micromanagement, but it does require directors to educate and interest themselves in company strategy, risk management, and talent development. And it calls for effective leadership of the board *by* the board. This may seem disconcerting to some chief executives used to more passive boards still focused on monitoring management, but we believe that most executives will come to embrace the principles of a leadership partnership.

"One of the Greatest Business Decisions of All Time"—by the Board

Our revised conception of corporate governance was early evident in one of the highest-payoff leadership decisions of the modern era, an atonement for an earlier, irresponsible board blunder. The Apple board had fired the wrong CEO.[6]

Pushed out in 1985, Apple founder Steve Jobs moved on to other start-ups, NeXT and Pixar. NeXT never took off, but by 1997, Pixar was prospering while Apple was failing. That is when one of the authors received a telephone call from Apple's board leader, Edgar S. Woolard Jr., who had joined the governing board in 1996.

The board decisions described at Apple, as for a number of boards in the pages that follow, are largely drawn from personal interviews that we have conducted with those in the boardroom, in this case primarily with board leader Woolard. He had been chair and chief executive of DuPont and director of Citigroup, IBM, and the New York Stock Exchange. A onetime army officer, he had become a consummate member of the inner circle of the business elite, including a period as chairman of The Business Council, one of the most select assemblages of corporate leaders in the country. He treated all with dignity, putting people first, though never at the expense of sound business judgment.

In the twelve years since the Apple board had forced Jobs out, the company had recruited three CEOs. One had been an advertising manager, another a cost-cutter, and the third a process engineer. Each had presided over a string of disastrous product releases. When one of us (Ram Charan) subsequently taught a business case on Apple, executive program participants almost always blamed the firm's decline on poor leadership in the corner office. But in our view, it was the board that had recurrently selected the wrong CEOs for the office—in effect, the chief executives were dead on arrival. A solid pedigree from past performance had made them attractive managers, but their skill set proved a poor match for the triage they actually had to perform.

Upon joining the board, Woolard spent hours with Apple's senior leaders to learn the specifics of the company's state of affairs. As CEO of DuPont, he had always made a point of having direct contact with people throughout the organization so he would not fall victim to information filters. He took the same approach as an Apple director, talking directly with the CFO, the head of HR, and the chief technical officer, because, he told us, "no matter how good the CEO might be, you're getting filtered information." His initial impression of CEO Gilbert Amelio was positive; the chief executive was a great talker and had big ideas. But the CFO was privately painting a gloomy picture of Apple's future, one that darkened in the months to come. At the annual meeting in February 1997, the disconnect between the CFO's acute concern and the CEO's rosy outlook came into sharp focus, and it clicked in Woolard's mind that the newest CEO was simply unable to confront a very grim reality. The chief legal officer conducted most of the meeting and fielded plenty of tough questions, while the CEO was conspicuously missing. Then Amelio took the stage and talked about how great things were going. Yet the arena was full of unhappy people lined up six deep behind four floor microphones, eager to voice their complaints about service, quality, and the lack of competitive products. It was the most disruptive annual meeting Woolard had ever seen. Amelio tried to respond, but his answers were far from confidence building. Woolard's wife leaned over to whisper to her husband a prescient observation of her own, "This guy doesn't know what he's talking about."

The company was nearly out of cash, having lost more than $800 million on annual revenue of $9.8 billion. Informed outsiders noted that Apple had a strong brand and a small band of die-hard customers, but many doubted if it had a future. Woolard, always probing, called Charan to ask if the company could be saved. There was no silver bullet, Charan replied. Then Woolard asked, could it be acquired? Would Dell Computer be interested in buying Apple? Though in the same industry, antitrust opposition was unlikely, since Apple was otherwise hurtling toward bankruptcy.

Charan checked with Dell vice chair Morton L. Topfer, only to hear back two days later that his company was not interested. Michael Dell would tell several thousand technology executives at an Orlando exposition that Apple should "shut it down and give the money back to the shareholders."[7]

Woolard then asked about Compaq Computer, and Charan's call to CEO Eckhard Pfeiffer yielded the same response. Others evidently shared similar appraisals. Nobody—not AT&T, not IBM—seemed the least bit interested in purchasing Apple. The only real prospect appeared to be a Taiwanese firm that might offer as much as $500 million, though mainly for the brand.

In the meantime, Woolard continued to dig into Apple's operations, reviewing in depth the firm's cash flow, product sales, and resource allocation with CFO Fred D. Anderson in weekly one-on-one meetings. The CFO's candid data-driven appraisals were dire in their implications. The company had too many products attracting too few customers, a licensing strategy was diluting its brand, and it felt rudderless at the top. Divestiture seemed the only way out. Woolard authorized the chief financial officer to retain Goldman Sachs, saying "Fred, we've got to find out if we can sell the company." By late May it was clear: they could not.

Woolard pressed the chief executive again and again to explain specifically how he would return the company to profitability. Around the same time, Woolard was learning from his private conversations with both the chief financial officer and the general counsel that Amelio rarely left his office or talked to people. In June 1997, the CFO warned Woolard that essential personnel were resigning or intimating they would soon be doing so. Woolard finally took the deepening crisis to a mid-June board meeting. In his estimate, if the board stayed with the same CEO, he warned his fellow directors, the probability of bankruptcy was near 90 percent, and even if they could find a buyer, it would nonetheless remain as high as 60 or 70 percent.

Despite three successive CEOs' dismal track records to that point, Apple's directors still believed that the company might be saved by the right executive. How to save it—or who could save it—had become the pressing question, and Woolard was flirting with a novel answer. Steve Jobs had become an adviser to Apple after its purchase of NeXT, so he had been on the scene talking to various people, including the CFO. In early May 1997 Woolard asked the board for authority to talk with Jobs about the possibility of his fully returning. "I think he'll come back," the CFO had already informed Woolard. "He is really getting involved in the company," explained the CFO. "He's got lots of ideas; he's talking to a lot of people."

Drawing on Woolard's own experience-honed instincts that the CFO had been offering candid advice without ulterior motives, Woolard told the board, "I think he's our only hope . . . I don't see any alternatives." Jobs was enthusiastic about the company, though he quickly added that it had way too many products and in any case they were all "crap." At Woolard's request, the general counsel arranged another board meeting in mid-June, and the directors then decided to fire the latest CEO and approve the rehiring of Jobs. Amelio resisted at first, but soon accepted his fate.

Jobs's mercurial and sometimes abusive behavior was already legendary. He had been out of the Apple game for a dozen years, and he could hardly have been more different from the lead director who was planning to recruit him. Jobs had dropped out of college, meditated in India, experimented with LSD, and clashed with virtually everyone he ever did business with. Woolard traveled the corporate byways with aplomb; Jobs broke china along the way.

But despite their vast personal differences, Woolard, with the board's backing, called Jobs: "We need you to come back." Woolard appreciated the gravity of the moment. The "grace of the Lord has dropped me down in the middle of this damn thing," he recalled, "and I'm just not going to let it go down if I have to piss everybody off and beg Steve Jobs to come back." Jobs refused to return as chair or CEO, saying only that he would return as an "adviser" until the board could find another CEO, but that was enough for the moment. He refused to accept any money or stock options. "I do not want anybody in Apple to think I'm coming back to make money," Woolard recalled Jobs explaining. "I'm coming back because I love this company, it's in big trouble, and I want to get it on the right track." He also stipulated that all the board members but Woolard resign, though he and Woolard settled on keeping one other, Gareth Chang.

The directors gathered in mid-July and invited Jobs, who had been sitting outside the room as the board met, to join them inside. After a pleasant "Hi, everybody" as he strode in, Jobs took a seat at the head of the boardroom table. Woolard said, "Okay, you know why we're here. Everybody has to resign except Gareth and myself." The other directors all confirmed that they would resign and walked out of the boardroom with no sign of rancor. They shook hands with Jobs as they left, some no doubt relieved to go, according to Woolard. Jobs wanted two new directors on the board—Oracle CEO Larry Ellison and Intuit CEO William V. Campbell—and Woolard wanted former IBM CFO Jerome B. York to join as well.

Bringing Steve Jobs back was an act of leadership that Woolard and the board should not have abdicated, and they did not. Then Woolard stepped forward to provide substantive guidance in the months ahead. Jobs came to Woolard for a discussion of what to do about the "clones," for instance, the computers that Apple had authorized other makers to produce that were now depressing the price of Apple's own Macs: "I've got to get rid of the clones," Jobs warned Woolard. "I can't get it going without that." Woolard cautioned against breaking long-term contracts with the clone makers, but Jobs insisted. "I don't care, Ed, I'll just have to pay whatever it takes to settle. But I need to call them to say they're out of business." Looking back on that decision, said Woolard, it was "pretty tough, but he was right."

Another week, Jobs sought advice on a plan to dismiss many of the company's engineers. "Ed, I really want to fire about half the engineers," he declared in a call. "I just can't see how we can do that," Woolard countered, but Jobs was adamant. "I've been here long enough now. I know who are really the talented ones."

Jobs and Woolard soon talked again about another Jobs proposal—to divide the company's remaining engineers into half a dozen teams in a way that would allow him to work one full day per week directly with each of the teams. "I can't work through a hierarchy," Jobs explained, "I know I can make that work because I need to put my personal involvement in everything that's going on." After an hour's discussion, Woolard finally OK'd the move. "Well, it's very unorthodox," he told Jobs, "but I do understand that you're the guy with the ideas, so go ahead. If the bureaucracy is weighing you down and this is the way to get to the best people and to get them functioning [then make the changes]."

At another point, Jobs came forward with an employee profit-sharing plan that would reward staff handsomely in several years but yield them little in the current year, a plan that Woolard strongly advised against (and that was eventually dropped). On several occasions, they talked about hiring a vice president from Compaq—Tim Cook—who had previously worked for a dozen years at IBM. They deliberated Cook's salary and title, and Jobs finally hired Cook with Woolard's blessing in 1998 (Cook would later become Apple CEO shortly before Jobs's death in 2011). In time, Woolard and Jobs would frequently engage around a host of other senior hires, their compensation, and their reporting relationships.

Later, Woolard and Jobs talked about the possibility of creating an Apple store. "I want to build an Apple store," Jobs asserted, but Woolard initially demurred: "Compaq's done that, others have done it, and everybody's failed." Jobs countered, "I've thought about it a lot, I think we can do a chain of Apple stores which would be unbelievable." They argued for another half hour, and Jobs finally said, "Approve for me to do four. Give me the money to do four. If you're right and I'm wrong, I'll quit," adding, "I'll take the medicine and say I was wrong." With Woolard's urging, the board approved the opening of four stores. "This is going to be a retail store like you've never seen," said Jobs.

Looking on their many weekly calls, Woolard observed that despite a few misses, "90 percent of his ideas were damned good." Other board members jumped into an active partnership with Jobs as well. For instance, new board member Larry Ellison provided feedback on computer design. In reflecting on the board's active relationship with Jobs, said Woolard, "It was not arm's length at all."

Through it all, Woolard had found Jobs to be respectful of those both above and below him. Though Jobs brought a strong point of view as to where Apple should be going and how it should get there, he worked well with the reconstituted board. Woolard had built relations with managers deep in the organization, but he heard few complaints from below about Jobs's behavior inside the firm and never personally witnessed his anger, arrogance, or imperiousness. Symptomatic of the special deference that Jobs had come to show Woolard himself, when the CEO telephoned the board leader's home and Woolard's wife would answer, she would sometimes call her husband to the receiver with the information, "Your *son*'s on the phone."

In the years ahead, Woolard found Jobs to be a "well-balanced, good CEO" of the company, and he noted that virtually none of the vital people hired by Jobs ever left the enterprise. "Steve Jobs is not just a creative guy," Woolard reflected of his work with Jobs, but he was also "a good leader of the board, he was a good leader of the company."

The company returned to prosperity, and Ellison declared at a board meeting several years later that the board was both the smartest and the dumbest in America. Directors had hired the best CEO in the country, and company stock had now risen by a factor of ten. But at the same time, they were still paying the CEO nothing—Jobs did, however, ask for a company-purchased Gulfstream jet because of his travel demands. Woolard and his fellow directors approved the aircraft and added that if Jobs could double the market cap of the company—it had by then already reached $16 billion—the board would give him a stock option grant equivalent to 5 percent of the increase, some $800 million.

In recruiting, coaching, and retaining Steve Jobs, Apple directors transformed a struggling $2 billion market value company on the verge of bankruptcy in 1997 into a company with a $500 billion market value just fifteen years later. Though they developed deep knowledge of the company and worked closely with Jobs, directors resisted the temptation to micromanage. The board's decision to hire Jobs has been ranked as one of the "greatest business decisions of all time," and Jobs would later say that the lead director who spearheaded it, Edgar Woolard, "was one of the best board members I've ever seen" and "one of the most supportive and wise people I've ever met."

When we asked Woolard about the most important lessons from his Apple experience, he reported that a board leader has to have regular access to the chief financial officer, deeply understand the company strategy and execution—and pick and partner with the right CEO.

Monitor *and* Leader

To appreciate the leap in board behavior that the Apple directors revealed—and the rising leadership content in the board's role at many companies—we take a step back to a brief retrospective on governing boards themselves.

For more than a century, American companies have been creating and sustaining boards of directors, a noble concept and one required by state laws and regulated by federal rules, to ensure that the controllers are controlled. Everybody needs a watchdog, if for no other reason than to be accountable to someone.

As the country's great franchises took form in the later part of the nineteenth century and early years of the twentieth century—General Motors, Johnson & Johnson, and Procter & Gamble among them—they initially filled their boards with family members, wealthy investors, and a liberal sprinkling of FOFs—friends of the founder. Not perfect overseers, but many if not most of them held a personal stake in the firm's commercial success and they predictably worked to achieve and protect it.

Until the 1930s, most American companies remained family owned, their boards dominated by owner-managers. It was often impossible to distinguish insiders—managing directors—from outside directors, but the distinction was largely moot in any event. If you were a director, you were likely a de facto insider because of your shares or investment in the company, or your position as a manager of the enterprise with a significant personal financial stake, as is the case with the boards of many private-equity-backed firms in America today. Or you were an insider by virtue of your kinship or friendship with the founding family.

Then came the celebrated "managerial revolution," chronicled by Adolf Berle and Gardiner Means in their landmark 1932 book, *The Modern Corporation and Private Property*. Rapidly growing companies in need of additional funds to stoke their engines took to the equity marketplace by going public, and the "modern corporation" emerged, defined by Berle and Means as the absence of "dominant owners," where "control is maintained in large measure apart from ownership."[8] Professional executives triumphed over the founders and their heirs. Expertise trumped pedigree. In the wake of the revolution, the locus of authority shifted from owner-managers to trained technocrats.

Boards were still adorned with what the British call "the great and the good"—individuals of great stature and impeccable reputation. But their powers had been upended, even eclipsed, by professional managers who now had their hands on the brakes and throttles. Directors met too infrequently, understood too little, and held too few shares to make, or even want to make, a difference. With stockholding widely dispersed among thousands of investors, none with sufficient clout to demand otherwise, boards became more ceremonial.[9]

Duties of Care and Loyalty

By the 1980s, however, dispersed shareholding was fast becoming far less dispersed, with public equity increasingly moving out of the hands of widows and orphans and into the hands of a relatively small set of mega-investors. In 1950, a mere 6 percent of US corporate equity was held by institutional investors; a half-century later, that fraction had grown tenfold. The growing concentration of shares in the hands of professional money managers became even more pronounced among large publicly traded firms. In 1987, institutional investors held 47 percent of the shares of the thousand largest American enterprises by market capitalization. By 2009, that fraction had risen to 73 percent.[10]

At first, massive investment-fund managers such as CalPERS, Fidelity, TIAA-CREF, and Vanguard chafed at their powerlessness, despite their massive holdings, to prevent companies from imploding—or even just plodding along. But then, as their assets accumulated and with an intellectual boost from financial economists, institutional investors sparked what came to be known as the "market for corporate control"—investor-driven takeovers and restructurings of poorly managed firms.[11]

These and a host of other investor pressures ranging from proxy fights to quiet negotiations rejuvenated the boardroom, bringing director oversight of executives—now on behalf of major institutional shareholders—back to life. The board's monitoring function had always been there in name. Now it was becoming established in fact.[12]

During the 1990s and the first decade of the new millennium, shareholders further strengthened their powers, but most major investors still dispersed their holdings across a large portfolio of corporations, leaving the institutions with little time or individual incentive to weigh in on the competitive challenges or operational shortcomings of any one of them. Some activist investors did begin to take on issues ranging from how to pay a CEO to whether the board should have a non-executive chair, but they often tended to focus more on standardized form and less on strategic function.[13]

Inevitably, investor demands for more independent boards that would be accountable to them, paid like them, and fiduciaries for them gave rise to litigation. To investors' dismay, challenges in the Delaware courts—where half of the country's largest firms are incorporated—even to what shareholders considered the most egregious violations of owners' interests, often did relatively little to force behavioral changes at the top. But the legal actions did help establish two standards for director obligation: *duty of care*, requiring directors to exercise reasonable caution in executing board responsibilities that could harm others if not performed well, and *duty of loyalty*, requiring that directors exercise good fiduciary judgment on behalf of the stockholders.

These dual obligations of care and loyalty were further strengthened by the Sarbanes–Oxley Act of 2002, new rules imposed in 2003 by the New York Stock Exchange, and the Dodd–Frank Act of 2010. Collectively, the three measures served to empower directors as overseers, with the goals of preventing executive self-dealing and excessive risk-taking, all in the name of better shareholder monitoring.

The Sarbanes–Oxley Act, for instance, holds directors responsible for ensuring that their company has internal financial controls in place and does not violate accounting rules. Dodd–Frank instructs the Securities and Exchange Commission to create procedures that make it easier for shareholders to propose and elect their own nominees to a board, facilitating stronger director oversight of managers on behalf of owners. And the New York Stock Exchange requires that all members of the board's audit committee be "financially literate" and "independent," and that their duties include "oversight [of the] integrity of the company's financial statements."[14]

Such regulatory measures, while their implementation has not always been smooth, have significantly sharpened the board's role as monitors of management. Plenty of evidence confirms that boards have in fact come a long way from the ceremonial status in the earlier era of managerial dominance. Though that status persists at some firms, it has been eclipsed at many.[15] To cite several key developments:

- The governing boards of more than nine out of ten of the S&P 500 (Standard & Poor's five hundred largest companies as ranked by market value) now have a lead or presiding director, as required under new listing rules.

- The percentage of company boards with separate board chair and chief executive had risen to 43 percent by 2012, though only 23 percent of the chairs can be deemed truly independent of top management.[16]

- The proportion of firms with so-called "poison pill" devices, designed to protect management from hostile investor takeovers, declined from 59 percent to 8 percent, while the fraction with *classified boards*—on which directors serve staggered terms, presumably making them less subject to shareholder pressures—declined from 61 to 20 percent.[17]

- Executive pay has been steadily migrating from fixed salary and benefits toward contingent compensation that varies with financial results that directly benefit shareholders. In 1982, a manufacturing executive arriving at work just after the New Year could expect to receive at least 63 percent of his or her pay by the end of the calendar year, regardless of company performance for shareholders. By 2012, that fixed fraction had dropped to 20 percent, and long-term incentive-based compensation, largely tied to shareholder value through stock-based pay plans, had jumped from 17 to 61 percent.[18]

Duty of Leadership

These and related trends have helped boards become far more effective monitors of management than they were a decade ago, and in doing so they inadvertently strengthened the board's leadership hand. And still other trends, we believe, are now helping boards become even more engaged in the task of leading the company, though it is a transformation still in process and one that will not happen entirely on its own. Indeed, one of the premier callings of both directors and executives now is to further facilitate the transformation, building on pioneering advances at other companies and market trends that are inexorably making board leadership more imperative. While the duty of care and the duty of loyalty have become critical to the directors' monitoring function, the additional responsibility, a *duty of leadership*, is becoming essential as well.

The most forceful underlying trend behind the intensifying obligation of leadership is the increasing complexity of company decisions across virtually every facet of doing business, from sales channels and product categories to price points and product markets. Consider wireless carriers. Early entrants focused on just several demographically distinct markets, but later incumbents came to distinguish some two dozen or more submarkets. The number of mobile phone plans rapidly expanded as well to include prepaid, postpaid, night, family, friends, family and friends, data, and text plans. Wireless carriers sold through as many as a dozen separate channels, ranging from company-owned stores to affinity partners and websites, and the industry embraced as many as a half-million distinctive price plans.[19]

A related challenge has been rising *information overload*, a condition in which the addition of ever more information leads to suboptimal company decisions rather than improving decision quality. Imagine an inverted U-curve: as data initially becomes more available, decision accuracy improves; but beyond an inflection point of increasing information, the amount of data diminishes management's capacity to process the information and thus its ability to reach optimal decisions.[20]

Yet another source of complexity: the increasing movement of enterprise operations or sales across national boundaries and the concomitant need for company managers to be conversant with multiple—and often widely diverse—regulatory regimes, consumer preferences, and cultural traditions. In 2001, foreign markets accounted for 32 percent of total sales of the S&P 500 companies. By 2011, that figure stood at 46 percent, approaching half of all sales and up 40 percent in a decade.[21]

That growing complexity has become increasingly of concern to company management. IBM has periodically asked a cross section of managers at a wide range of companies to identify their greatest challenge. In the surveys of 2004 and 2006, managers gave top place to coping with change. By 2010, however, the more than fifteen hundred managers that IBM surveyed in sixty countries reported in the aggregate that "complexity" had emerged as their leading concern. What is more, nearly four of five anticipated even greater complexity in the five years ahead, and only half said that they felt "prepared for the expected complexity." Four out of five of the polled executives also responded that the most important quality of leadership for the next five years would be executive "creativity" in dealing with that complexity.[22]

While some of these developments are more operational than strategic—and thus for executives rather than directors to address—they reflect an ever-broadening challenge for board members. With increasing complexity in how markets operate and with sharper bends ahead, a greater premium is placed on understanding how these uncertainties can create opportunity or, conversely, destroy value.

Still other evidence suggests that boards are, in fact, rising to this challenge. Spencer Stuart periodically surveys corporate secretaries and general counsels at S&P 500 firms regarding the areas that require the greatest board attention. In 2008, "shareholder concerns" nudged out "company strategy," but by 2012 the results had flipped: company strategy topped shareholder concerns by better than two to one.[23]

The directors' duty of leadership as a result is ascendant at many companies. We delve into this in greater detail as we go along, but here are four starting points:

- Directors and executives increasingly view the boardroom as a place where they can mutually engage in reaching critical decisions for the company.

- While boards are still obligated to the duties of care and loyalty—their vigilance on behalf of investors must be honored—

many boards have been adding a new obligation, focusing director attention on company strategy, capital allocation, executive
succession, management compensation, talent development, and
enterprise risk. That does not mean wandering into the weeds—
micromanagement is decidedly *not* the point—but laissez-faire is
no longer an acceptable posture at many boards either.

- In selecting a new chief executive officer, boards are becoming more mindful of both their monitoring and leadership roles.
  This points toward selecting a new CEO who has a tangible
  record of creating shareholder value, either within the company
  or in another firm, though not necessarily as a chief executive.
  And it also points toward a new CEO who has also displayed a
  capacity for working hand in hand with governing boards.

- In building the leadership at the top, executives are increasingly
  furnishing directors with the information from both inside and
  outside the firm required to reach strategic decisions, and directors are increasingly conveying their strategic intent to guide
  executives in taking clear-eyed actions.

That last item in particular points to the key ingredient in making this
new model work. In certain leadership areas, such as selecting a new chief
executive, directors tend to drive the process, as we have seen at Apple.
In other realms, such as setting strategy and developing leaders, directors
and executives often work collaboratively with executives more at the
wheel. And in still other areas, directors wisely avoid any involvement.

When to Lead, When to Partner, and When to Stay Out of the Way

Each company board will want to fashion its own unique blend of the
components of direct and collaborative leadership. "Boards should sit
down" annually, urged Ford's lead director Irvine O. Hockaday Jr.,
"and say, OK, what are we really doing here, what really is our role
given the situation of this company at this time, what are we doing
to incarnate that role, how are we going to function with the lead

FIGURE 1-1

Boards take charge, partner, or stay out of the way

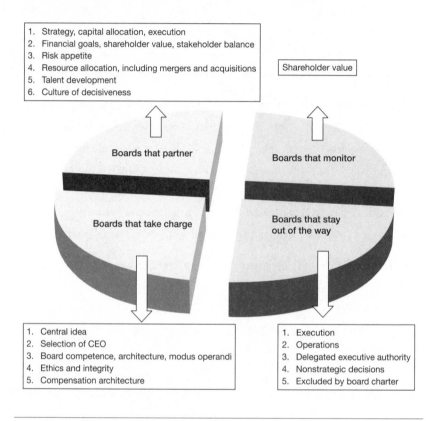

1. Strategy, capital allocation, execution
2. Financial goals, shareholder value, stakeholder balance
3. Risk appetite
4. Resource allocation, including mergers and acquisitions
5. Talent development
6. Culture of decisiveness

Shareholder value

Boards that partner

Boards that monitor

Boards that take charge

Boards that stay out of the way

1. Central idea
2. Selection of CEO
3. Board competence, architecture, modus operandi
4. Ethics and integrity
5. Compensation architecture

1. Execution
2. Operations
3. Delegated executive authority
4. Nonstrategic decisions
5. Excluded by board charter

director, and what are our priorities?" Finding the right balance among the board's leadership components—knowing when to lead, when to partner, and when to stay out of the way—is one of the premier tasks of the board's leader.

Our road map, and the foundations for this book, are shown in figure 1–1.

A duty of leadership also implies that directors should remain steadfastly detached from the products of their labors. Though now far more deeply engaged in the company's strategy and other practices than ever implied by the monitoring function, directors nonetheless must also be able to back away from a path that they have had a direct hand in mapping. That is never easy of course, but the prescription here is clear: leadership by its very definition implies that directors resolutely focus on what is right for the enterprise, regardless of personal pride or sunk investment. A useful dictate to keep in mind: *mission first*, or in Peter Drucker's well-known phrasing, "Leadership is doing the right thing"—regardless of commercial interest or personal pride.

Our assessment does not imply that executives are any less in the driver's seat. But the way that they drive at many companies is now markedly different—a shared or distributed leadership model that is better suited, in our view, for guiding companies that are facing more uncertain, more changing, and more complex markets.[24]

The Director's Checklist

We believe that executive leadership can be mastered and that a leader's checklist can focus mastery on the most vital principles for navigating through virtually any leadership challenge. We have similarly come to conclude that much the same kind of director's checklist can be important for boards to lead as well. A set of enduring checklist principles can furnish directors with a road map for leading through the most challenging moments that boards inevitably confront.[25]

From watching dozens of governing boards in the United States and elsewhere, we are convinced that their experience points to a relatively modest number of emergent mission-critical leadership principles. Albert Einstein said that the calling of physics was to make the natural universe as simple as possible—but not simpler. The director's checklist is likewise at its best when it is as bare bones as possible—but not more so.[26]

Here is our first checklist for the decisions that directors will want to lead, the decisions where they will want to partner, and the decisions where they will want to stand clear. The chapters that follow conclude with additional director's checklists, and we gather all of these mission-critical templates, as well as some valuable extras, in "The Complete Director's Checklists" at the end of the book.

DIRECTOR'S CHECKLIST FOR LEADERSHIP DECISIONS

When to Take Charge

✓ Central idea

✓ Selection of chief executive officer

✓ Board competence, architecture, and modus operandi

✓ Ethics and integrity

✓ Compensation architecture

When to Partner

✓ Strategy, capital allocation

✓ Financial goals, shareholder value, stakeholder balance

✓ Risk appetite

✓ Resource allocation

✓ Talent development

✓ Culture of decisiveness

When to Stay Out of the Way

✓ Execution

✓ Operations

✓ Areas of delegated authority

✓ Nonstrategic decisions

✓ Excluded by board charter

Companies vary greatly in how they specifically work to enhance the board's hand, customizing their architectures and practices around their own specific histories and mind-sets. Within a given board, directors also vary in their conversational intelligence—their ability to advance the boardroom dialogue in ways that serve company leadership. We see a broad spectrum across boards and even within boards, with some boards and some directors more drawn to the direct-leadership calling, others to more collaborative leadership, and still others to neither.

A distinctive feature of this emergent governance model is that one size does not fit all. Rather than trying to cram square pegs into round holes, directors and executives are crafting their own way forward. And the way they will do so in good times can be quite different from hard times. Running through it all, however, is the common thread of boards more forcefully leading, not just monitoring. We believe that this is an important and welcome development. Publicly traded companies, in our view, deserve no less.[27]

With directors increasingly at stage center—responsible for leading the enterprise along with monitoring management—they will want to begin with the central idea, the cornerstone for a company's mission and strategy. Chapter 2 takes up the central idea, what makes it compelling, and how its absence can cause a company to flounder. We will appreciate the former in a look at the power of a central idea at India's mobile phone operator Bharti Airtel, and we will see the latter in an American company whose board was pulled apart by the absence of a central idea.

PART ONE

BOARDS THAT WORK

2.

First Things First:
Define the Central Idea

The central idea of a corporation is the seed that blossoms into a clear framing of the company's full-blown strategy and the many implications for how to execute it. It is the animating force from which hundreds of strategic and operational details emanate. The central idea references why the company exists, whom it serves, how it should be nurtured, why it will flourish, how it will make money and manage risk, and where it must be going if it is to sustain a competitive presence and achieve its broader purpose. The central idea is the bedrock on which the enterprise is raised and how its resources are spent. The central idea is practical, readily translated into action. It is simple—no more than several hundred words—tangible, graphic, not lofty. One can feel and picture it.

Boards need to be sure the central idea is clear and compelling and that every board member understands it. Directors should internalize it so that it becomes a natural, instinctive frame of reference against which to gauge strategies, external information, and board decisions. Repeated reference to the central idea is vital. At one company, the central idea thus appears on a slide displayed at every board meeting. At another, the chief executive updates the operational implications of the company's central idea at each board gathering.[1]

No company succeeds linearly without setbacks, and most face growing complexity in their markets. The central idea provides a rudder that lets the board and management navigate through the choppy waters ahead. This can be particularly important for large global companies that operate in an array of multifaceted markets.

Centripetal DNA

To see how the central idea serves as a kind of company DNA, take a look at Bharti Airtel, a rapidly growing Indian telecommunications company with global ambitions. The private telecom industry in India first found traction in 1991, when the government began allocating the communications spectrum to private enterprise, part of a broader effort to deregulate a tightly constrained economy. Large business houses, extremely wealthy and superbly connected in government circles, jumped into what was seen as a huge and profitable market in its infancy. Because so many comers were entering the fray, the government opted to ensure that spectrum applicants could win only a portion of the country's coverage, with no one telecom spanning the subcontinent.[2]

Creating a new telecom company is a capital-intensive sport. It can take years from the time a license is first obtained to produce profitable revenues. Yet, despite the daunting task of securing short-term cash to build a telecom, an unknown entrepreneur, Sunil Bharti Mittal, decided that he would create an entry as fast as possible to become a dominant provider. Mittal founded Bharti Telecom Ltd. in 1996 and later renamed it Bharti Airtel. The seed of his central idea, initially conceived by him but formulated and approved by his directors, boiled down to its essence was: *Grow faster than others; scale it up to become number one far ahead of competitors.* The idea is measurable and benchmarked against regular milestones.

Airtel's central idea can be summarized as follows:

- Create primary demand for telephone services as fast as possible by making the services affordable to even the country's lowest-income families. Reduce prices enough that demand can explode.

- Scale up more quickly than the competition and achieve national coverage faster than others by building out from an initial small geographic territory through licenses, acquisitions, or horse-trading with other carriers.

- Make the cost structure as variable as possible. Achieve the lowest capital intensity by creating an ecosystem of long-term partnerships in which equipment and other suppliers link with Airtel so that they provide all the hardware and software and ride with the growth of Airtel's revenues. When revenues go up, suppliers earn more; when down, they see less.

- Construct and own transmission towers through joint ventures with competitors and later consider public offerings of them.

- Build the most recognized mobile telecom brand in the nation and beyond, and do so more quickly than others.

- Divide the country into thirty-eight geographic circles. Staff each circle with the best available managers, who are aggressive in managing profit and loss, generating new demand, and scaling up the largest number of customers annually. Build the brand locally, gain market share in each geographic area more rapidly than competitors, and then lock them in through superior customer service.

- Instill urgency and speed as company principles. Collect data daily and act on it instantly, eliminating decision layers and delays.

- Recruit top talent from around the world and link performance indicators and compensation to the central idea.

- Establish an exceptional capability for managing supplier partnerships with vendors such as Sweden's Ericsson and the United
  States' IBM.

Note how clear-eyed yet ambitious this central idea is, with measurable goals implied along with implementing actions, strategic alliances,
and defined objectives. It is simple in conception, stated on a single
page, innovative in thrust, and potentially game changing. It was not
developed by Airtel executives during a weekend retreat but instead
emerged from repeated refinement of its elements through executive
testing and director engagement over many months. Airtel directors
served as a sounding board for the central idea, working with executives to clarify, crystallize, and cultivate it. They did so in both formal
boardroom dialogue and informal give-and-take at Mittal's home. The
directors were never passive or reticent; they offered real-time feedback, whether sought or not—although it often was. As a testament
to its resulting power, Airtel's central idea became so compelling that
many would-be competitors in India soon sought to mimic it. The
central idea and its strategy alone, though, would not have carried the
day. What also gave the idea sustainable advantage was a corresponding
set of execution components—vetted by directors, though not created
by them—that others could not so readily replicate.

In collaboration with the board and in hands-on fashion, Sunil Mittal and another executive who also served on the board built up the
enterprise in one of the fastest ramping ups of a telecom start-up ever.
To do so, they collaborated, concentrating on the top line, seizing the
early-mover advantage, and accepting the risks that always come with
speed.[3]

"One of the burning things in my story has been [to grow] the
top line as fast as you can," Mittal explained. "I have always believed
that the bottom line will come if there is a top line." As a result, he
says, "Speed and always speed has been what we have done: launch
things in the marketplace, get ahead of competitors, be there, get the
market share, get top line." Mittal urged his managers, often to their

surprise, "[If] you are caught between speed and perfection, always choose speed." Manoj Kohli, who became Airtel's president in 2006, added, "We will always be a start-up venture in our mind in terms of our hunger [and] passion to win in terms of agility."

To achieve both scale and speed, the essence of the execution task, Mittal shocked the telecommunications industry by farming out the operation of his entire phone network in a $400 million contract to Ericsson, Nokia, and Siemens. He would no longer have to acquire and maintain equipment. He would instead simply pay the European vendors according to the traffic they handled and the quality they provided. He also contracted out most of Airtel's information technology services, ranging from customer billing to the company's own intranet, in a $750 million deal with IBM. So comprehensive was the outsourcing that it left virtually no IT staff on Airtel's payroll—although information technology is the very foundation of wireless telephony. Even Mittal's own desktop computer was given over to IBM management.

Airtel's outsourcing moves defied conventional logic. Since core competencies are widely viewed as the value drivers of a firm, peripheral functions ranging from property management to employee benefits—so goes the reasoning—could be handed over to other firms for which such functions are their core competencies. But in outsourcing its telephone network and customer infrastructures, Mittal appeared to be placing Airtel's value drivers outside the company. "People gasped in horror," he told a reporter. "I got calls from around the world saying, 'You've gone nuts! This is the lifeline of your business, something you can't afford to lose!'" But outsourcing was simply necessitated, Mittal concluded, by the imperative of scale and speed—that is, by the central idea that launched the enterprise and controlled the entire highly successful chain of events that followed.[4]

By 2012, Bharti Airtel had become India's largest carrier by customer number, brand recognition, revenue share, and market value, but India was only the beginning of the story. Now operating in twenty countries, Airtel is likely to add another hundred million customers to its vast Indian base during the next several years, and in so doing could become one of the world's largest telecoms, ranking behind number-one China Mobile but ahead of some of the giants of America and Europe. South America and the Middle East could be next, and if the global telecom industry consolidates, as is anticipated, Airtel's distinctive and aligned combination of central idea plus strategy plus execution could well position it to be not only an Indian leader but also a world player.

Challenges and setbacks are sure to be encountered at home and abroad as regulatory barriers rise and competitors' prices fall. Still, with a firm grasp on the central idea, Airtel's directors and executives have a compact foundation to make their moves in a reasoned and consistent fashion.

Centrifugal DNA

Bharti Airtel provides a powerful example of the *centripetal* force of a great central idea—the way it draws and melds strategy, execution, management, and the board onto a common ground and overarching purpose. A bad central idea has just the opposite effect—it pulls the enterprise apart, scattering strategy, execution, and capital and decoupling them from one another. To see this destructive *centrifugal* force field in action, we turn to a wrenching conflict within the boardroom and between the directors and executives at one of America's premier consumer-goods companies.[5]

During its seventy-year history, Centrifugal Corporation had built a widely admired brand. (Names and some details are disguised in this and other accounts; events are actual.) Centrifugal had come to dominate shelf space for its product category at big retailers like Walmart, and it demonstrated strong North American market share, annual profits, and cash flow. No surprise that its owners, including a family that held more than two-fifths of the shares, were satisfied, even pleased, with the company's sustained performance, though market share had begun to falter.

The company's long-serving and very successful chief executive retired, however, and the seeds of decline were inadvertently sown when the board hired John Scott as the new chief executive. An outsider, Scott had been the right-hand man to the widely respected CEO of another company that was also highly regarded in the consumer-goods world. He exuded confidence, communicated persuasively, and arrived with high aspirations for Centrifugal. And he believed that he would be a game changer for the company.

In his first few years, Scott set about cutting costs by streamlining product mix and reconfiguring manufacturing. He also tapped into a new market segment with aggressive advertising for a fresh set of products, but he was not prepared to move beyond the company's almost exclusively North American footprint. The board supported those stratagems, and the stock price ticked upward as investors took notice of Scott's successful steps to reinvigorate the company. It seemed that he was proving to be the game changer that he had aspired to become.

But the greater game had been changing faster than Scott had been able to change the company. One of Centrifugal's biggest rivals had gone on an acquisition spree, including a major purchase that created cost-saving synergies in its product distribution. Global players were expanding and making inroads into the United States, progressively chipping away at Centrifugal's market share. And the costs of raw materials for Centrifugal were incessantly rising, steadily narrowing its margins.

Scott decided in response that the time was ripe for a big expansion by taking the company into a whole new product category. Geographic enlargement, he concluded, would be too challenging because of differences in local consumer tastes. Better to remain in North America, he reasoned, and expand by entering adjacent domestic markets.

Although the directors expressed mixed feelings about his diversification plan, Scott proceeded to launch a new set of products and acquisitions. Financial results, however, bombed; shareholders lost patience; and directors began to grouse about the loss of shareholder value as the stock price steadily eroded. Scott suspended the diversification strategy, and directors now pressed him to devise a new strategy that capitalized instead on growing opportunities outside the North American market that he had so far eschewed.

By a coincidence of timing, the membership of Centrifugal's board changed significantly just as the results of the CEO's newest new strategy were proving meager. Three non-executive directors retired, and three new outsiders took their seats. The newcomers joined six incumbent directors, including three representatives of the family that held the large majority of Centrifugal's shares.

The new outsiders each brought extensive business experience and expertise and, on the face of it, added the kind of substance that the board seemed to need at the moment. But their ability to bring that content into a working relationship with the CEO was only as good as their ability to work well in the boardroom, and here their personal baggage might have been a warning sign, had anyone been looking. One of the new directors had been a senior investment banker but had been let go by his firm a few years earlier. The second had served as head of a major division of another major consumer-goods company but had resigned after being passed over for the CEO job. The third had been chief executive of still another consumer-goods corporation but had been forced out because of poor performance.

The reconstituted board had barely gelled when the chief executive informed them of yet another dramatic new plan—this one to go global by merging Centrifugal with a non-US company twice its size. The three family representatives on the board openly objected, complaining that the merger would dilute their holdings and cede control of the merged company. Other directors expressed their disapproval by asking probing questions and making critical comments, and still others implied as much through their silence around the board table. The three new members, by contrast, reacted enthusiastically to the proposal and openly encouraged the CEO to pursue it.

Scott incorrectly interpreted these mixed signals, viewing the directors on balance as supporting the plan, and the non-executive board chair did not disabuse him of this misreading. Nor did the CEO or board chair seek to more fully bring out, let alone resolve, the underlying disagreements in the boardroom.

The unaddressed fissure would worsen when two more directors retired, and their replacements—one a former chief executive and the second with experience in the federal government—further exacerbated the schism by throwing their weight behind the merger plan. Nearly half the board now advocated the merger, while the other half was more against it than ever.

The contentious issue of whether to merge the company arose at nearly every bimonthly board meeting over the next year as Scott pressed his case and opposed board members who continued to challenge it. Several directors repeatedly asked Scott to develop an alternative strategy for growth, whether domestic or international, that would not result in the loss of the family's control.

Almost inevitably, the tone in the boardroom declined from civil to cool to quarrelsome, even on subjects that had little to do with the proposed merger or company strategy. Still, the chief executive opted to double down, and he furnished the skeptical directors with reams of numbers purporting to demonstrate the financial merits of a merger. When it became apparent that his spreadsheets and appeals were budging none of the skeptics, however, the CEO let his frustration show, and his board supporters became increasingly aggravated by the continued intransigence of the other directors.

The non-executive board chair belatedly began to work behind the scenes, calling each of the directors privately to better understand views that had not always been so candidly expressed in the boardroom. He communicated frequently with Scott about the objectors' reservations; in particular, why the three family-directors were so adamantly opposed. Scott himself had opted to engage in one-on-one conversations with the newer directors who favored his plan, but those conversations, unfortunately, only reinforced his own ongoing efforts to persuade the other directors.

With the board unable to resolve its contentious debate, Centrifugal's stock price languished as equity analysts began to question whether the immobilized company could stay ahead of its rivals in a fast-changing and highly competitive industry, especially after the earlier attempt to diversify its product lines had faltered. The board's failure to bridge its own divisions finally convinced directors that they would have to force Scott out. Even his own supporters concluded that this was the only practical way to repair a fractured partnership at the top and to reestablish a compelling central idea.

The directors replaced Scott with the firm's chief financial officer, James Franzen, who had already demonstrated leadership skills beyond the finance function. Franzen took several immediate actions to bolster the firm's share price, including an increase in product prices. Board meetings became less fractious—for the moment, until it became apparent that boosting margins through higher pricing came at the expense of market share and shelf space, and that strategy soon proved unsustainable.

Alarmed at still another strategic initiative gone awry, the new CEO boldly suggested selling the company to a large European competitor, but this plan divided the board as instantly as his predecessor's merger plan had. Two directors backed the idea, but others were skeptical, and the three family-directors adamantly opposed it. A whiff of cynical distrust of the CEO could now be discerned among the opposed directors. Without quite saying so, several board members began to question Franzen's motives, noting that because of his own large equity holdings in the company accumulated over time, he would stand to receive a financial windfall if the sale went through.

Frustrated that the governing board was still splintered, strategic direction unclear, and company performance unsure, the board chair finally asked Franzen to prepare a presentation for the next board meeting that laid out a long-term international strategy for the company, theorizing that directors would find common ground by looking at a more distant horizon.

Instead, the CEO sandbagged the chair's suggestion, refusing to bring a strategic plan to the board at either the next meeting or even several that followed. At wits' end, the board chair finally concluded that the board itself would have to fill the leadership vacuum—one of its own making. As a precondition for doing so, the chair decided that a first priority was to create more unity of thought among its badly divided directors. To do so, he determined, the most immediate step was to resolve the company's ownership question one way or the other, getting it off the table. He decided to bring the matter into sharp focus at the next board meeting by forcing the question.

Once the directors had settled around the boardroom table, the chair brought the matter to an up-or-down vote after brief discussion: Should we sell the company or not? He asked the directors to raise their hands rather than permitting a secret ballot, and a strong majority visibly voted against selling the company.

Privately consulting with several of the directors after the meeting, the chair concluded that for the board to restore its leadership and re-commit to its central idea, the two most dissident directors who had been advocating the company's sale should be forced off the board, since it appeared that their differences with the majority were irrec-oncilable. The chair also concluded that the chief executive did not have the skill set or temperament to forge a strategy that would keep the company independent and healthy. The chair asked the dissident directors to resign, and with his urging, the board forced the CEO to depart as well.

Centrifugal's costly malfunctions offer numerous lessons, many of which we will take up in subsequent chapters: for example, the critical role of the board leader; the need to bring deep-lying conflicts into the sunlight so director differences can be reconciled and the enterprise can move forward; the imperative of clear and direct communication on the part of both the board and the CEO; and the hard-nosed deci-sion to jettison both CEOs and nonperforming directors when no bet-ter alternative presents itself. But at the heart of Centrifugal's dilemma was one inescapable fact: It had no central idea.

Instead of drawing the enterprise together in common purpose, as Mittal's simple and straightforward central idea had done for Airtel, Centrifugal's CEOs lurched wildly about, searching for some way—any way—to restore profitability. Strategy was inconstant, execution impossible, solutions unachievable. Changing chief executives achieved no greater clarity or consensus because ultimately Centrifugal's direc-tors had no road map for moving ahead. The same centrifugal forces that pulled the business apart eventually pulled management and the board apart, and pitted directors against each other as well. Meanwhile, the recurrent and unresolved revisiting of the central idea questions consumed so much time over so many months and distracted the directors and executives so deeply that Centrifugal's downward spiral became a self-fulfilling prophecy.

In Centrifugal's case, the board leader finally recognized the root cause and was able to reconcile director differences and forge a common point of view that paved the way toward a timely board decision on the merger. But pulling out of steep dives is never guaranteed. To get where you want to go, it is far better to know where you are trying to go all along, as seen at Bharti Airtel.

Focusing boardroom time recurrently on the central idea—not just at an annual retreat but reiteratively, time and time again—helps make both directors and executives more comfortable with the idea and the resulting strategy and plans for execution. Conversely, the absence of a central idea is a sure sign that the directors have failed to meet one of the most significant obligations of their leadership of the company.

To ensure that the firm's central idea is clear and compelling, a wise board will author a short but definitive document with clear and persuasive language setting forth the central idea of why the company exists, how the company will compete ethically and win, and linkages between the resulting strategy's components, including specific and sequenced actions that will be taken to execute it consistently. *That* is the core of a central idea, and that is one of the board's premier duties of leadership.

Direct leadership by the board in creating and sustaining a company's central idea serves three complementary functions. First, it reinforces an expanded view of company leadership, seeing it as the exclusive province of neither the executive suite nor the boardroom, but rather a considered relationship between the two. Second, it brings directors irreversibly into leadership of the company. Boards that wrestle with the questions of strategy, succession, execution, and evaluation implicit in a powerful central idea along with the idea itself are unlikely to retreat to the passive posture of old. And third, it creates a logic for recruiting new directors, the focus of the next chapter. Before we delve into that, we offer a checklist of eight questions for directors to pose in partnership with company executives for assessing whether the firm's central idea is sound, a driver of strategy, and capable of execution.

With the central idea in place, the company will also want to ensure that it has the right directors on board. In the chapter that follows, we take up the capacities that directors should seek in their fellow directors if they are to lead and partner with management. Executive experience and strategic requirements are important here, and we will see them instructively evident in companies as diverse as America's Delphi, Brazil's RBS Group, China's Lenovo, and India's Infosys.

DIRECTOR'S CHECKLIST FOR THE CENTRAL IDEA

✓ Is the central idea clear and compelling?

✓ What is distinctive and compelling about the central idea?

✓ How sound is the central idea's value-creating proposition?

✓ What is the company's advantage over each of its primary competitors?

✓ What are the risks, and how will they be mitigated?

✓ Has the chief executive considered all the viable alternatives?

✓ How good is the strategic fit between company and leadership?

✓ Is the central idea tracked and measured?

3.

Recruit Directors Who Build Value

For the new model of a board that leads to work, a new breed of executives and directors—or at the least, an altered mind-set among existing executives and directors—is required. Company executives must be able to actively collaborate with their directors, and they must be ready for directors to exercise leadership in areas that may have been the sole prerogative of management in the past. Directors, in turn, must bring not only a monitoring eye to the boardroom but also real content to the executive suite, and they must appreciate where and when to exercise full leadership, collaborative leadership, or no leadership at all.

Recruiting for Fit

In recruiting directors for a board that can lead with executives, eight questions, in our experience, become mission-critical:

1. Does a prospective director have the capacity to think strategically and clearly about the firm as a whole, the customer value proposition, and its competitive position, and thus contribute to the ongoing evolution of its central idea?

2. Will the candidate be able to contribute tangibly to the board-room discussion without veering into operational detail?

3. Is the board candidate familiar with and experienced in the specific strategic and execution issues stemming from the central idea—and capable of helping to formulate a new direction when market disruptions dictate?

4. Does the would-be director have a proven track record of working collaboratively with executives at other companies in developing business practices stemming from the central idea?

5. Will the prospect add intellectual and experiential diversity to the board, plugging weak spots and adding bench strength for guiding the central idea, strategy, and execution?

6. Will the candidate be ready to stand tall and engage construc-tively when vital issues are on the line, the stakes and stress are high, and leadership of the company becomes even more essential?

7. Will the candidate help the board become more effective? Will the candidate, for instance, be asking the right questions with courtesy and respect and not draining energy by calling up ex-periences that do not relate to the items under discussion? Does the candidate come with conversational intelligence?

8. Finally, does the prospective director add real value not only to the boardroom but also to the executive suite?

To be sure, such vetting represents a greatly increased obligation for a board's governance committee, the entity normally charged with finding and vetting director candidates—a burden far bigger than in days past when a chief executive could slide insiders or others onto the board without much director review at all. To see why this extra effort is so clearly worth it, we turn to four enterprises: one based in India, one in China, one in Brazil, and one in the United States. The

Indian, Chinese, and Brazilian cases show how three fast-growing, emerging-market companies matched their board-member qualities to their market ambitions and central ideas and then forcefully drew on their directors' experience. As for the well-established US company, it completely repopulated its governing body, recruiting directors who brought other company leadership experience, not just shareholder vigilance, to the boardroom, and then it too capitalized on the new directors' expertise.

Expanding India's Infosys

Infosys Technologies, India's premier information technology firm, with more than 150,000 employees in 2012, provides a textbook example of the role of leadership in defining who is brought on to the board. Founded in 1981 by N. R. Narayana Murthy and six engineers and cobbled together on a shoestring budget—start-up capital came to a grand total of $250—Infosys was built on the central idea that it had to be close to its customers and available to them around the clock. From that simple and compelling premise eventually grew a sprawling network of more than sixty offices and an almost equal number of development centers in India, the United States, China, the Middle East, and pretty much everywhere else in the developed world.

To help govern this rapidly growing and highly successful enterprise, Infosys went looking for directors with extensive experience in corporate strategy, consumer goods, life insurance, financial services, economics, and accounting, as well as a balance between its roots in the Indian subcontinent and its new global reach. To its core of six executive non-independent directors—including four of the cofounders—the company by 2010 had added David L. Boyles, a former executive of American Express and Bank of America; Omkar Goswami, the former top economist for the Confederation of Indian Industry; Sridar Iyengar, former chairman and chief executive of KPMG, India; K.V. Kamath, the highly regarded former chairman and CEO of ICICI Bank, India's largest non-state-owned bank; law professor and former Cornell

University president Jeffrey Sean Lehman; Claude Smadja, former director of the World Economic Forum; and M.G. Subrahmanyam, a finance professor at New York University. For lead director, the board picked Deepak Satwalekar, chief executive of HDFC Standard Life Insurance Company.

This is an all-star lineup by any reckoning, but the point is that this team of heavy hitters could pull its weight because the directors were substantively engaged with the enterprise's central idea, strategic plans, talent development, and execution goals. Narayana Murthy reported in an interview for another study by one of us and others that the primary value of his firm's directors to the company was not in shareholder monitoring but in asking questions that "make us rethink our assumptions." That, he said, "makes us look at issues we may have missed and think about alternatives."[1]

At one Infosys board meeting, for instance, the executives and directors debated the synergistic merits of several acquisitions and alliances for the better part of three hours. The board deliberated the strategic issues: What were the downsides to combining different company cultures? Would management have the "bandwidth" to manage a proposed acquisition? If completed, would the two firms be able to cross-sell their services to the other's customers? As characterized by the board chair, a central role of the directors in that and prior board meetings had been to provide substantive guidance on the company's business strategy. In this instance, the two-way dialogue served to crystallize the directors' thinking about the acquisitions and the executive thinking behind them, allowing the board to effectively own the acquisition decisions by the end.

In India, Infosys has been a trendsetter. Traditionally, corporate boards have played a primarily ceremonial or modest role at most in company decisions, with monitoring ideals often playing second fiddle to the more parochial interests of family owners. China had much the same tradition for a different reason. There, enterprises controlled by the state took the place of family-run enterprises. The sustained growth of both economies, however, has forced regulators, shareholders, and companies to reexamine their governance practices for two reasons. First, international investors increasingly moved cash across country lines and as they took greater ownership in publicly traded companies outside their home countries, they also brought home-country biases for independent, informed, and engaged directors. Second, Indian and Chinese executives increasingly moved their operations across national boundaries—witness Infosys and, as we are about to see, China's Lenovo—and as they entered demanding international markets, they also learned that independent, informed, and proactive directors can constitute a source of company advantage. In the end, globalizing their governance as they globalized operations just made good sense.

Integrating China's Lenovo

China's Lenovo offers both a case in point and a sample of the boardroom changes that, we believe, companies worldwide will increasingly pursue in the years ahead. Recruiting a new set of directors to lead a global expansion had become imperative in the wake of Lenovo's game-changing acquisition of IBM's personal computer line, and other companies are likely to face similar necessities in the years ahead.[2]

Founded in 1984, Lenovo had emerged two decades later as China's largest computer maker, with 27 percent of the nation's rapidly expanding computer market and annual revenue exceeding $3 billion. By then, though, sales were beginning to flag, in large part because of strong domestic inroads by American competitors Hewlett-Packard and Dell. Company executives concluded that long-term growth depended on Lenovo becoming an international player, just as many American and European companies had concluded in years past. "In our world," explained executive chairman Yang Yuanqing, "a high growth rate is hard to sustain if you only try to maintain your position in the China market."[3]

Coincidentally at nearly the same time, IBM approached Lenovo about the possibility of acquiring IBM's personal computer division, and Lenovo's management swiftly embraced the offer, even though

IBM's operation drew four times the revenue of Lenovo. To be sure, IBM had been losing money on its PC sales, but Lenovo's due diligence convinced executives that it could turn the much larger IBM operation around. "We finally came to believe that in IBM's hands, the PC division would continue to suffer annual losses," reported Liu Chuanzhi, then executive chairman of Lenovo, but he felt that in his own hands the IBM operation "could be profitable." That conclusion was partly based on an analysis of the overhead that the IBM parent allocated to its PC division—the division would have been profitable were it not for its high headquarters costs. And it could have been even more profitable had it adopted Lenovo's lean manufacturing methods. Assembling a PC in the United States at the time cost $24, compared with $4 in China.[4]

On December 7, 2004, at a Beijing news conference attended by some five hundred Chinese and Western journalists, Lenovo announced that it was acquiring IBM's Personal Computing division for $1.75 billion. It wrapped up the acquisition in April 2005, and Liu almost immediately began an aggressive retooling of the directors' monitoring and leadership roles. In 2003, non-independent directors outnumbered the independent directors four to three. The post-acquisition board, by contrast, was divided between five executive and non-independent directors, three private equity directors, and three independent directors. Prior to the acquisition, all seven of the directors were Chinese or of greater China origin. After the acquisition, four of the eleven directors were Americans.

Before the acquisition, board meetings had always been conducted in Chinese; after the acquisition, because all but one director spoke English and several spoke no Chinese, English became the medium of expression. Going into the acquisition, the executive chairman and chief executive were both Chinese; coming out of the acquisition, the executive chairman was Chinese and the CEO American. Of the top management team in 2004, all were Chinese; of the eighteen members of the top management team in 2007, six were from greater China, one from Europe, and eleven from the United States. Ma Xuezheng, the company's CFO at the acquisition moment, declared at the time,

"This is going to be very much an international company operated in an international fashion."[5]

A large part of that new determination involved forging an active partnership between the board and top management. "The IBM PC acquisition is a watershed," observed Liu. "Before that point," he said, "the board of directors did not play much of a role." The board had mainly been concerned with company audit and executive pay. Independent non-executive directors prior to the IBM acquisition were viewed by the company as largely present to protect minority stockholders—in this case, investors other than the Chinese Academy of Sciences. Liu and Yang reconstituted the board to go well beyond that limited focus, adding the international directors, improving board capacity to render guidance to the executive team, and more generally, creating a governing body that is more globally informed, independent, and proactive— important prerequisites for leading on top of monitoring.

The decision to add international directors was largely driven by the reported need for the board to bring global "vision" into the boardroom. "Now," said Yang, "internationalization is our key consideration as we are taking on international business." This required directors who would bring fresh insight into how Lenovo could make inroads into the worldwide market share of its larger rivals—Dell Computer at 18 percent and Hewlett-Packard at 16 percent in 2005—and at the same time hold onto the home market share against its smaller rivals, including Acer at 5 percent and Fujitsu at 4 percent in 2005.[6]

The restructuring of the Lenovo board following the IBM purchase also brought the directors into guiding the integration of two distinct operating styles. IBM had built up strong, enduring relations with its select corporate customers; Lenovo, by contrast, had created a mainly "transactional" exchange with its many retail customers. Although large enterprise relations had been the staple of IBM's PC sales, management anticipated greater growth among small consumers. But identifying the optimal areas for growth outside of China and identifying effective ways of reaching them were uncertain and risky judgment calls, encouraging management to seek director guidance.

To facilitate the board's collaborative leadership, the company formed a strategy committee, charged with vetting mid- and long-term decisions on behalf of the board. As a step toward internationalization, the company placed two Chinese directors—Yang Yuanqing and Liu Chuanzhi—on the strategy committee along with two Americans—private equity investors James Coulter and William O. Grabe. The board met quarterly, but the strategy committee met monthly to focus on issues ranging from competitive strategy to cultural integration.

Lenovo's board also became directly engaged in decisions on executive succession, an arena that had not previously been its prerogative. At the time of the purchase, the IBM executive responsible for the PC division, Stephen Ward Jr., had been the logical candidate for the role of chief executive, with Yang to serve as executive chairman. Their dual appointment was largely an executive decision, but within months it became evident to the board's strategy committee that the former IBM executive was not the right person to lead the combined enterprise, given the specific challenges it faced, starting with the need for greater supply-chain efficiencies.

Yang and Liu worried, however, that the unexpected exit of the top American executive so soon after the acquisition could cast a shadow over their effort to internationalize the firm. Neither knew the international computer industry well enough to identify a strong replacement. Thus, it fell to American non-executive directors Coulter and Grabe to identify several candidates for succession, including William Amelio, then head of Dell Computer's Asian operations, who eventually became the successor. Nor were Yang and Liu familiar with the process of replacing an American chief executive, but the private equity directors on the Lenovo board represented firms that had often done so. Through the strategy committee, the board had early detected the need for change at the top and acted quickly on it.

Soon, a host of other major issues was laid before the directors for vetting and decision making: among them, how long to retain the IBM logo; what acquisitions to make; which adjacencies, such as servers, to consider; and whether to build devices that bridge laptops and telephones. Lenovo subsequently considered acquiring personal computer makers Packard Bell, for instance, and the directors took an active role in deciding on whether to proceed and what to pay. "Everybody was involved," reported non-executive director Shan Weijian, "because this is a large issue for the entire company." Lenovo decided to back off—another PC maker, Gateway, was later acquired by Taiwan's Acer—and the board's deliberations proved critical in reaching that decision.

None of this happened of its own accord. Informed directors who trust one another and have faith in their executives constitute an essential platform for board leadership, and Lenovo worked to build it. The directors and executives adopted a rule, for instance, that all directors must attend all board meetings, which were rotated around the world, or send a predesignated alternate. Liu Chuanzhi frequently flew to the United States to meet with the American directors, especially when the board faced contentious issues. The reward, however, has been crystal clear: directors played a company leadership role in the wake of the IBM acquisition by quickly replacing the chief executive, deciding against an acquisition, and facilitating cross-cultural integration of widely different entities. Eight years after the IBM PC acquisition and remake of its board to better lead the company, Lenovo's global market share of PC sales had become second only to Hewlett-Packard's, having edged out Dell and dozens of other makers.[7]

Preparing Brazil's Grupo RBS

In many parts of the world where economic growth is newly energized, founding families work to retain control of their firms even as they grow large. Yet in doing so, some have also worked to construct a vibrant board that goes beyond the family to help ensure the firm's continued growth. This can be seen at Grupo RBS, one of Brazil's premier multimedia companies. Founded in 1957, it employs more than

six thousand and provides content and services through a host of television stations, radio networks, newspapers, internet portals, and even
management education.[8]

Maurício Sirotsky had forged a partnership with Rádio Gaúcha
in southeastern Brazil's Porto Alegre to create the company in 1957.
Brother Jayme Sirotsky joined the enterprise five years later, and the
two brothers together rapidly expanded into the nascent television industry and later into newspapers. In the wake of Maurício Sirotsky's
unexpected passing in 1986, Jayme Sirotsky and their other siblings
created two holding companies to govern Grupo RBS and ensure its
continued growth as a professionally managed but family-controlled
enterprise. They formed a board of directors in 1991 and initially filled
the room with consultants and lawyers close to the family. Jayme Sirotsky became chairman of the board and Nelson Sirotsky, son of the
founder, became chief executive of the group.

As the company's challenges evolved over the years, the board sought
directors who had expertise in corporate finance and risk management.
But a seismic event in 2008 forced a far greater change in the board's
composition. Gávea Investimentos, a private equity fund led by Ar-
minio Fraga, former president of the Central Bank of Brazil, acquired a
minority but significant stake in RBS. A representative of Gávea joined
the board, and the board in turn expanded its scope to include active
oversight of support for the management team. CEO Nelson Sirotsky
became chairman of the board, but he was also committed to a separation of board and management and had begun to plan his own exit
from the CEO role.

When RBS chief operating officer Pedro Parente, who had served
as chief of staff for Brazilian president Fernando Henrique Cardoso and
who had been seen as the logical successor, unexpectedly resigned for
personal reasons, the board chair led a search that ended in the anticipated appointment in 2008 of Eduardo Sirotsky Melzer. His pedigree
was impeccable: he was a grandson of the founder and the board chair's
nephew. And he had come with extensive prior experience in digital
media, mergers, and acquisitions; he had an MBA degree from Har-

vard Business School; and his performance after joining RBS had been strong. He was not yet ready for the corner office, but Nelson mapped out a three-year developmental path for Eduardo, including Nelson's personal coaching of the heir apparent. In July 2012, Eduardo took over the CEO reins.

In the meantime, directors and executives were already concerned about a rapidly evolving and technology-disrupting media market. Since its inception, Grupo RBS had focused on traditional media, but growth opportunities were coming in adjacent areas, such as digital platforms and management education, and traditional vehicles were being upended by Google and other internet powerhouses. RBS established an investment company in 2011 to lead its diversification through the acquisition of small and medium businesses, but the chair also concluded that he needed a different set of directors to serve as source of wisdom to help the company navigate the rough waters.

The board reconstituted itself not only to monitor the business but also to work with the executive team. To that end it retained founding-family members Jayme Sirotsky, Marcelo Sirotsky, Pedro Sirotsky, Carlos Meltzer, and Nelson Sirotsky as chair; and the representative of Gávea continued. But it also expanded to include new directors who brought five areas of expertise seen as key to the company's growth decisions:

Entrepreneurship: Regis Dubrule, founder of a furniture and accessories company acquired by private equity firm Carlyle Group

Finance: Israel Vainboim, former CEO of Brazil's Unibanco

General management: Claudio Sonder, CEO or director of several Brazilian and multinational companies, including Hoechst

Human resources: Betania Tanure, a prominent academic expert on people management

Technology and digital business: Nelson Mattos, Google's vice president for products in Europe

In addition to their specific areas of expertise, the new directors as a group brought experience with a variety of business sectors, international companies, and market disruptions. Google's Nelson Mattos, for example, had had extensive research and development experience in Europe with Google, and before that with IBM, where he served as worldwide vice president for information and user technologies. To optimize use of the directors' expertise, the board created committees focused on talent, finance, and risk, each led by one of the new directors with expertise in the area. While management remained accountable for daily operations and developing company strategy, the board took responsibility for setting management guidelines and long-term strategy. The board retained its focus on financial discipline and shareholder value, but now it added a working focus on company values, competitive strategy, capital allocation, executive coaching, management succession, and executive performance. The board, in short, came to lead the company along with the top management team.

Reimagining America's Delphi

Supplying major automakers worldwide is a grueling business with demanding buyers, thin margins, tough competitors, and cyclical markets. Visteon, a parts supplier spun off from Ford Motor Company in 2000, had plunged into bankruptcy in 2009. Delphi Automotive, a parts supplier separated from General Motors Corporation in 1999, had suffered the same fate in 2005. Executives of auto-parts manufacturers could use all the help they could muster for navigating a very hazardous landscape, and Delphi executives found it in a governing board newly constituted to lead the firm after its emergence from bankruptcy in 2009.[9]

During Delphi's radical remake from 2005 to 2009, spearheaded by turnaround CEO Robert S. Miller and then successor CEO Rodney O'Neal, the company slashed costs, shed obligations, and tightened supply chains. It also diversified its customer base globally (more than two-thirds of its sales had been to General Motors, but now less than a quarter), focused on growth areas such as safety, green technologies, and new electronics (e.g., the internet), consolidated business units (from 27 to 10), cut manufacturing floor space (by 60 percent), and trimmed product lines (from 119 to 33), reducing its employee rolls from 185,000 to 100,000.

Delphi recruited an entirely new board of directors in 2009, and in populating the boardroom it drew on much the same leadership criteria that we have already seen at Infosys, Lenovo, and RBS Group. It first recruited former DuPont CEO John A. Krol as board chair, and then with his guidance and that of debt holders General Motors and several hedge funds, Delphi methodically recruited a new breed of directors with the background and experience not only to avert relapse but also to rekindle growth.[10]

When the new board met for the first time in November 2009, it included four directors who had served as chief executives of other major companies. What better directors to lead and work in collaboration with the executive team to rebuild the company than those who themselves had experienced the tribulations of being a CEO and had also worked with several boards?

Over the next three months, the board wrote a charter on how to operate and the values to stress—in essence, Delphi's central idea— formed its key committees, reviewed and approved the company's annual business plan, created a fresh compensation package, and appraised the management team, retaining all except the chief financial officer. With the new board organized and executive team reorganized, the board turned in 2010 to harvesting the directors' own extensive know-how by instituting an intense process for learning about the auto-parts business and Delphi itself.

Working with the executive team, directors drilled down methodically, typically in teams of two or three with a designated leader, periodically reporting back to the full board. One team led by Lawrence A. Zimmerman, former chief financial officer of Xerox, focused on the company's internal controls and financial risks. Another team led by Mark P. Frissora, CEO of Hertz Global Holdings and formerly CEO of

Tenneco (itself an auto components maker), concentrated on making the firm's reporting systems more concise and focused so that directors and executives could readily track progress on their financial and operational goals.

A third team led by Rajiv L. Gupta, former CEO of chemical maker Rohm and Haas, included members of the firm's compensation committee. Its assignment was to develop a one-page map for capturing the company's competitive strategies, operational objectives, financial goals, and basic values, including safety, environment, and integrity. The purpose was to consolidate the commitments by each of the senior executives, allowing the board to review their performance in a single source.

Another team, led by J. Randall MacDonald, who served as senior vice president for human resources at IBM, worked to strengthen the company's evaluation of talent, development of high-potential managers, and movement of executives into new assignments. Still another group, led by Nicholas M. Donofrio, who had served as executive vice president for innovation and technology at IBM, focused on Delphi's technical innovation to ensure that Delphi maintained technological leadership over the coming decade. One more team, led by chairman John A. Krol and including members of the governance committee, focused on tightening the firm's compliance systems and ensuring that it was followed in plants around the world. (The company had been accused of improper accounting practices as it hurtled toward bankruptcy in 2005.)

With the firm's internal architecture restructured, the board turned to restructuring its outside ownership. In preparing to reenter the public equity market in 2011, three directors—Mark Frissora; Sean O. Mahoney, who had served as a partner at Goldman Sachs and on the post-bankruptcy board of Lehman Brothers; and Michael McNamara, who was CEO of Flextronics—worked with the executive team on the complex path for an initial public offering. But before reentering the public-equity market, John Krol and new CFO Kevin P. Clark shouldered the equally complex task of simplifying its equity holdings: General Motors owned about 35 percent, and several hedge funds—including Paulson & Co.—held the remaining 65 percent. Seeking a clean slate before the IPO, Delphi bought out the GM stake for $4 billion and reacquired the hedge funds' governance rights. It also bought out a $600 million stake held by the Pension Benefit Guaranty Corporation.

Through all this, Delphi's directors at times took the lead, and at other times partnered with the executive team. When the board replaced the chief financial officer, directors drove the search, identifying, interviewing, and recruiting the successor. After deciding that more specificity was needed in the strategic and operational goals of CEO Rodney O'Neal and his lieutenants, directors crafted a process for this. When the board became focused on succession planning, directors delved into the management ranks to identify and elevate potential CEO candidates. Feeling that a culture of integrity and compliance required articulation at every opportunity, directors asked executives to beef up training globally and to talk ethics along with safety at the start of every employee gathering. And when the board became concerned that potential risks to the company had not been fully identified, directors turned executive attention to enterprise risk management.

Similarly, when the board concluded that the company needed to be on the cutting edge of very rapid technological change, directors established a new position of chief technology officer and added a board committee on innovation and technology, chaired by Nicholas Donofrio and including three directors who came with extensive auto manufacturing executive experience: Gary L. Cowger, former group vice president of global manufacturing and labor relations for General Motors; Thomas W. Sidlik, former CEO of Chrysler Financial Corporation; and Bernd Wiedemann, former CEO of Volkswagen Commercial Vehicles and Truck Division. In a host of other areas, too, the board worked collaboratively with management to effect a range of improvements.

As Delphi was coming out of bankruptcy, the hedge funds representatives on the board were outspokenly out of sync with other directors in how they judged the chief executive. They saw the CEO as a strong operating executive who could deliver great results but was not quite ready for prime time with Wall Street investors and analysts. Other directors took it upon themselves to coach CEO O'Neal on strategy presentations and investor relations. Later, the directors invested time in helping O'Neal and his team build a talent-development and coaching program with regular feedback on individual performance, and a structure to ensure that future CEO candidates would become directly visible to the board.

The fruits of the directors' leadership and that of the CEO and his team had become evident by late 2012, when Delphi's annual revenue had risen from $9 to $16 billion. Just three years out of bankruptcy, its financial metrics came to rank in the upper quartile of the industry. Delphi's price of $22 per share at the initial offering in 2011 had increased by more than $15 less than two years later.

India's Infosys, China's Lenovo, Brazil's RBS, and America's Delphi all bear witness to the value of finding and holding on to directors who can exercise leadership at the top. All four companies recruited directors who were comfortable with the central idea, worked well with company executives, brought vital content to the boardroom, and were ready to lead both directly and collaboratively. In all four instances, the benefit of engaged and active directors became evident in the bottom line.

This chapter shows how mission-critical it is to get the right directors on board. In the following chapter, we examine the flip side: how to deal with less effective or even dysfunctional directors who may already be on the board. What can the board do to make faltering directors more effective or to rein in disruptive outliers?

DIRECTOR'S CHECKLIST FOR RECRUITING DIRECTORS

✓ Does a prospective director have the capacity to think strategically about the firm's competitive position and thus contribute to the ongoing evolution of its central idea?

✓ Is the board candidate familiar with and experienced in the specific strategic and execution issues derived from the central idea?

✓ Does the would-be director have a proven record of working collaboratively with executives at other companies in developing and implementing business practices stemming from the central idea?

✓ Will the prospect add intellectual and experiential diversity to the board, plugging weak spots and adding bench strength for guiding the central idea, strategy, and execution?

✓ Will the candidate be ready to stand tall when vital issues are on the line, the stakes and stress are high, and direct leadership of the company becomes essential?

✓ Does the prospective director generally add real value not only to the boardroom but also to the executive suite?

4.

Root Out Dysfunction

Almost all directors look promising before they enter the boardroom, but not all perform equally well once inside. Sometimes a prince in other realms can even turn into a petty gabber at the table, the very opposite of what English novelist George Eliot had championed: "Blessed is the man who having nothing to say abstains from giving wordy evidence of the fact."

Consider the case of director Frank Whyte (as we'll call him): "You show a 3 percent increase in productivity," Whyte snapped at the executive vice president of the largest division of a very successful consumer-goods company and likely CEO successor. The executive was in the middle of a routine presentation to the board. "You're sandbagging," barked the director. "You ought to have at least 6 percent."

The chief executive and the rest of the board rolled their eyes, but no one intervened to rescue the highly regarded but now hapless executive. Their mad-dog colleague was off on one of his rants. Not surprisingly, executives at the company hated making presentations at board meetings. Whyte kept them on the defensive by peppering them with personal opinions and demanding lofty goals that could not be met.

He never listened, executives complained. He never asked questions or made constructive suggestions. He just declared in an intimidating tone, implying he knew others were wrong, whatever their clarification or explanation. And he always delved into minutia.

Whyte considered himself an expert on productivity management, but his condescending attitude and disproportionate use of airtime made the entire board unproductive. He sapped energy from other directors and executives who entered the room. Worse, he detracted from critical problems that the board should have drilled into and resolved. He was a dysfunctional director.

Let us be clear. We are not critical of directors who disagree with management strategy or voice alternative directions. We are not even talking about hostile directors sometimes forced onto the board by a hedge fund trying to take control of a company or about partisan factions that have formed for whatever reason. Dysfunctional directors have their own modus operandi. Some see themselves as the smartest person in the room, others seek recognition, and still others are frustrated would-be CEOs. Whatever their personal motives, they tend to micromanage or take boardroom discussions down dark alleys. We have seen a director interrupt the first five minutes of a CEO's boardroom presentation and sour the mood of both board and management for the remainder of the day. The result is to impair, even negate, a board's capacity to lead the firm. As in any group, a dysfunctional member can sabotage the entire team.

In our experience, as many as half of *Fortune* 500 companies have one or two dysfunctional directors. Not infrequently, an intimidated management ends up kowtowing, fine-tuning its presentations in the boardroom to anticipate the difficult director's reactions or consulting with the director in time-consuming ways accorded to no others. It becomes a drain for everyone involved—except the dysfunctional director.

If such directors were recruited too quickly, however, many boards still respond too slowly. One would think that a board chair or lead director would be quick to call out a dysfunctional director for disruptive behavior. In fact, though, that rarely happens, largely because of the traditional decorum of the boardroom. Collegiality and comity still prevail; board members are still reluctant to criticize a fellow director. Directors focus on reasons to be respectful of one another, few want to be known as a director who told others to rein themselves in, and fewer still feel strong enough to openly call a troublesome director to account. Boards often find it easier to fire a CEO, itself a hugely daunting task, than to remove a director.

Yet it does happen. In one instance, when the chief operating officer of a major company was making a presentation to the board, Charles Smith, a recently elected director trying to make his mark, kept interrupting the presentation with minor questions and a caustic tone. Finally, after unsuccessfully suggesting that Smith defer his issues to a later executive session, the lead director acerbically inquired, "Charlie, do you want the job?" So ended the disruptive interventions, and the directors and executives got on with the board's business. Such interventions are rare but also indicative of what a lead director with spine can do to bring the mood of a board discussion back to the right level.

Conversational intelligence—an ability to read the moment and to contribute agenda-advancing comments—can be vital here. Its occasional absence underscores its essential presence. In the case of one large manufacturing firm, for instance, a new chief executive joined the board for his first meeting. One conversationally unintelligent director dropped an overtly disrespectful comment not long into the meeting, as was his habit, questioning the CEO's authority. The new CEO respectfully but firmly pushed back, isolating the director's clumsy interruption and averting the derailment of an otherwise productive dialogue—an act of courage for which the majority of directors later expressed their appreciation. Other unintelligent behaviors include a domineering style or a boardroom ethos that suppresses dissent or diversity. Whatever the source, most dysfunctional factors are subject to redirection by the board leader's intervention. Overt standards can help here. "We are putting together a short list of board values," offered the chair of Lloyds Banking Group, Sir Win Bischoff, and "they will be largely behavioral."[1]

A director's blocking behavior can be subtle. The chief executives of two *Fortune* 500 companies, for example, privately complained that their board's governance committee was dominated by subpar directors who tended to recruit others like themselves to the board. Though articulate and expert, they had no real experience in running a large enterprise, and worse, they were drawn to board candidates who also did not bring much heft to the company's leadership.

Dealing with Disrupters

The most complete solution for dealing with unresponsive directors is to remove them from the board, but such a course of action is not readily undertaken. For the same reason directors avoid correcting a director's behavior during board meetings, they can be even more reluctant to push out a dysfunctional member. Sometimes it is done, but always with distress, or worse.

A US company at the top in its industry, for instance, had a foreign director who had been the chief executive of a similar company overseas. He spent years as a board net-energy drainer, pontificating on issues in ways that other directors found pretentious or irrelevant, before a newly elected lead director took the initiative to force him out. The shocked director wept when he was voted off the board, and he fired off an indignant letter to his fellow directors, accusing them of underappreciating the unique value of his European network and business knowledge. He was out, though not without much hand-wringing all around.

Whatever the particulars, a mission-critical team is only as strong as its weakest link. If directors are to effectively exercise their leadership of the company, boards must work to create a dysfunction-free zone.

Evaluate the Directors

Dealing with a director who requires remedial assistance or should be encouraged to depart is, in the words of James E. Nevels, founder and chairman of The Swarthmore Group and a former chairman of several boards, "a gentle art form" and a board leader's obligation. "I firmly believe it is one of the primary functions of the chair to assist the CEO, so the CEO can discharge the principal responsibilities people have agreed upon," he explained. "When the dynamic between a director and management is not going well, it is incumbent on the chair to confirm with other board members that the person is disruptive and enlist their understanding and aid. That consensus gives the chairman the moral suasion and explicit authority to remedy the situation."

The remedy, as Nevels prescribed it, comes in three stages: First, a board leader's private conversation with a disruptive director, starting with the director's strong points, opens an opportunity to reference weak areas requiring improvements. Asking the director how he or she sees the role of a director can identify areas in which the director may not even appreciate that the behavior requires change. A next step is intervention, coaching included, a second stage that Nevels has seen work with directors who were simply unaware of their disruptive behavior. But if that effort fails, a third stage calls for the board leader to simply say, "I'm sorry," since real improvement has not occurred, "it may be time for you to opt out."

"People get on boards because they have exceptional qualities," Nevels said, "so opting out should happen in a dignified way." And if it comes to that, a board is wise to have an able replacement already in the wings.

Rather than resorting to an ouster, we believe that boards would benefit by installing a corrective process that regularly and meaningfully evaluates the contributions of directors. Such a process can assist the lead director and chair of the governance committee in providing feedback to each director privately—to avoid the onset of dysfunction or to correct it—while at the same time reinforcing the behavioral norms of the well-functioning directors.

According to data gathered by The Conference Board, whole-board evaluation has already become a standard among American companies. In 2000, directors at only one in four companies evaluated their own board's performance. A decade later, such appraisals were conducted annually at more than 90 percent of companies. The even more valuable evaluation of individual directors is still to catch hold on a widespread basis, but the practice is gaining traction. The portion of companies that asked directors to appraise each of their fellow directors rose from 11 percent in 2000 to between 34 and 38 percent in 2011.[2] Though board and human-capital audits are on the upswing, the trend should not be overinterpreted. Efforts to improve poor director performance or remove dysfunctional directors have remained, in our experience, tepid at most.

Two veterans of board evaluations, Davis Polk law firm partners David L. Caplan and William M. Kelly, confirm from their work with both well-established enterprises and Silicon Valley start-ups that, while the precise contours of the evaluation process vary from firm to firm, virtually all boards have come to embrace some form of annual evaluation. Among the more actionable questions in such evaluations: "Do we have the right set of talents around the boardroom table, and if not, what talents are still missing?" and "If you had a blank sheet, how would you want the board to spend its time?" They find that directors are generally comfortable identifying areas where additional expertise would be valuable and where board protocols should be strengthened. One of the more common director urgings: the board should devote more time to grappling with strategy issues and less time listening to formal reports.

Even better, in our view, is an annual cycle for each director to meet privately with the lead director or governance committee chair to confidentially offer an appraisal of the board or even individual directors. As noted, some boards still balk at individual appraisals, principally on the premise that they could undermine collegiality, but the right process can help make everyone more comfortable. For example, a matrix with performance criteria down the left side and director names across the top allows board members to assess the value of each director, akin to peer evaluations in 360-feedback exercises.

Actionable questions here include whether each of the other directors: (1) brings useful skills and experiences to the boardroom, (2) comes prepared to board meetings, (3) understands the central idea and the company strategy, (4) poses useful questions, (5) helps with business development, (6) moves discussions forward, and 7) facilitates relationships within the board and between directors and executives. A bad grade on several such criteria can be enough to alert a board leader that intervention may be in order. By way of example, we have included in appendix B one such evaluation used in 2012 by the board of a publicly traded US technology firm.

One pragmatic way to overcome resistance to feedback on individual director performance is to invite a trusted third party—for example, outside counsel, governance consultant, or external auditor—to privately ask each director about the behavior of the boardroom peers. From our own familiarity, we know that it can be particularly useful for the third party to ask not only what one or two steps other directors could take to strengthen their monitoring and leadership roles in the boardroom but also what one or two actions they should *stop* taking.

We have found, as have the Davis Polk partners, that executives welcome board self-appraisals to the extent they can be tangibly used to strengthen the board's leadership. And for the same reason, executives also welcome actionable feedback to improve their own engagement with the directors and board committees. Regardless of the specifics, Caplan and Kelly advise their clients to be sensitive to the legal risks involved in potentially creating a record that could later be used against the board by disgruntled directors or investors.

Director evaluation is not an evaluation in the traditional sense. It is a matter of gathering information from directors and executives on how an individual director can best contribute to the effectiveness of the board and, through the board, the effectiveness of management. The clearer the information, the more it is given in the spirit of improvement, and the earlier it is delivered, the better.

Sometimes boards equate director performance with the amount of airtime a director takes—rather than their real value to the company's leadership. The directors who recruited Alan Mulally as Ford CEO made a real contribution to the enterprise, for instance, whatever their share of boardroom discussion. Or consider the director who said little

over the course of a year but then raised three show-stopping objec-
tions to a proposed acquisition—resulting in the proposal's withdrawal.
Many evaluations of directors are still focused on inputs like attending
meetings and coming prepared. Better that they focus on the director's
outputs, whether helping to recruit the right chief executive or stop-
ping an ill-fated acquisition.

Some boards resist evaluations because of the word itself. Or they
are concerned about the confidentiality of their appraisals. But in our
experience, most directors take feedback well from their peers when it
is specific and constructive.

Facilitating that two-way flow is yet another challenging task for
the lead director, one that must be prudently taken up, since mutual
criticism within a team of equals—each accomplished in his or her
own right—can seem unfitting. To that end, consider the path of the
board chair of a $15 billion manufacturer. In his experience, direc-
tors take pride in the quality of their board—"every director wants
to be on a great board"—but he also appreciates that they would be
uncomfortable if building a great board entailed singling them each to
improve their individual performance on it. To avoid going down that
rabbit hole, the chair opted to personally ask each director—nothing
to be written—to name the two or three directors who already did an
outstanding job on the board, as well as to identify any directors who
could do a much better job. The board leader was then able to em-
ploy offline follow-ups with individual directors to suggest where each
could become a stronger performer.

Most directors will take feedback to heart, but for the few who do
not, the lead director—with the backing of the governance committee—may want to suggest they remain on the board until the next
annual meeting. At one financial services company, to better pinpoint
those who might best be rotated off the board, the lead director asked
each director annually who among the fellow directors were "keepers"—or not. In effect, the lead director was asking the board to hit
a yearly refresh button, singling out the one or two directors whose
contributions others saw as falling below the line. He then asked

those who came up short to remove their name from the next proxy ballot.

To be sure, it does not have to end that way. One chief executive, with whose board one of us was personally conversant, spoke privately to a dysfunctional director about his behavior at board meetings. The CEO pointed out that the director too often referenced what his own company had done instead of asking what this company should do. The CEO subpar director noticeably changed his ways, and the CEO later reported that he became one of the best on the board. Two years later, other directors even told him to be ready to become the next lead director. What is key is for the evaluative process to be in place *well before* a director's dysfunctional behavior begins to poison the room, and we have seen this work at several companies.

A special case is that of dissident directors invited onto the board in response to investor demands or elected to the board through a proxy fight. They are in the boardroom to redirect the company, and while restructuring may be very much in order, they can still serve as a disruptive or even counterproductive presence if their dissident voices are not managed well by the lead director. In the case of one $4 billion company, for instance, the directors decided to add a 5 percent owner to the board on the premise that you hug your friends but "hug your enemies even closer." In the candid appraisal of one director, however, though "we hugged him," he became "a royal distraction in the boardroom" with a self-serving agenda focused on just "maximizing short-term results so he can exit with a profit." Ensuring that a board can exercise its company leadership even if deeply riven by dissidence depends much on its board leader's conflict management skills—and an iron constitution.

Upward Evaluations of Directors

A handful of companies have taken evaluations a logical step further, asking their executives to assess the work of each of the board members. The consistency of the executive appraisals of their directors was, in our experience, quite striking. We typically find that most executives are already in quiet agreement that one or two directors are draining energy from both the boardroom and management. On the affirmative side, directors usually welcome upward feedback, in our observations, since they appreciate that they must exercise their leadership through management and that ability will be badly impaired if executives do not follow or are disrespectful of them.

By way of example, look at the process that the chief executive of a $5 billion-plus manufacturing firm instituted for executive feedback on his directors' performance. He first informed the board that he planned to initiate an annual review of the directors by his executive team. Perceiving no overt resistance, he then retained a third party to confidentially interview him and his direct reports, including business heads and the general counsel, chief financial officer, chief human resource officer, and strategy director.

Working under the guidance of the CEO and the chair of the governance committee, the outside consultant asked each of the executives to appraise the board's several committees, focusing on what worked and what could work better, and the relative contributions of each of the directors to their committees and full board. The outside consultant compiled responses so that no individual executive could be identified as a specific source.

The first time through the process, the CEO reported, much "heartburn" was evident in the boardroom, since directors had never before had their service appraised from below. By contrast, the CEO's direct reports were energized by a procedure that not only sought their own views of the board's behavior but also could result in tangible enhancements in the board's work with them. Executives reported, for instance, that a recently formed special committee of the board was proving unproductive and even burdensome to them. This came at a time when the chair of the committee, a long-serving director, had actually been intent on increasing its purview. Not surprisingly, he took umbrage at the executives' suggestion that the committee be eliminated altogether.

For such upward feedback to have real impact, the chief executive found, it was essential that the board leader and the CEO carefully explain the reasons for the upward evaluation and secure the directors' buy-in ahead of time. Otherwise, he warned, it could feel to some directors like a "witch hunt." The greater the two-way information flow and willingness to act on it, the more effective the directors' leadership.

Identifying the Keepers

Honing strategies for evaluating directors—and exiting directors when necessary—becomes especially important when mergers force boards to make hard choices about which directors to keep and which to drop so that the board itself will not become an unwieldy roster. Consolidating a boardroom can be especially vexing, since few directors readily exit on their own accord.

Consider the case of one *Fortune* 50 company. Among America's premier technology and service firms, the company had built its market dominance through a half dozen mergers and acquisitions. In the wake of one of its largest mergers, the board temporarily numbered more than two dozen directors, a powerhouse of experience but also a bloated entity, and one that the lead director and chief executive concluded would have to be cut in half. Rather than imposing their own judgment or that of the governance committee on which directors to retain or let go, the lead director and CEO asked the combined directors to identify who among their colleagues should remain on the fused board, taking into account not only the experience of each director but also the collective composition of the survivors.

The lead director and chief executive confidentially polled each director (who was not allowed to self-nominate) on this question—and also asked with which directors they would be most uncomfortable should those directors be retained on the consolidated board. The lead director and CEO found that the post-merger directors consistently singled out about a dozen keepers. Though one might fear that this could reduce the board's demographic diversity, with an old-boy network insidiously favoring its own, the retained directors came to constitute one of the more diverse boards in the *Fortune* 500.

The mergers gave the lead director and chief executive an excuse to click the board's reset button and helped legitimate regular reappraisals of which directors to retain. As a result, the board came to annually assess the performance of each of its members, asking who among them were contributing the most to the firm's central idea and business strategy. The board even invited the CEO to add his own evaluation of what the directors were bringing to the boardroom and where they fell short. The chief executive candidly informed the directors, for instance, that they were sometimes distracted or even misdirected in board meetings. Over time, in the metaphor of the CEO, the retained directors came to function as the firm's "fifth infielder," preventing "grounders" from bouncing into the outfield.

The Right Line for Engagement

Appreciating the line between leading and overreaching is an acquired understanding. Most boards create an implicit norm, evident to virtually all—except the oblivious transgressor—when it is breached. Personal motives are often at the heart of such overstepping, even if the act is more self-defeating than self-enhancing.

One of the more commonly witnessed drivers of such transgressions is a director's determination to prove that he or she is as knowledgeable as anyone about the business. The director might assume that delving into company operations demonstrates a deep grasp of detail—how product pricing should rise in China, when drilling platforms should be retired in the Gulf—that matches management's and even exceeds fellow directors' and shows the director to be one of the smartest in the room, or at least the one who has best mastered the homework.

Sometimes, too, directors will dive into detail to demonstrate that they can make a special contribution in one area when their lack of broad-based executive experience gives them too little to contribute otherwise. These are often individuals who have been invited onto a board because of special expertise, perhaps with government, science, or technology. In the experience of a chief executive of a biotechnology firm who has witnessed this in several boardrooms, specialist directors sometimes "gravitate toward topics where they are comfortable, but they quickly get down to a low altitude," ending up "three or four clicks" too deep. In one case, for instance, the chief executive had raised the issue of sustainability with the board. A director who happened to be exceptionally passionate and informed about the issue suddenly began pressing issues that were in specifics even below the operating levels of the company's vice presidents, let alone those of the chief executive or senior vice presidents.

A third animating force is occasionally evident in board chairs who had earlier served as company chief executive. They know too much, it seems, to remain silent when discussions veer into operational detail. "They don't leave their [former] CEO role at the boardroom door," warned the chief executive of a large health-services firm who had served in several boardrooms. On one of those boards, for example, a former CEO who had transitioned to non-executive chair never gave up his CEO persona and was consequently "never able to back off." Mindful of his unhappy boardroom experience at other companies, the active CEO insisted on making the boundary between chair and CEO clearer at his own firm. "It's very important to define where the line is," he said.

Still, the chief executive carries an associated responsibility to keep operational details out of the boardroom, according to many boardroom veterans. When directors pose questions that would seem to imply they are missing their operating days, a polite but firm hand by the chief executive can help: "If we need to go further into this," the biotechnology chief executive would tell his directors, "we need to schedule another time" outside the board meeting. This can become particularly important when a former CEO, long out of office—sometimes for a decade or more—delves into operational areas that have long since evolved from their own time at the helm.

A fourth motive that we have witnessed among a small number of directors is an unexpressed desire to actually move from the board-room into the executive suite. These directors might feel that proving themselves to be masters of operational detail, even more so than some of the executives, could better position them to replace a top executive.

Finally, a fifth driver appears occasionally: excessive anxiety about the unknown. A few directors push incessantly for additional informa-tion—far more than they require for governing—to allay their per-sonal fears that they are insufficiently in charge or might be blamed for a blowup on their watch.

Many of these unhappy motives were evident when an executive-search firm interviewed several dozen directors in Australia on what made for an exceptionally effective director. Inevitably, the interview-ers also heard much about what made for the opposite, and several strains of micromanagement were at the top of the list. In the report's colorful labeling, "nonstop talkers" sought to demonstrate their ex-ceptional knowledge, "hobbyhorse jockeys" overly focused on the one topic they knew well, "hand-grenade throwers" were contentious and obstructive, "captives of compliance" stressed rules over judgment, "egocentrics" were ever self-referential, and "in over their heads" di-rectors simply did not understand their firm's real challenges.[3]

That such excesses emerge in even the bluest of the blue-chip board-rooms is not surprising. Directors bring the same array of human foibles to the boardroom as do people to any room, though one would expect that the oddest of the oddballs would have been screened out. What is more surprising is that so few steps are taken to limit the damage. A boardroom norm on acceptable discussion and personal behavior can be of special value here, guiding directors on where their leadership ends and management begins.

The boardrooms of large private equity controlled firms often have strong behavioral norms, and their experience is useful to examine. Consider Blackstone, a publicly traded private equity firm that has a long history of acquiring, strengthening, and then profitably selling companies. With more than fourteen hundred employees, $3 billion in yearly revenue, $20 billion in assets, and $1.5 billion annual income, it evaluates a thousand investment opportunities every year, carefully vets a hundred, and finally invests in just four or five. During the two decades prior to its public offering in 2007, the firm had placed some $20 billion in 109 private equity transactions. An important factor for ensuring the investments' success has been assessing the quality of the recipient board, and for that Blackstone brought in Sandy Ogg, who had served as the Leadership, Learning and Performance senior vice president for Motorola and then as chief human resource officer for Unilever.

An operating partner in Blackstone's Private Equity Group, Ogg works actively with directors at firms where Blackstone has taken a major stake. He presses the directors "to be active" with management—but at the same time "not too active." In his experience, overdoing is just as bad as "underdoing." The art of directing is to navigate the right path between the two. When a director fails to find the right path, Ogg often joins with the board chair to force a too-active or overdoing director off the board. In one case, for instance, he bluntly informed the offending director that he was an "energy-sucking, horrible force on the board." The CEO had been warning Ogg that he found it hard to get out of bed on a morning when he was scheduled to meet the offending director.

At the same time, Ogg warns directors against too little engagement, reminding them that Blackstone has invited them onto the board for the experience and judgment they will be drawing on—and not for their résumé or renown. And, of course, Ogg has great clout behind him: Blackstone's large ownership stakes enable it to wield exceptional influence on director behavior and their reputation within the business community.

A Damaging Insurgency

The disruptive power of a dysfunctional director and the need for careful screening are well illustrated at a manufacturing company, one of

America's *Fortune* 50 blue-chip companies, where the corner office had suddenly become vacant. A chief executive had unexpectedly decamped to another firm, and the directors quickly concluded that no executive within the firm was quite ready for prime time. One of the directors, however, thought he himself would be a worthy candidate, even though he lacked relevant executive experience. The manufacturing company board had elected him interim chief executive and chair for the company while it searched for an outsider, and that had only whetted his appetite.

Although the board made clear at the outset of the search that it was looking for a specific set of skills that the interim chief executive did not possess, the aspirant approached the lead director, who was also chair of the search committee. The lead director rebuffed the query, since the interested director was not sufficiently qualified even to be considered. Taking the rejection as an affront, the director licked his wounds momentarily but soon raised the issue again, now proposing that he become executive chairman of the board, or at least non-executive chair. When the lead director turned away that request too, sparks flew, and the ambitious director and lead director dropped all pretense of civility. Though regularly in the boardroom together, they refused to speak to one another for the next several years. But that was only the start.

A new chief executive was soon recruited from the outside, and the disgruntled director became hypercritical. Finding fault with almost everything the CEO did with the company, even questioning the executive's moral compass and personal ethos, the dissenting director worked to cultivate other critics on the board. As chair of the governance committee, the director also recruited a like-minded ally to the board despite the CEO's objection and bonded with the new director to form what the new chief executive came to feel was "an axis of evil."

Often poisonous in commentary, sometimes disrespectful in demeanor, these two dissident directors quietly but effectively intimidated other board members, including the lead director. We have seen this elsewhere, and a contributing factor in most cases, evident here too, was the subtlety of the dissident's challenge. The ambitious director in this case played down his aspirations to avoid the appearance of self-serving motives. Instead, he distributed his poison in small doses, sometimes even with a dollop of sugar. Since most directors did not expect or want a fight with other directors, this subtly inappropriate behavior was tolerated by the board in a way that in retrospect should not have been permitted.

The director's guerrilla warfare gained traction, and the board soon split into factions, with some supporting the dissidents, others opposing, and still others indifferent. The lead director was a person of character and integrity, but he was also conflict averse. He had little stomach for confronting the two dissenting directors openly in the boardroom, preferring to allow their insults to simply dissipate into the ether when the gavel sounded. In the past, a powerful chief executive might have intervened to right the listing ship, but with the axis of leadership now shifting to the boardroom itself, that duty now fell to the lead director, who could not bring himself to intervene.

Little restrained, the dissident directors took their toll on the firm in the years that followed, even though the firm was otherwise performing well under the new CEO's leadership. No great damage was done, but the costs added up. The new chief executive and his staff devoted extra time to preparing for board meetings, making sure their documents were always above censure and directors were well briefed ahead of time. For their part, the dissident directors brought no constructive guidance to the boardroom, creating a vacuum where different directors would have contributed. The new CEO later departed, partly for this reason, and a talented senior executive resigned soon afterward, saying he could no longer work with a company where a few board members displayed such unprofessional conduct and drained out so much energy. The behavior was obvious to most senior managers, and in time they lost respect for all of the directors because of their unwillingness to confront the disruptive conduct. Without a lead director prepared to rein in or a review process to force out the two dysfunctional directors, the board dramatically underperformed its leadership role. Though a relatively rare case, it stands as a warning for the costs that dysfunctional directors can impose on a company.

Every situation is of course unique, but to avoid leadership shortfalls of this kind, directors would generally be wise to ask one of their own to step off the board if that director seeks to become an executive candidate. Sometimes boards do draft a member to serve as CEO, but if a director raises a hand without being asked, exiting that person from the board forthwith should be seen as an act of good governance. Otherwise, such a director's continuing presence can morph into dysfunctional governance. Boards would do well to carefully vet prospective candidates in the first place for their proven record of adding value to a boardroom rather than potentially sucking air out of it.

When we asked the chief executive of the manufacturing firm discussed previously what he would have done differently with the benefit of hindsight, he said he would have insisted on removal of the difficult director from the board *before* accepting the offer to become CEO. Alternatively, the CEO could have laid down the gauntlet within six months of his appointment and worked through the governance committee process to have the director removed, even if it meant putting his job on the line, a course that we have seen successfully mastered at two other *Fortune* 100 companies. Instead, the dysfunctional director became a thorn in the CEO's side throughout the years of his tenure, and his board could not come close to fulfilling its leadership potential.

We have seen companies build capabilities for giving individual directors personal feedback from both executives and fellow directors. We have witnessed board leaders coach dysfunctional directors away from disruptive behavior and remove them altogether when they could not. Bottom line: redirecting, deselecting, or not recruiting dysfunctional directors in the first place have become far more important tasks for the board in an era when its leadership has become far more important to a company—and its ineffectiveness far more damaging.

With a good central idea and competent set of directors in place, the board leader now has a critical role to play, as we see in the following chapter. A sound chemistry among the directors can catalyze a boardroom, and identifying a director with the personal and professional qualities to serve as board leader and to create that chemistry becomes a pivotal decision.

DIRECTOR'S CHECKLIST FOR DEALING WITH NONPERFORMING DIRECTORS

✓ Does the director bring few useful skills and a lack of relevant experience to the boardroom?

✓ Is the director often unprepared for board meetings?

✓ Does the director fail to grasp the firm's central idea and business strategy?

✓ Are the director's questions distracting or inappropriate?

✓ Does the director bring few ideas or leads on business development?

✓ Has the board established norms on what is expected of directors in the boardroom?

✓ Has the line between leading and staying out of the way been made clear by the lead director and chief executive?

✓ Have directors and executives been asked for confidential feedback on a dysfunctional director?

✓ Has the lead director privately coached a director whose behavior has been disruptive?

5.

Wanted: A Leader of the Board

A *New Yorker* cartoon some years back captured it well: A ferocious-looking chief executive sits at the head of the boardroom table, leaning menacingly toward a cowering group of directors. "That is my gut feel," says the CEO in the caption, "now I'll recognize any other guts!" Amusing, but the cartoon also captured a fundamental truth about many US boardrooms at the time. The chief executive was in charge, and the directors, mostly handpicked by the CEO, were there to do little more than nod agreement with the CEO's pronouncements. That was the age of the imperial CEO, responsible for major decisions and accountable to none. And it was the age of the ceremonial board. Separate leadership in the boardroom by directors and for the company would have been an oxymoron.

As we saw earlier, however, this CEO-dominated model has long been on the wane. Boards have brought on more independent-minded directors, thinned the back-scratching network of directors who served on one another's boards, discouraged outside CEOs from serving on their compensation committee if their own CEO sat on the other's compensation committee, and vested more authority in their governance committee for recruiting new directors.

While the impetus for these governance reforms was primarily to strengthen the board's monitoring function, in large measure driven by investor pressures and regulatory requirements, the changes have had the unintended but useful effect of also strengthening the board's leadership function. Investors came to target individual directors, and regulators began to demand face-to-face meetings with boards. Directors got the message that they were deemed accountable for both the firm's financial performance and its management practices. As boards became more independent of management, smaller in size, more populated by veteran executives, and better led, more director time has focused on central ideas, competitive challenges, and value drivers.

Intensifying demands for better monitoring of managers thus paved the way for stronger leadership by directors. This is likely, in our view, to have more tangible and lasting impact on business performance than many of the monitoring improvements themselves. Directors and executives embraced necessity and out of it came better leadership of both the board and the company.

Priority: The Right Board Leader

Good-governance advocates such as Institutional Shareholder Services (now a subsidiary of MSCI Inc.) have long pressed for separating the role of chief executive and board chair—the model championed by Britain's best-known governance panel, the Cadbury Commission of 1992, and a model more prevalent in the United Kingdom. The stated impetus was to fortify the directors' oversight function and strengthen their leadership role.[1]

That campaign has found less fertile ground on the American side of the Atlantic, however. At issue is a long-standing and deep-rooted American corporate norm that such a separation would cast a shadow on the CEO's authority within the company and credibility with the investors. Still, the CEO as de facto leader of the American boardroom is being replaced by either an independent board chair or a designated board leader.[2]

Most major American companies have opted to create the role of *lead director*, or what some companies prefer to call the *presiding director*. Much of the impetus for this hybrid came from the decision by the New York Stock Exchange in 2003 to require that non-executive directors meet at least annually without executives in the room and that, if a specific director is designated to preside at such meeting, his or her name be publicly disclosed.[3] Since then, the trend line has been remarkable: from no takers in 2000, to a decade later with more than 90 percent of the S&P 500 having designated a lead director.[4]

The precise definition of the position varies from firm to firm, but the essence is to designate an independent director who can congregate, speak for, and otherwise organize the other non-executive directors apart from the chief executive or board chair. Among the lead director's most important prerogatives is the power to convene the board without the chief executive present and to review management behavior and performance outside executive earshot.

Compared with the lead director, some argue that a separate board chair still enjoys the edge in setting agendas and controlling deliberations. The *chair* designation also generally carries more clout with institutional investors and equity analysts and has considerably more legitimacy in areas such as Asia, where major customers prefer to deal with—and in fact, expect to meet with—a CEO who is also board chair. Disparities in compensation between lead directors and board chairs are, as a result, substantial. Among S&P 500 companies in 2012, for instance, those with a lead or presiding director paid the director an extra annual fee averaging just over $26,000, but those with a separate chair compensated his or her service with an additional stipend of more than $168,000.[5] This reflects in part the fact that a significant number of the separate chairs are recently retired CEOs who have stepped up to the executive chair role.

Such a pay discrepancy might seem only fair. Board chairs draw media interest that exposes them to public scrutiny and personal heat when things go sour. If the compensation and media gaps between the two positions remain significant, however, the authority gap has been steadily narrowing over the past decade. Non-executive chairs, lead directors, presiding directors—whatever one chooses to call the board leader—have emerged (and are still emerging) as one of the most important new forces in corporate governance and leadership, which makes the issue of selecting the *right* board leader one of the single most important decisions any board can now take.

Far more important than the board leader's specific title is the relationship between the designated leader and the chief executive officer—and, more broadly, the other directors and officers. This constructed rapport is a vital foundation, in our view, for effective leadership by the board, whether direct or collaborative, and it is one that is tucked between the titles and boxes on the organizational chart. Here, the personalities and temperaments, experiences and skills, and relations between the key players become the critical ingredients.

Get that chemistry wrong, and even great directors can fall victim to destructive patterns of behavior that undercut their company leadership and cast a shadow over enterprise performance. Momentum is slowed, opportunities dissipate, competitors move ahead. Ill-led boards are not only draining for members but also costly to stakeholders.

Past conflict between the directors of Hewlett-Packard comes to mind here—conduct that included bitter disputes, illicit investigations, angry resignations, forced departures, and even criminal indictment of the board chair (later dropped).[6] A damaging consequence was HP's continued inability to install the right chief executive, in stark contrast to IBM's succession experience. Between 1999 and 2012, the HP board hired and fired no fewer than four chief executives. Technology archrival IBM, a model of CEO stability and succession, forced out none.

One of those passing and disappointing HP chief executives, Léo Apotheker, proposed to acquire British software giant Autonomy in 2011 for $11.1 billion. At twelve times annual revenue, the price raised eyebrows, especially when comparable firms, according to one investment bank's appraisal, were selling for more like three times revenue.

Equity analysts and market rival Oracle were openly critical, but so was HP's own chief financial officer, Catherine A. Lesjak, who had briefly served as interim CEO prior to Apotheker's arrival. She was reported to have boldly advised at a board meeting that the deal was "too expensive" and "not in the best interest of the company." Despite the many warning signs, the CEO pressed for approval and the board unanimously backed his buy.

Just a year later, Apotheker's CEO successor Meg Whitman wrote off $5 billion of Autonomy's value after forcing out its top managers and then finding "serious accounting improprieties," including evidence of inflated sales figures. Several directors confided in retrospect that they should have more carefully vetted the proposed purchase, though the Autonomy losses came in the wake of an earlier $885 million write-down for HP's purchase of Palm Computing and $8 billion for its acquisition of Electronic Data Systems (EDS).

Whitman, who had served as a non-executive HP director when the board unanimously approved the Autonomy deal, explained that "you rely on the recommendations of management." That is certainly true, since directors cannot conduct their own due diligence, and even management is forced to depend in part on the guidance of its own special advisers. HP had engaged two of the top accounting firms to review Autonomy's books before the purchase. Still, the leadership calling places the burden of informed judgment on the directors' shoulders when a company is reaching its most important decisions. In this case, the board's role presumably should have included careful listening to the critical voices on the outside and the dissident CFO on the inside.

And the literal price of the failed liaison between board leader and CEO—or multiple CEOs, in HP's case? Here's one way to look at it: At the start of the decade of the 2000s, Hewlett-Packard and IBM had reached similar market valuations. By early 2013, HP, with 2012 revenue of $120 billion, had achieved a market capitalization of $33 billion, while IBM, with annual revenue of $104 billion, had reached a market value of $225 billion. And a significant fraction of the difference can be traced, we believe, to their respective boards' actions.

The Right Chemistry

Get the board chemistry right, however, and its leadership can flourish. The question, of course, is how to accomplish that. Irvine O. Hockaday Jr., whom we met in chapter 1, has served as presiding director at Ford and lead director at Estée Lauder. At both organizations, he had to become, in his own words, "the connecting rod to the rest of the board." In his experience, the board leader must define the board's modus operandi, ensure a bridge across the no-man's-land separating board and management, and orchestrate the work of the board's audit, compensation, and governance committees. The board leader works as a sounding board for both directors and executives, he advised, and, as needed, a reconciler.

Another seasoned boardroom inhabitant, Richard L. Crandall, offered a similar appraisal. He has founded a venture capital firm, built and led several enterprises, and joined the boards of a number of firms, some private, others public. He served, for instance, as non-executive chair of Novell Inc., a large enterprise software provider. The board leader "is the ombudsman between the CEO and the board," Crandall said. "You have to know how to work well with all the independent personalities in the room. And you have to make sure that anyone who has something to say has the opportunity to do so without being clipped."

For that to work, Crandall cautioned, it becomes vital for everyone to know what to say. Each "director must do the work to understand" the central idea, he counseled, "and internalize it so that the central idea becomes the template against which the board can evaluate and approve decisions and the deployment of capital, assess acquisitions, and even set executive compensation." But he found that some directors might not have done the necessary work. "In my experience, it is usual to find one or a few directors who 'don't get it' and don't do the work to internalize the concept." He added, "if a director avoids the work and remains in the clueless state, [that director] must go."

Finding the right person for board leader requires looking well beyond the monitoring skills expected of all directors. Being a board leader demands capacities that we typically associate with individual and team leadership at the highest level, including an ability to think strategically, communicate persuasively, and act decisively. Board leaders should be deft at creating cohesion among directors and executives, and bridging the formal gulf between them, while also focusing directors on strategic content without edging into micromanagement. Also critical is an ability to work hand in hand with the CEO and other top executives on company issues. That, in turn, relies heavily on the informal rapport that the board leader is able to construct with them.

We have worked with many board leaders and company executives who collaborate well, but we have also seen or witnessed other pairs whose business skill sets were equally strong but whose relationship was weak and sometimes even poisonous. A toxic match was evident, for instance, in the resignation in 2010 of the non-executive board chair of AIG, Harvey Golub, who had served as the highly successful chief executive of American Express when it required a turnaround in the 1990s and as non-executive chair of Campbell Soup Company. As AIG's active and engaged non-executive chair in its post-debacle era, Golub sought to work closely with Robert Benmosche, a strong-willed chief executive at a time when the company's recovery required draconian measures, including the disposal of major assets. Each chafed at the other's will, however, and their kinship never gelled. According to Golub, AIG's CEO had reported to the board that their relationship was "ineffective and unsustainable." Benmosche had even threatened to quit after Golub successfully led the board to reject Benmosche's plan to sell one of the company's divisions. Instead, Golub resigned from the board because of the unworkable association with Benmosche, saying "It is easier to replace a chairman than a CEO."[7]

Six Qualities of a Board Leader

Our collective experience has uncovered six personal qualities that have become particularly critical when directors are considering which of their colleagues to elevate as board leader. None of the following qualities is sufficient, but all taken together can help to define what should be sought in a board leader: executive experience, respect and confidence, collaboration and restraint, personal bonding, personal comfort, and resilience.

1. Executive Experience

At the top of the board leader's skill set list is executive experience itself. Collaboration depends on speaking the language and appreciating the management concerns facing any chief executive. Keen business judgment and deep understanding of the strategic, operating, and people issues of a business are prerequisites. Directors themselves evidently have this much in mind when they cast their lots for a board leader: three-quarters of the non-executive board chairs of the hundred largest market-capitalization companies in 2010 had served as chair, president, or CEO of another company. Executive experience with crises or even calamities is helpful on the résumé as well. It should be noted, however, that the capabilities needed by a chief executive are not identical to those needed for board leadership. For reasons we will soon explore, many successful CEOs would not make successful board leaders.[8]

2. Respect and Confidence

A close second is exceptional respect and confidence from other directors. Most directors are highly accomplished in their own right, and engaging them in productive dialogue and decision making in ways that further a company's central idea, strategy, and even execution requires standout facilitation skills, including the ability to first draw others out and then draw them into judicious decisions, the essence of a seasoned diplomat. Performing the role effectively calls for hearing what is said as well as reading between the lines to uncover reservations that directors and executives are sometimes loath to express openly. In moving directors across a sometimes uncertain terrain, replete with landmines, directors will want a board leader who is a transparent and trusted partner.

3. Collaboration and Restraint

Strength and effectiveness as a board leader are also expressed by the ability to hold back so that intelligent conversation can flow and collaboration can result. Conversely, board leaders standing too tall on their own soapbox can inhibit a free flow of ideas. At the same time, it is important for a lead director to exercise individual and collective restraint so that board directives do not tread on management's toes.

When one of Home Depot's cofounders retired from the board in 2008, the directors elevated Bonnie G. Hill, a former executive at the *Los Angeles Times* and chair of Home Depot's compensation committee, to serve as lead director. From that experience and her service on several other boards, Hill warned of the need for collaboration and restraint in a board leader: "A lot has to do with the person, and how they handle the role." The danger, she said, "is that someone with a strong personality may inhibit open and honest discussion among board members." She stressed that a board leader's primary obligation is to make certain that all directors had an opportunity to contribute to the firm's collective dialogue. To that end, she sought to ensure that each of Home Depot's non-executive directors felt "that their opinions were important and that they had the opportunity to be heard" at each of the board meetings.

At the same time, Hill cautioned, it is vital for the board leader to respect the implicit boundary between the boardroom and executive suite: "It is important to make certain that the board does not usurp the authority of the CEO in front of the management team." Directors, she warned, "should feel free to ask questions and get additional information if needed, but they should not 'direct' the management team. That is the CEO's job." If directors harbor serious reservations about the team, she advised, "the lead director's job" is to set up a process so that further discussion with the CEO can take place in executive session.

Prior to her first board meeting as a lead director, Hill held discussions with both the chief executive and the general counsel to clarify the "rules of engagement." The board "interfaces so much with the management team and other associates at Home Depot," she explained, "I felt it was important for us to be reminded of the fine line between our respective roles." She had the same discussion with the full board, since several of the directors were new to Home Depot and she wanted everyone to have "a chance to weigh in." That, she said, "set the right tone going forward."

Ensuring director engagement was just one of a host of obligations that Hill shouldered upon becoming lead director. She met personally with Home Depot's largest investors, talked with each of the company's non-executive directors before board meetings, privately asked each director for an assessment of the others as part of the board's annual evaluation of directors (she in turn asked to be evaluated by the board chair or the compensation-committee chair), served as mentor to several company executives, and regularly consulted with the chief executive.

4. Personal Bonding

A fourth quality for a board leader is the ability to create personal connections. As board leader Irvine Hockaday described it, "So much about being an effective lead director has to do with your ability to establish relationships and work well in the context of the DNA of a particular board." Personal relationships facilitate a board leader's ability to hear from all and, in turn, credibly communicate the board's mentality.

Consider the experience of Mark D. Ketchum, who served in senior roles with Procter & Gamble, the corner office with Newell Rubbermaid, and as lead director for Kraft Foods, a $50 billion behemoth of the consumer products industry. Soon after he joined the Kraft board, chief executive Irene Rosenfeld encouraged him to become the lead director, and the board chose him to do so. Ketchum accepted, he recalled, because the CEO "and I had a good rapport, and she knew she could talk to me. As a [former] CEO, I identified with the need to have a peer to use as a sounding board. I know that being a CEO is a lonely job."

Ketchum's value as lead director was tested in mid-2009 when Kraft sought to acquire Cadbury, the world's second-largest confectioner. An icon of British business, the two-hundred-year-old Cadbury flatly rejected Kraft's initial offer of $16.7 billion, on the grounds that "the proposal fundamentally undervalues the group and its prospects." With Rosenfeld deeply immersed in the details and tactics of the resisted takeover and worries about other would-be acquirers who were circling, Ketchum took it upon himself, he said, to "represent the range of views on the board, including the minority viewpoint, which can be hard to pull out, especially from quieter board members, but their opinions can be critical." In early 2010, Ketchum's well-versed board approved Rosenfeld's enhanced offer of $19 billion, a price that Cadbury finally accepted.[9]

5. Personal Comfort

Yet another factor defining the board leader is a sense of comfort in one's own skin and place in life, with nothing yet to prove or still to achieve, most often the product of a long and successful career as a corporate leader in one's own right—no coveting of the chief executive's office, no longing for operational control. As Mark Ketchum offered from his own experience, "There is a certain sort of personality, a level of self-assurance, that is part of the makeup of many CEOs" serving on boards. But, he warned, "That can get in the way—not necessarily intentionally—of achieving what is best for the company." Authentic leadership comes to mind here: self-effacement, consistency, and commitment to the mission with no trace of private agenda.[10]

Though first among equals, the board leader is called to pull others' views together for concerted action. "There is a lot of synthesis involved so that the board leader can crystallize the viewpoints of the board and communicate those to the CEO," observed Novell's Richard Crandall. "The chair has to be totally straightforward and honest," he added. "You can't have someone in the board leader position who wants the CEO's job." The rapport between the CEO and board leader lies, in his experience, at the heart of the partnership. In building that relationship, said Crandall, "it is important to spend sufficient time together, offline, so that you can virtually read each other's minds."

6. Resilience

Last but not least is the bounce-back factor. Board leaders can anticipate at least one major crisis during their tenure—an oil spill, a product recall, a failed takeover. A board leader's personal resilience and drive to confront and surmount a crisis count for much. In some ways, this sixth quality counts most of all. Rising to the task of board leader is like any other challenge—far harder and more impactful in bad times than good. The board leader's job is to head off those terrible moments if possible, or at the least not let them paralyze the organization once they emerge. After all, board leaders are chosen by their fellow directors precisely because they have demonstrated the perceptiveness and persuasiveness required for aligning others at the top when it really matters. A board leader is also the person who most feels the tensions that can infuse a boardroom as divisions emerge between directors and executives. Here too resilience—now in the face of internal conflict—can be essential.

From Division to Decision

Like it or not, deep disagreements within the boardroom are quickly sensed by the curious world. Without necessarily knowing the specific divisions between directors, equity analysts and business journalists often find out when a CEO is stymied by lack of board agreement, or when a lead director is acting as just another layer between a CEO and chair, or when a board is unsure of whether it even has the right CEO. Employees sense it, too, in stilted messages, shifting priorities, and ambiguous strategies.

This is when board leaders must be on their toes: bridging the divides, whether between directors or between the board and management; hearing unspoken reservations; and conveying the particulars.

In times of crisis or great upheaval, the board leader will want to bring both facts and intuition to the table, ensure that options are defined and debated, and move the board from division to decision. When Procter & Gamble's earnings stumbled in 2012 and hedge fund manager Bill Ackman's $12 billion Pershing Square Capital Management complained about the corporation's languishing performance, the board's presiding director stepped forward to say that the board will "actively oversee" a new restructuring "plan's implementation to ensure effectiveness."[11]

That was precisely the course that the lead director of another company pursued in seeking to redirect his enterprise from consolidation to expansion. The chief executive had complained to the lead director that the company was frittering away precious time that should have been used to create footholds in emerging markets. The lead director, in turn, talked offline with other directors about the expansionist vision but soon realized that there was more opposition in the boardroom than support for it. The lead director also learned, however, that the directors' resistance had less to do with the concept than with the CEO's failure to explain it. Directors had received ample financial information from the CEO to appreciate the case, but too little business rationale to accept it. Communicating the essence of what he had learned from other board members, the lead director worked with the CEO to develop a more compelling long-term rationale for the expansion strategy, and the chief executive, with the full board's approval, was finally able to move toward implementation.

Indeed, so important is this role of trusted communicator that we would include one more quality in the board leader's essential toolkit: *a capacity for complete candor and a willingness to ask the same of others.* If directors perceive that management is filtering the information that goes to the board or is making it hard for directors to have their questions answered or information requests fulfilled, they will come to wonder what else is hidden. The chair of Enron's compensation committee twice asked Enron's senior human-resources executive for detailed information on the CFO's compensation package, which the director suspected, correctly in retrospect, was improperly structured to allow self-dealing. Neither request was honored, leading the director to question management motives, though alas not in time to avert the train wreck that was coming down the tracks.[12]

If the chief executive believes directors are less than candid, the CEO may in turn withhold data or lose confidence in the partnership. Board leaders will thus want to keep the chief executive well informed about where the board stands on important subjects, including the directors' view of the CEO's performance and company results. Updating the CEO after every executive session of the board can help ensure that no skeletons remain in the closet.

A Social Scaffolding

As companies have built up their leadership in the boardroom, they have also created an architecture to underpin it. Among its central features is a suite of board committees and their executive liaisons. By 2012, all of the S&P 500 companies had established audit, compensation, and nominating/governance committees (hereafter termed the governance committee), a product of regulatory and stock-exchange requirements. Their chairs have come to work closely not only with the chief executive and board leader but also with second-echelon executives who report both to the CEO and the board.[13]

For the chair of the audit committee, the primary liaison is typically the chief financial officer; for the compensation committee, the chief human resource officer; and for the governance committee, the general counsel. This second tier has become particularly important in an era when a majority of boards among the S&P 500 include only a single executive, the CEO. As a result, chairs of the board committees have to be better prepared to act in their specific arenas, and they are generally compensated for doing so. Compared with a decade earlier, for instance, the audit committee is now more likely to be chaired by an outside chief financial officer, financial executive, treasurer, or public accounting executive.[14]

Company leadership is thus not only exercised more by the board as a whole but also more spread across its key committees. Alex J.

Mandl, presiding director for Dell Inc. and chair of its audit committee, summed up a shift reported by many: "When I think what the work of the audit committee was like" when he had much earlier served as chief financial officer for AT&T, "we had one-hour meetings where we would flip through the financials and the external auditor would present a five-minute summary. This is in stark contrast to today where we go into all sorts of detail."

The board's key committees are also more actively supported by the top management team. Consider the enhanced role of Campbell Soup's Nancy Reardon when she served as the company's chief human resource officer. "The work of the compensation committee shouldn't just be a numbers exercise of benchmarking," she said. "Part of my job was to make [its members] more knowledgeable about high-potential people in the organization, in whatever way is easiest for them. It's all about people. We need world-class people in every position, so we have to make sure we spend more time on that than the process stuff. The more the better when it comes to the board getting to know our people and our culture."

The role of the general counsel has expanded as well; it now often includes directly advising the board and its governance committee on a host of issues ranging from ongoing litigation and proxy challenges to intellectual property, global risks, and director candidates. The general counsel increasingly views the position as directly reporting to the board along with the traditional line to the chief executive, a hybrid status that is being embraced by the chief financial officer and chief human resource officer as well.

Directors more often have a hand now in vetting executives for these second-echelon positions, including an interview with the finalists. And occasionally they force a vacancy when an executive has lost their confidence.

What It Takes—in Their Own Words

To learn more about how the new board leader role has evolved, we asked eleven current and former board leaders of large US companies to share their experiences.[15] Our panel generally reported that there was now little difference in how their companies utilized the board leader whether he or she carried the title of non-executive chair, lead director, or presiding director, though a few still viewed the title of chair as carrying symbolic clout.

The board leaders uniformly described a role that had grown well beyond that mandated by listing requirements. The board leader, they said, had come to serve above all as a collaborator with other directors and the chief executive on strategy formulation, as well as on functions that the CEO had historically embraced alone, including setting board agendas, focusing the CEO and directors on the right issues, recruiting new directors, and assessing company risk. They have learned how to exercise lateral influence within a group of powerful peers.

Clearly, not all directors are capable of serving as board leaders. Our panel reported that the process of selecting a board leader has evolved from an unstructured and haphazard approach toward one that sometimes resembles the complex procedures often followed in CEO succession, though they also cautioned that at some companies it remains a work in progress or still just ad hoc. Board-leader replacement, they advised from experience, should start with a formal document that specifies the professional duties and the leadership capacities that a prospective leader must embrace or bring to the boardroom, recognizing that both the duties and the capacities will also evolve over time. The document can then furnish the criteria not only for directors to identify who among them would best serve as their leader but also for directors to conduct periodic appraisals of the board leader's performance. Still, relatively few boards conduct regular performance appraisals of their board leader, though many directors believe they should.

Drawing on their own boardroom experience, our panel advised that the board leader's responsibilities, best embodied in a written document, should at a minimum include chairing executive sessions and presiding over annual evaluations of the board and individual directors. The duties should also entail collaboration with the chief executive in selective communication with shareholders and other stakeholders, appointing and working with board committee chairs; acting as liaison between directors and executives; ensuring that a succession plan is in place for both the CEO and the board leader; and above all, bringing directors into a working relationship with the chief executive and top management team.

All of the board leaders on our panel emphasized the need for close collaboration and trusted communication with the chief executive and fellow directors to focus boardroom discussions on the central idea and value creation. Some also stressed the need for the board leader to work personally with directors who are seen—or formally identified through the annual evaluation of directors—as subpar performers and, in extreme cases, to galvanize an effort to remove them.

Given the focus on meetings and conversations, our panelists also stressed the need for the board leader to be an exceptional facilitator. "A skilled board leader can wring a lot out of these discussions," reported James G. Cullen, the lead director of Johnson & Johnson and non-executive chairman of Agilent Technologies. That function, he added, "lies at the heart of what a board leader can bring to the governance process and to the successful strategic momentum of the business." Doing one's homework on the business is also key. "You have to stay current," Cullen said, and "understand the priorities of the business, the strategy, and the direction of the business, especially if you are going to have candid one-on-one discussions with the CEO." All these board-leader capabilities take on special salience, panel members noted, when a company confronts a crisis or turning point.

These strands point to three director's checklists for defining the personal qualities, professional capacities, and leadership obligations of the board leader.

With a central idea and a board leader well in place, the directors are ready for their most fateful decision, selection of their chief executive. In the next chapter, we draw on the experience of America's Ford Motor Company and 3M, Australia's BHP Billiton, and the United Kingdom's GlaxoSmithKline to identify what goes into the demanding task of recruiting the proper CEO.

DIRECTOR'S CHECKLIST FOR PERSONAL QUALITIES IN SELECTING A BOARD LEADER

✓ Extensive business leadership experience, including crisis leadership

✓ Respect and confidence of other directors

✓ Collaborative and restrained in style

✓ Personally bonded with other directors

✓ Comfortable in own skin and place in life

✓ Resilient with a drive to confront and surmount setbacks

✓ Complete candor and expectation of the same in others

DIRECTOR'S CHECKLIST FOR PROFESSIONAL CAPACITIES IN SELECTING A BOARD LEADER

✓ An experienced mentor of business leadership in others

✓ Shows mastery of the company's central idea, strategy, and operating issues, and applies seasoned and judicious judgment

✓ Downplays self-interest and serves as a trusted counselor and partner of the CEO

✓ Displays a passion for corporate governance, including both monitoring and leadership

✓ Brings the personal time and emotional energy to devote to board leadership

✓ Listens well and draws out ideas, learns what other directors have on their minds, crystallizes directors' diverse views, facilitates expression of underlying concerns, and focuses deliberations

✓ Displays effective influence, corporate diplomacy, and constructive guidance

✓ Embodies integrity and expects it in all directors and executives

DIRECTOR'S CHECKLIST FOR BOARD LEADER OBLIGATIONS

✓ Works with the board to guide management on the central idea, strategic issues, and long-term planning

✓ Serves as liaison between directors and executives

✓ Presides over regular and special board sessions without executives present

✓ Determines who attends board meetings, including members of management and outside advisers

✓ Consults with executives and directors on meeting schedule, agenda, and materials

✓ Responds in alliance with the CEO to shareholder inquiries and approves company responses to investor communication

✓ Works with the chair of the compensation committee on CEO performance evaluation and compensation

✓ Works with the chair of the governance committee on the selection of committee chairs and board members, and presides over an annual board and director evaluation

✓ Works with the chair of the audit committee to ensure compliance with laws and regulations and appropriate risk management

✓ Ensures that a succession plan is in place for both the CEO and the board leader, and that a backup for the CEO is in place in case the CEO unexpectedly exits

PART TWO

LEADING THE LEADERS

6.

CEO Succession: The Ultimate Decision

Leaderless teams are not unknown. The Orpheus Chamber Orchestra performs Beethoven symphonies without a conductor. Special forces conduct combat missions without a commissioned officer. Yet these are the rare exceptions. Virtually every team—whether a rowing crew seeking a championship or a company executing a strategy—requires a capable leader. Even in an era of enhanced board leadership, picking the right replacement for a departing chief executive remains critically important at the corporate apex. That said, chief executives are often not inclined to place succession at the top of the boardroom agenda. In some cases, they are too consumed with day-to-day affairs; in others, succession seems too far ahead to worry about now. And, like all humans, they are not eager to contemplate their own professional mortality.[1]

Directors, too, have their own reasons for delay or deferral. Many appreciate that selecting a new CEO can be laborious and contentious, some may secretly aspire to the post themselves, and most recognize that it is the most weighty decision that they will have to face during their tenure, making it easier to opt for more proximate and less portentous issues at the next board meeting. Some directors believe it is best in any case to give the benefit of the doubt to a new or seemingly effective chief executive.

Yet while adopting a succession mind-set is difficult—maybe even unnatural—it is also essential, though too often underincentivized. John England, the managing partner of Pay Governance, a consulting firm that provides advisory services to compensation committees of a number of large corporations, has found that succession planning is not rewarded sufficiently by many boards, partly because it is not readily quantifiable. "It would be unusual for a CEO to be 'bonused' on how well succession planning is going," he explained, "because that is something that is measured more qualitatively than saying, for example, that 10 percent of your bonus will be tied to successfully meeting [financial or operational goals]."

So while many boards and CEOs devote some time to the succession question before the eleventh hour, a robust benchmark for doing so does not usually find its way into the CEO's annual objectives and bonus plan. "That doesn't mean that succession planning and grooming is not on a short list of, say, three to seven objectives that are evaluated as a whole," England continued, but "they are just not assigned a separate weight."

A number of boards have shown that the job can be done, and done well. In the case of one company, for example, the board had focused in concert with the chief executive on developing a CEO successor even though the transition was still five years away. The directors and chief executive expanded their attention from just the company's top tier down to its upper ninety managers. To give that technique teeth, the board inserted succession metrics into the incentive formula for annual progress by the chief executive and his seven lieutenants. When the succession moment finally arrived, the transition was predictable, not panicked—a telling sign within the company and beyond that not a beat would be missed.

Taking the Wheel at Ford

To further appreciate the leadership that directors play in executive succession, we turn to Ford Motor Company's recruitment of a new chief executive in 2006.[2] Founded by Henry Ford in 1903, the company had risen to great prominence in the American auto market, but in 1998–2001 it was jolted by a massive recall of the Firestone tires it had installed on its vehicles. In the wake of the disastrous setbacks, William Clay Ford, Jr., the great-grandson of the founder, who already served as chair of the Ford board, moved to become chief executive. By 2006, three chief operating officers had come and gone, and the company's financial condition and market share had steadily deteriorated to a critical-care condition.

Ford's manufacturing costs were outpacing its rivals; its acquisitions of Jaguar and Volvo had sidetracked management; market share was slipping to Volkswagen, Toyota, and even Hyundai; and operations were badly balkanized. Ford's earnings skidded more than $12 billion into the red.

Some of Ford's travails could be traced to structural declines afflicting the American auto industry as a whole. Analysts were already suggesting that archrivals General Motors and Chrysler might even be forced into bankruptcy, and while on first glance that might have seemed favorable to Ford's own fortunes, William Ford and the board anticipated just the opposite. If GM and Chrysler were to go through bankruptcy or even garner a government bailout, Ford could end up at a competitive disadvantage, since its rivals would no longer have to honor labor contracts, pension obligations, or supplier agreements. These perilous possibilities led company directors to wonder whether Ford could survive this worst-case scenario. To prepare for the threats, the board engaged law firm Davis Polk and investment bank Goldman Sachs to offer an independent appraisal of Ford's financial viability and bankruptcy possibility.

The old governance model would have kept Ford's directors mostly on the sidelines while management worked to save the company. After all, management ran the business, and responding to competitive challenges was part of its manifest. But the board had already evolved an understanding with management that would now result in directors stepping forward to take more active leadership. Holding the reins was Irvine O. Hockaday Jr., who had run Hallmark Cards for fifteen years and who now served as Ford's lead director. William Ford had earlier warned Hockaday that it was becoming increasingly difficult for him to direct the enterprise in the deteriorating environment: "No single individual can run this company effectively under the current circumstances," said the CEO. "I need help and I cannot do this all by myself." In the name of his fellow directors, Hockaday responded, "That's what we are here for."

Hockaday turned to fellow directors Robert Rubin, former co-chairman of Goldman Sachs and former secretary of the US Treasury, and John L. Thornton, former co-COO of Goldman. They agreed that William Ford was indeed stretched too thin to lead on his own through the gathering storm. But they also soon concluded that no internal candidate would bring the requisite skills to the corner office to surmount the crisis they feared ahead—and ultimately to restore Ford to its glory days as an icon of American industry.

Recruiting a chief executive from the outside, however, would require an extremely discreet search. With the company visibly on the ropes and a stock price already fragile in an anxious equity market, openly seeking a new chief executive could signal that the company's problems were far deeper than those already disclosed. "You guys must have the best Rolodexes on the planet," William Ford said to Hockaday. "You should be able to get anybody to come to the phone. Why not talk among yourselves first and come up with some ideas?"

Hockaday, Rubin, and Thornton did just that. They pooled their personal networks, asking who among their acquaintances might bring the skill set required to turn Ford around and ready the company for the crisis ahead. They did not constitute a formal search committee, but through dialogue inside and outside the boardroom, they built an informal consensus that an ideal candidate would bring a strong vision for the firm's future, an exceptional ability to strategize and execute, an appreciation for the power of current and future technologies, and an experienced hand in harnessing complexity. A viable candidate would also have to be CEO-ready, prepared to run the enterprise from the first day for the long term—in other words, both a sprinter and a marathoner.

Though not personally acquainted with him, John Thornton already had his eye on a prominent Boeing executive, Alan Mulally. For more than three decades, Mulally had been designing, engineering, and building aircraft, including the workhorse 737, the massive 747, and the popular 777, and now he oversaw all of the company's manufacturing. He had also been passed over twice for the top post of Boeing itself, including just a year earlier when the Boeing board brought in then-CEO of 3M and fellow Boeing director James McNerney Jr.

In assessing Mulally's credentials, Hockaday turned to a fellow director on the Sprint board, Gordon Bethune, who had served as CEO of Continental Airlines, one of Boeing's major customers. Bethune was extremely enthusiastic about Mulally, and Hockaday and Thornton arranged to meet secretly with Mulally at Hockaday's home in Aspen, Colorado. All were instantly impressed with Mulally in ways that added up, and he was impressed with the company's potential and the board's capability. Still, prying him loose from Boeing would be no easy task, since its executives knew that he had been so central to its biggest product launches.

A subsequent discussion with William Ford concluded with a meeting of the minds. Ford even offered to step down as board chair if Mulally required that as a precondition for coming to Dearborn, Michigan, Ford's headquarters. Mulally, however, insisted on the opposite—that Ford stay on as executive chair to provide the collaborative leadership with the board that he as chief executive would need to get the job done.

To ensure that the board had missed no shortcomings that might derail a candidate, Hockaday asked one of us to conduct a discreet vetting of Mulally, an important step in its own right but also one that was called for when another search professional raised red flags about Mu-lally's capabilities. Our interviews with a range of individuals who had worked with the candidate yielded only positive assessments. Hocka-day then presented Mulally's candidacy to the full board, a choice that came as no surprise, since Hockaday had regularly updated the board in real time as the vetting unfolded. No surprise for William Ford either, since, as Hockaday explained, during a period of stress "the last thing you want to do is to allow any air to go into the seams of the relation-ship between executive management and the board. I really worked on that."

With the board's full backing, Mulally became chief executive of Ford in September 2006. In the years ahead, he would steer the com-pany through a collapse of the US auto market after Lehman's failure in 2008, the bankruptcy and bailout of Ford's two archrivals in 2009, and the restoration of Ford's reputation and earnings by the end of the decade. In 2011, Ford's income soared to $20 billion, and *Chief Execu-tive* magazine named him CEO of the year.[3]

Ford's recruitment of its new chief executive offers an instructive ex-perience for other boards faced with thorny succession issues. First, the governing board actively directed the process. Three highly ex-perienced directors took charge, but all board members pitched in to help. Each of the directors had already served on several boards, each had extensive experience in evaluating CEOs in diverse industries, and each was acquainted with a large pool of potential candidates. Hocka-day and his fellow directors concluded that new talent was required at the top, crafted the new CEO's job description, sourced and vetted candidates, and recruited their first choice. "I knew all these people," recalled Hockaday. "Many were higher-profile individuals than I, all of them had their own views and were smart folks, and my job was to play to the attributes and advantages that they individually and col-lectively offered." Seasoned boardroom troopers, they had learned to operate collaboratively. "A number of us had been together on that board for quite some time," Hockaday said, and since "we were all used to working together," the informal norms and social architecture guiding the search process "just happened naturally." All this was done in consultation with chief executive William Ford, but in selecting the new chief executive, the board unambiguously drove the vehicle.

Second, the board's leadership did not follow a formally designated process, nor was its foundation visible to the outside world, including the rating agencies. Hockaday had long been "coalescing and constructing a direction for what the board does," he said, so that he and several fellow directors could aggressively go after an outsider when it came time to do so with the full backing of the board. The process was less a matter of formal rules than active direction within the particular boardroom. As Hockaday found, "Effective leadership at the board level will relate to the particular state of the company and the dynamics of the board at a given point in time. A written-in-stone template about board governance is a distraction and maybe even risky."

Third, and critically, the recruitment process that had served the company well in 2006 also provided a foundation for the board's search for a replacement of Alan Mulally as he approached his own retirement in 2014 or beyond. The directors had pioneered a leadership process of trust and transparency among themselves and with the executive team that had served the company well in 2006, and now they expected to build on those same leadership principles in searching for Ford's next chief executive.

Ford's directors had masterfully resolved the most momentous issue confronting any board: installing the right person to run the show. In getting there, having the right directors on the Ford board proved providential. Hockaday, Rubin, and Thornton had each served as chief executive or chief operating officer of other large enterprises where they had selected and deselected executives many times over. In bringing their acquired but rare talent to the boardroom, they added the human capital essential for reaching the board's biggest decision of all. Ford's directors and the understandings among them had served as a critical driver.

Directors Own It

Good succession habits start early in a new chief executive's tenure and go well below the top of the organization, particularly in a large firm. Such habits will be strongest if not only driven by the chief executive but also sanctioned by the directors. As a case in point, consider the experience of George W. Buckley, recruited as CEO of 3M in 2005 after serving as chief executive of Brunswick Corporation and as a top executive at Emerson Electric Company.[4]

In one of his first meetings with the 3M board—even before his official start as chief executive—Buckley talked with directors about the importance of his own succession and, more generally, leadership development at the seventy-thousand-employee company. On the premise that, in Buckley's own words, "great companies produce great leaders, and you don't get one without the other," one of his earliest decisions, taken in consultation with the directors, was for the next chief executive to come from inside 3M, unlike himself. That, Buckley and the board concluded together, would require strengthening and aligning the management development process around company strategy.

Buckley and the directors dug into the company's recent experience and soon discovered that, despite its reputation for creativity and innovation in its scientific and engineering people, development practices in the past had not been producing the kind of executives required for the future. In Buckley's words: "We concluded that while Six Sigma may be a great process to drive out variability in manufacturing and supply chain, it does not produce the desired effect when applied to management development in R&D."

You have to be careful not to kill the goose that lays the golden eggs, warned the 3M CEO. "In a creative company, you can't have forces that dictate creativity. Innovation by system just doesn't work," said Buckley. "Creativity is random, like the weather, not a linear process." Management development in such a company should not be one-track or single-minded. "If there were a precise process for management development and succession, everyone would be doing it, and everyone would be average."

Buckley believed that "the seedlings were good" at 3M and that a more creative approach to succession geared around the firm's specific way of generating value would better prepare the next generation. As one component, he restored a practice that had earlier been ended in the name of efficiency—allowing R&D employees to devote 15 percent of their time to pursue whatever creative tack they preferred.

As a second component, Buckley slowed management rotation around the company to ensure that managers would stay in key positions long enough to experience both success and failure. He asked that high-potential leaders remain in key assignments for five years, rather than moving every two or three years. As a third component, he pressed for managers who understood local preferences, tastes, marketing, and design. Critical to developing the best global leadership, in his view, was "putting local people in charge of local operations, but with enough rotational space to be able to move great people to other positions around the world. We want the best people everywhere."

To improve the CEO succession process itself, Buckley concluded that there had to be stronger director understanding of "where the fault lines are" at 3M and where things can go wrong. More generally, directors had to devote more attention to the talent in the ranks. He was also concerned about the effect that federal legislation, listing requirements, and rating agencies might have on management development. In a rules-based governance environment, boards are often pressed to focus more on monitoring management than partnering with it. With director attention pulled in the wrong direction, Buckley worried, the company was likely to be less capable of identifying and developing the creative executives it required.

To ensure the right kind of due diligence by the directors, Buckley concluded that the entire board should be involved in succession planning, but with a select committee—composed of committee heads and the board leader—serving as the working group. "If you leave it up to the entire board, everyone is in charge so no one is in charge, and it never gets done," he explained. "There is never enough time to cover such an important topic in executive session at the end of board meetings."

Given their always-limited time, directors can be excused for want-ing to retain an outside consultant—but here, too, Buckley pressed for full director ownership of the process. "Sharing ideas" with a consul-tant, he said, "can be of tremendous value, but no one is an oracle, and boards cannot abdicate their responsibility or accountability."

When Buckley finally stepped down as CEO of 3M in 2012, his successor came from the inside, as intended by both the chief execu-tive and the directors. Inge Thulin, a native of Sweden, had joined 3M in sales and marketing more than three decades earlier, steadily working his way up, with stints in Asia, Europe, and the Middle East, and most recently as the company's chief operating officer. He had also served on another board, a role encouraged by 3M directors and Buckley. Mentored, tested, and developed by the CEO and directors over the years, Thulin's readiness meant that no outside search was required.

Work the Inside Options

As well executed as 3M's succession process was, not every leader is—or should be—selected from inside a company. As the Ford experience suggests, identifying external candidates can also be an important ele-ment of CEO candidate searches. At the very least, exceptional out-siders can serve as benchmarks for directors to review along with an insider slate.

Still, the best scenario in our view is for companies to grow their own and have at least several successors who are both leadership-capable and personally aligned with the company's central idea and strategy. By way of example, we turn to the experience of Mark Frissora, who became chief executive of Hertz in 2006 and had served as an outside director for Delphi Automotive, NCR, and Walgreens. From his time as both executive and director, he became convinced that a disciplined development process—pressed by both the directors and chief execu-tive—can help ensure that able homegrown prospects do emerge.[5]

"I think it is important to surface at least two internal candidates as early as possible," Frissora said. "The board should ask the CEO to

identify appropriate candidates through the company's people development system. They might be as much as five years away from being
ready and two to three layers deep in the organization," he maintained.
The company "should think in terms of those with the raw aptitude
to be CEO, as opposed to ready-now candidates." Once the high-
potentials with the right "DNA" have been earmarked, a carefully tailored development plan for them should kick into action.[6]

Vital for that development process is planning and coaching. "We
put a great deal of emphasis on development planning at Hertz," said
Frissora, "and we do an awful lot of coaching. We meet every week
with the management team, and every two years we put everyone
down to the [mid]-level through 360s." For Frissora, that process included no less than the top six hundred managers. But he also drew
on several separate sources of data on his top managers, looking for
consistent patterns. With more than one instrument to identify how
managers' leadership is perceived by their boss, peers, and subordinates,
the results become more reliable and thus more actionable.

Triangulated data can prove invaluable for the directors as well. Impressed with individual managers they have met, directors sometimes
ask, "Why isn't Joe or Mary on the high potential list?" Chief executives might feel the same way, but unless they can back their instincts
with facts, their views of successor prospects are likely to carry less
weight with the directors. "You need to give the board more than simply the CEO's opinion," explained Frissora. "Boards need evidence,
and the more data points the better." Without a system that yields
strong internal data, boards can end up turning to the outside when,
in fact, the CEO and directors have simply not recognized their own
home-grown talent.

Beyond 360-Degree Assessment at GlaxoSmithKline

For an illustration of the value of strong internal data, consider the anticipated retirement of the UK's GlaxoSmithKline (GSK) CEO Jean-
Pierre Garnier, who had led the company since 2000.[6] Three years
before his exit, the board began to work closely with chief human

resource officer Daniel Phelan and Garnier himself on succession. According to company policy, Garnier would be leaving within six months of turning sixty in 2007, but the CEO had raised the succession issue with the board far in advance to ensure that he and the board would have the inside information required to make a well-informed judgment call.

The GSK chief executive and directors let the strategy drive the search for a successor by first assembling a comprehensive picture of what the industry would look like going forward. Garnier produced a strategy paper on industry trends, reported Phelan, with reference to "cost pressures, growth trends, productivity, drug safety, and reputational issues, and how they might affect GSK." The company's annual report articulated four priorities for its strategy in a well-regulated and highly competitive industry. "We are well positioned relative to our peers," said the report, as a "broad-based, geographically diverse and well-balanced business" that emphasized "improved pipeline productivity" and "innovative programs to reduce expenditure and work more closely with customers." The company was also well positioned to "take advantage of opportunities in the growing health-care economies."[7]

Three company managers emerged as CEO prospects because their thinking and experience fit the company's current imperatives. With that, the company launched a succession process that included twice-annual board meetings at which Phelan reviewed potential successors. The CEO and directors also identified three quantifiable leadership capacities required in the next chief executive, given that all three candidates fit with the company's central idea and strategy:

- *Business acumen:* Intellectual resourcefulness, sound judgment, industry knowledge, adds value to the R&D process, ability to drive innovation, ambassadorial skills

- *Leadership qualities:* Sets high standards and gets exceptional results, communication skills, drives change, develops and empowers a high-talent team, creates a sense of urgency, and is a role model to the organization

- *Personal characteristics:* Understands one's own strengths and weaknesses, has stamina, demonstrates competency and leadership, is resilient and a continuous learner

Working through three separate channels, GSK used this template to make a comparative assessment of three finalists. First, the chief executive and directors arranged for the finalists to take on yearlong CEO-level projects under their discerning eyes. They intended through this channel to gather comparable data about the candidates from watching their leadership in real time. But because no two of the strategic projects were alike—one candidate was tasked with rethinking supply-chain management, the second with improving product safety, and the third with redefining sales and marketing—this turned out to be the least useful of the three data-gathering techniques. While Garnier, Phelan, and the directors had high hopes, Phelan cautioned that the technique was "a little like comparing apples and oranges."

A second channel provided sharper comparative insight. Phelan requested evaluations from GSK employees who had worked closely with each potential successor. The company believed that having someone outside the company conduct the comparison would elicit greater candor on each. At a neutral, off-site location, the CEO and fourteen of his top deputies—themselves not candidates but all with extensive work experience with each of the aspirants—were interviewed by one of us. Several of the three finalists' direct reports were interviewed as well. Each interviewee was asked to appraise the three candidates on eight behavioral components associated with each of three leadership capacities and to rate the three finalists on a 1–5 scale.

This proved labor-intensive, requiring two to three hours for each of the fourteen executives interviewed, but the extra effort proved informative. When the non-executive chair of the board, Sir Christopher Gent, subsequently conducted his own independent interviews with many of the same executives and others, the appraisals emerging from his discussion aligned closely with what came to be known as "the 450," an extension on the customary 360-degree assessment. (The extra 90 degrees represented comparative information on the final candidates gathered from those who had worked with them all.)

The company utilized a third channel as well, arranging for each of the contenders to have a private lunch or dinner with each of the directors, sixteen in all—another time-intensive process that brought still more comparative insight.

"It was a somewhat unusual process at the time," recalled Phelan, "scientific and very structured. We put a great deal of thought into it with the board, and it produced great results. Given the increased emphasis on the board's succession duties, I think more boards are going in this direction. Ultimately, the most important decision the board makes is to decide on who the CEO will be. Our board understood the magnitude of the decision and the importance of their involvement, and that they would have to live with the decision for quite a while."

In the end, the three-channel successor-evaluation process led GSK to select its European pharmaceuticals director, Andrew Witty (later Sir Andrew). He had been considered an unlikely winner, in part because he was the youngest—he became chief executive at age forty-three. Garnier himself had anticipated that another of the three candidates would emerge as the top finalist, but the CEO and his directors had been turned by their bottom-up evaluation.

The two capable but unsuccessful contenders were offered additional shares in the company and seats on the board as inducements to stay, though both left within a year. Yet the CEO and directors were confident about their decision, and vital to reaching it were the three separate channels they had used to make it. An added bonus: the rigorous analysis conducted by the board provided insight for the new chief executive to guide his own further self-development.

Preemptive Action

Rather than waiting for the chief executive to bring the succession issue to the boardroom, directors are increasingly opting for preemptive ownership of it. This can be seen at Humana, a $33-billion company that sells and administers health insurance.[8] Chief executive Michael B. McCallister, who had led the company for a decade, had decided to step down by 2013, and director William J. McDonald, an executive at Capital One Financial Corporation and chair of Humana's organization and compensation board committee, offered an early call to action. Succession, he said, is all about "lead time, lead time, lead time." "The board is accountable for the succession process," he observed, "and must stay out in front rather than waiting to hear from the CEO. If the board waits for the CEO, it is too late."

Two factors proved important for Humana's directors in designing the succession process. The first was staying abreast of the company's evolving market and strategy and, equally, its talent pipeline. "Even if the news isn't good" about either, said McDonald, "determine what the circumstances are and what to do about it." The second was assessing prospective internal candidates well before CEO turnover was anticipated. To that end, directors are wise to anticipate how those in the pipeline are likely to grow or stall in the time ahead. "I think one of the biggest mistakes boards make is to assess people only in the context of their current job," warned McDonald. Judging people on present performance is easier but it will not necessarily uncover the best talent, since "people can change dramatically when they get the brass ring."

But without a ready candidate to take that brass ring at Humana, the chief executive and directors reached outside the company for a candidate. After extensive due diligence on prospective candidates, they tapped Bruce Broussard, who was serving as chief executive of a $9-billion subsidiary of McKesson Corporation, a distributor of health-care supplies, systems, and pharmaceutical products. The board brought Broussard, who had served as CEO of US Oncology, aboard as Humana's chief operating officer and CEO designate. Broussard, in turn, brought extensive experience with Washington regulation, vertical integration, and product diversification, three strategic areas that Humana sought to strengthen.[9]

The ownership of CEO succession by company directors can also be seen at BHP Billiton, an Anglo-Australian mining, oil, and gas company with headquarters in Melbourne and roots dating to 1860. Its operations are global—ranging from Australia and Chile to South Africa and the United States—and by 2011 the company's annual revenue had reached over $50 billion and its market value $200 billion.

When the board had appointed Marius Kloppers as chief executive in 2007, he had indicated that his tenure should not exceed five to seven years. The directors began to focus on succession soon after the new CEO took office, and by 2011 they had laid out a detailed month-by-month map of their key decisions and major milestones. The board's adherence to its timeline, witnessed by one of us who followed the process from beginning to end, was methodical.

The board prepared a forty-six-point profile of what would be required in the next CEO, seeking to articulate the company's needs before identifying potential candidates. The successor would certainly have to understand the "big picture," with special appreciation for emerging opportunities in China, India, and Brazil; have a record of creating sustainable shareholder value; bring executive experience with both minerals and oil, including operational safety in each; and demonstrate an ability to build teams and work with boards.

The directors updated the profile in meeting after meeting as the company's market environment evolved and competitors changed. As the selection criteria became clearer and the priorities more evident, the directors came to concentrate on just a handful of criteria that were most likely to distinguish the CEO they sought.

The directors considered several external candidates who had been running natural resources or large capital-intensive global companies. But the board chose to focus more on a handful of internal prospects on the premise that it would prefer—all else being equal—to promote an insider. Board chair Jacques Nasser worked with the chief executive to identify and prepare their home-grown candidates. They discussed with the inside candidates their ambitions, and they arranged for 360-degree assessments, professional coaches, and added responsibilities to minimize any gaps that remained in their work experience. Through it all, the directors and chief executive worked to modulate expectations, repeatedly stressing there was no "pre-ordained outcome or timing." Mindful that one or more of the candidates might be approached by other companies, they also devised contingency plans and continued to track external prospects.

Near the end of 2012, the directors took one more hard look at the CEO requirements and sought to learn how well each of the final candidates would fit. Recognizing that the candidates were already well known to the board—they had been regularly attending its meetings— the directors gave the candidates a set of questions for response and discussion at a subsequent board meeting. The questions focused on how the executive would modify the company's strategy; what forces were most likely to affect the company, including changing markets and community expectations; how the executive would enhance shareholder value; and whom the executive would recruit around him or her to optimize the decision-making process.

From the board presentations, coaching reports, and the incumbent CEO's separate assessment, the directors concluded that the finalists were all solid but that one brought a better fit for what the company faced. The board decided in early 2013 to hand the tiller to Andrew Mackenzie, who had earlier worked with BP and mining-giant Rio Tinto, and who had been running one of BHP Billiton's largest divisions employing 50,000 people.

The directors informed Mackenzie that he would take the helm on May 10, 2013, and they gave him detailed guidance on what was expected of their new captain. They worked with him to identify strategic priorities and immediate areas for focus and delivery.

The board chair met with each of the other candidates to explain the directors' decision. The outgoing CEO, incoming CEO, and board chair also met with major company investors to explain the succession and transition. And the chair worked with the CEO-elect to ready his leadership hand for the demands ahead.

Through it all, more than five years in the making, the directors, with the advice and support of the incumbent CEO, had driven both the leadership development and the succession plan. The process had been meticulously planned, but it also remained fluid and adaptable. The board chair had taken responsibility for keeping the moving parts coordinated and diverse parties informed over the years. Succession management and leadership development had been viewed as an ongoing function of the board rather than a punctuating event.

The Dangers of Inadequate Due Diligence

When selecting a new chief executive, boards of directors will want to demand in-depth data on their final choice. If the CEO begins to fail, the recriminations and the questions always seem to begin with, "Why didn't you uncover this in the referencing process?" Better to solve the problem at the front end than pay the price at the back end, as some enterprises have painfully learned.[10]

The high cost of delaying due diligence played a key role in the 2012 proxy challenge to the Yahoo! board mounted by hedge fund activist Daniel Loeb, manager of the $9-billion Third Point fund, which had amassed a 6 percent stake—about $1 billion—in Yahoo!'s stock. Loeb was unhappy with the company's declining fortunes and executive turnover. The board had appointed six CEOs in eleven years. To remedy matters, Loeb proposed a slate of four dissident directors to implement a strategic redirection that he had already been advocating, including greater focus on the firm's media and advertising business.

The current directors, in Loeb's view, did not have the talent to help the firm grow its revenue from advertising. While the company still drew large numbers of viewers, its ad sales had declined compared with those of Facebook and Google. Loeb's filing with the Securities and Exchange Commission argued that "key elements of a balanced strategy remain unaddressed at the Board level" because "the Board's current strategic direction is to emphasize the technology aspects of [Yahoo!'s] business at the expense of advertising and media, which accounts for the vast majority of the [Yahoo!'s] revenues." As a result, Yahoo!'s "core revenue generating capability [is] at substantial risk," and "directly results from a dearth of essential expertise in media and entertainment at the Board level."[11]

What Daniel Loeb singled out about his own nominated directors' capabilities was not their record of management oversight, but rather their direct familiarity with the market challenges faced by management. Loeb advocated, besides himself, Jeff Zucker, the former president and CEO of NBC Universal, for his building of Hulu, a website with ad-supported streaming videos; Michael J. Wolf, founder of media consulting firm Activate and former chief operating officer of MTV Networks, because of his familiarity with "talent" in the industry; and Harry Wilson, a restructuring specialist who helped engineer the turnaround of General Motors. While ultimately advocating for investors, the four dissident directors were viewed by Loeb as bringing to the board the kind of strategic thinking that company directors and executives presently lacked.[12]

Then came a startling revelation. While performing its due diligence on Yahoo!, Third Point discovered that then-Yahoo! CEO Scott Thompson had listed two college degrees—in accounting and computer science—from Stonehill College (near Boston), but had in fact only earned the first. Next, Third Point found that the director who had led the CEO search that had selected Thompson—Patti S. Hart—had herself incorrectly stated her own college credentials, reporting that she had earned a degree in marketing and economics instead of business administration. The chief executive resigned and the director announced that she would not stand for reelection. In May 2012, Yahoo! agreed to bring three of Third Point's director nominees—Loeb, Wilson, and Wolf—onto its board. Two months later the board recruited Marissa Mayer, who had long served in senior positions and the inner sanctum of Google, as its new chief executive.[13]

This and other misfires share a common root: inadequate due diligence on the part of the board. CEO referencing is a central responsibility for directors, one in which they are directly and personally involved. The board's role in risk mitigation has been much discussed but linked primarily with financial risk. Preventing human capital shortfall by ensuring the selection of the right CEO—one whose capabilities and skills properly align with the job to be done—is among the board's most fundamental risk management responsibilities. Nothing can fully make up for the choice of the wrong CEO.

Ten Principles for Finding the Right CEO

When determining suitability to be CEO, directors will want to remind themselves of an obvious premise: no candidate is perfect. The goal is to understand the relative trade-offs among the candidates' strengths and weaknesses, and to ensure that the prospects' deficits are not in areas that are especially critical for company performance. While candidates' visible accomplishments are prerequisites, rigorous referencing goes deeper, exploring how the results were achieved, including leadership style and capacities—all essential inputs. From the directors, executives, and specialists whom we have witnessed, worked with, and interviewed, and from our own search and consulting experience, we draw ten principles for executives and directors to guide the executive succession process.

1. People set strategy.

American baseball legend Yogi Berra warned, "If you don't know where you're going, you might not get there." Berra was famous for his "Yogi-isms," but this one contained an essential truth: inchoate strategies and ineffectual leadership generally go hand in hand. Conversely, directors and executives who know where the company should be going will be best equipped to guide it there.

2. Implement a CEO and successor evaluation methodology.

Link an evaluation system to the company's central idea, its competitive strategy, and prospects' individual capacities and performance, with the latter focusing on their integrity and ethics, team building, execution excellence, shareholder return, and personal gravitas—and ability to work in the boardroom. More generally, the board leader will want fellow directors to be clear-minded and in agreement about the leadership criteria used to compare candidates.

3. Include in the CEO's evaluation an assessment of how well the company is building a succession plan for the next generation of company leaders.

On this issue, much work is yet to be done. When we asked the chief human resources officers at a number of major companies whether they had a coherent system in place to evaluate and compensate the CEO's succession performance, most reported that their firm had none. And even those who did have at least the rudiments of such systems in place said that the reward system was still too weak to effectively guide the CEO's actions.

4. Place the board leader in charge of the succession process.

By tackling the job in partnership with a still-effective chief executive, the board leader can help root the process deeply in the company's management development, preventing succession from becoming an event-driven crisis. It is also helpful to consider both short-term disaster scenarios—are one or two lieutenants ready now to replace the chief executive if an accident or illness suddenly disabled the top executive?—and long-term outcomes—will a handful of executives be ready candidates to replace the CEO after a planned exit five years in the future?

5. Retain a high-performing chief executive, but also work to keep capable successors.

Able executives who have learned how to run an enterprise are likely to be itching for a CEO opportunity. Effective succession also requires offering incentives to these potential chief executives—including extra compensation—to retain their presence as CEOs-in-waiting if a well-performing chief executive still has ample energy in the battery.

In the wake of Johnson & Johnson chairman and CEO William C. Weldon's decision to step down as CEO in 2012, for instance, the directors and CEO first settled on two final candidates—Alex Gorsky and Sherilyn S. McCoy—and then arranged to appoint them both as company vice chairs of the executive committee, pending a final succession decision. In the end, they opted for Gorsky, who had returned in 2008 from a stint as head of Novartis's North American pharmaceuticals, in part because his execution credentials were deemed particularly important at time when the company had been plagued by execution shortfalls. Whichever way the board went, it had cultivated two strong successors well before the succession event.[14]

Efforts to retain prospective successors do not necessarily end when the succession itself concludes. Those who are passed over are still among the firm's topmost talent; after all, they had just been considered viable corner-office candidates. Both the new chief executive and the directors have their work cut out for them to retain an executive who has been visibly passed over, especially with executive search firms perceiving a recruitment opportunity.

6. Seek candid comparative data on inside CEO candidates from those who have worked with all of them.

GlaxoSmithKline's 450-degree assessment, which confidentially vetted the views of all company executives who had worked with the three final candidates, is a useful illustration of this data-seeking process. Administered by either a trusted insider or a third party, the 450 yields comparative data on finalists, all of whom are obviously very strong leaders in their own right. Using such data sometimes yields surprising results. At GSK, the dark horse emerged as the best choice by a wide margin once the additional comparative data was compiled.

7. Make direct contact with both sources and candidates to verify information.

Even when engaging a third party, boards cannot fully hand off the vetting process. Directors will want to personally check on references, especially valuable where they have a preexisting tie with referees. A few trusted sources can yield far more useful data than a large number of less certain sources. In the absence of a trusted relationship, references can sometimes reveal little inside information or, sometimes, false information. As an example of the latter, one source claimed that a top candidate was an alcoholic, but when further vetting with more trusted sources confirmed no such behavior, the company chose the falsely accused candidate as its chief executive. In the end, a personal meeting of directors with the finalists can yield still further information, especially around whether the candidates are likely to prove strong partners with the directors.[15]

8. Review outside consultants carefully to prevent conflicts of interest.

Intentionally or not, executive search consultants hired to help with a CEO search can sometimes offer an overly affirmative view of a candidate they have sourced or an overly skeptical view of one they have not had a hand in finding. In one instance of the latter, a board's external search led directors to identify an executive at a *Fortune* 100 company who was ready to accept the job. As a final step in the process, the board retained an outside consultant to make one last evaluation of the candidate that the board, not the consultant, had identified. This consultant, however, reported a serious defect in the candidate and urged against the executive's appointment. When the board then turned to one of us, we found no evidence of the alleged shortcoming and recommended the executive's appointment. We also found reason to believe that the first consultant had hoped for a new CEO search assignment if the candidate he opposed was rejected. The company finally went with its initial preference, and the new chief executive performed exceptionally well over the next five years.

9. Maintain confidentiality.

We have seen stellar CEO candidates drop out of consideration when their identity is inadvertently revealed, especially if they are serving as a chief executive elsewhere. Journalists inevitably circle during a high-profile external search, and communicating orally and avoiding media contact can help preserve confidentially. One way to prevent a damaging revelation is to ask outside references for guidance on a candidate not for a CEO position but rather for a board seat. Now that boards increasingly partner to lead the enterprise, not just monitor management, many of the same leadership qualities that make for an effective director also make an effective chief executive. Thus, board-seat evaluations can provide a veiled but useful appraisal of CEO-related competencies.

10. Embed succession planning in corporate culture.

Creating a culture of executive succession entails many steps, including performance incentives for executives to build the system, a development capability that repeatedly reaches large numbers of managers, coaching and mentoring by both directors and executives, and an openness to both inside and outside candidates. Above all, it requires an active partnering between the directors and the chief executive to preemptively ensure that their pipeline is full and its occupants are developing in the upward direction.

Selecting a new chief executive has become more critical because so much rides on a positive outcome. Uncertain times, complex markets, and the need to scale up to compete globally all raise the ante on leadership at the top—and raise the obligation of directors to assure that the best fit possible is at the helm. Is this the right person to lead the company in this particular business at this particular time? Will he or she collaborate with the board, or fight it? Do his or her talents make a strong match with the strategic requirements of the moment? Is there a process in place for cultivating, identifying, and appointing not just the next CEO but the one after that? These have become critical director obligations for one simple reason: the fate of an enterprise depends heavily on the right answers.

While many of the qualities that define an effective chief executive are almost universal and are essential for virtually every organization, not all are. In the following chapter we look at finding the fit between what the company requires and what a potential chief executive offers. It is a matter of making a match between the several most critical company requirements and the several most critical candidate talents.

DIRECTOR'S CHECKLIST FOR CHIEF EXECUTIVE SUCCESSION

✓ Are company strategy and executive succession explicitly linked?

✓ Is a board process in place for evaluating the CEO and potential successors?

✓ Does the board explicitly assess the CEO's management of a succession plan for the next generation of company leaders?

✓ Is the board leader driving the succession process for the CEO and direct reports?

✓ Is the board working to retain a high-performing chief executive—but also to keep capable successors?

✓ Does the board have a member who could serve as CEO in the wake of an unexpected exit if no insider is yet ready for succession?

✓ Has the board compiled comparative data on the inside CEO candidates from those who had worked with all of them?

✓ Have directors had direct contact with both the CEO candidates and the information sources to verify information about them?

✓ If executive search consultants are retained, have they been vetted to ensure that there are no conflicts of interest?

✓ Does the board ensure candidate confidentiality?

✓ Has the board gathered independent references on the outside candidates?

✓ Is succession planning embedded in the company's culture?

7.

A Question of Fit

We believe that the concept of the *universal chief executive* is as misleading as the idea that a gifted athlete should be able to excel at more than one position on the sports field or even several kinds of fields. Strategic fit between a candidate and the shoes to be filled is the crux. Gauging that calls for a vital focus on two facets:

Leadership requirements: What are the two or three most critical requirements for executive leadership given the company's expected competitors and future opportunities?

Candidate capabilities: What are the two or three most distinctive leadership talents the candidate has demonstrated?

Consequences of a Mismatch

The absence of a tight fit between the leadership requirements and candidate capabilities can be seen in the aftermath of the Citigroup's board's decision to pass the CEO baton to its chief operating officer, Charles O. Prince III, and to move Robert B. Willumstad up to chief operating officer under Prince. The plan was for the new number-two to use his extensive operating experience to run the company on the inside—Willumstad had served as CEO of Citigroup's Global Consumer Group and president of Citibank North America, among its biggest operations—and for Prince to shoulder the external work. The plan fell apart when Willumstad left the firm in 2005 and Prince decided to absorb the COO's inside responsibilities as well.

While the CEO and COO had worked well together, the chief executive was now by himself at the top of a multisegment business in a wide array of financial markets that were becoming increasingly volatile. The CEO did not bring the entire range of capabilities required to fully lead the complex firm on both the inside and the outside in a more unpredictable climate, and after surprisingly poor company performance, the board forced him out in 2007.[1]

Consider yet another disappointment in CEO selection that also came down to a failed fit. Founded by two pioneers, Retailer Inc. (a pseudonym) grew with giddying speed into the largest company in its category in America. One founder, John Riley, became the CEO, while the second, Mary Stanton (both pseudonyms), remained on the board but pursued other interests, including service on the board of Industrial Inc., a large multinational company that primarily sold heavy equipment to manufacturing customers. When the time came for CEO succession at Retailer, the chief executive had given little attention to the capabilities of internal candidates, nor much thought to the leadership requirements that might be compulsory in the next CEO. Customer service on the stores' floors was still considered legendary, but the firm was encountering significant problems, including cash crunches, excessive inventories, and shrinking margins.

Fortunately, or so it seemed at the time, Michael Cicerone (as we will call him), the runner-up among two top candidates for succession at Industrial Inc., had become available. Mary Stanton had known Cicerone for seven years from board presentations, site visits, and private dinners, and had acquired further information about him when he was competing for the top slot at Industrial.

Stanton knew, for example, that Cicerone had overseen expansion of an equipment-making unit at Industrial from $4 billion to $8 billion in just three years, largely through bold acquisitions with effective integration. Cicerone was also considered one of the best operating executives in America, his stamina legendary. Few could match his ability to ratchet up productivity year after year. Other boards and headhunters were circling.

Both of the Retailer cofounders considered Cicerone's availability a rare opportunity to recruit a top executive with a proven record. Though other board members questioned his lack of experience in a consumer business, the board gave Cicerone the keys to the kingdom.

As new CEO, Cicerone immediately began to implement the tactics that had made him so successful at Industrial, quickly bringing in two former associates to head human resources and acquisitions. They, in turn, each recruited a dozen of their own ex-associates to build their own departments.

With familiar personnel in place, Cicerone set out to implement the same strategic planning system that he had used at Industrial. He fired the two most senior executive vice presidents, centralized the organization to wring out costs and generate cash through better inventory management, and commissioned bankers and the new acquisition executive to plan for inorganic growth, including acquisitions in adjacent markets. His announced goal: to outperform his previous employer in revenue growth, operating margins, and cash generation. To that end, he increased product prices, toughened supplier terms, and tightened labor discipline in the stores.

Within a year, the company had expanded cash reserves, improved margins, and increased revenue. But store associates and retail consumers began complaining that retail floor services had deteriorated. At the same time, Retailer's chief rival accelerated refurbishment of its own stores to make for a better shopping experience. Despite great financial results at the outset, Retailer's stock price took a tailspin compared with that of its main rival.

Cicerone never acquired a feel for what the company and its customers really needed. He neglected investment in the core business model, and customers began migrating to the rival's more appealing stores. When year-over-year same-store sales declined, the CEO argued that the metric was no longer relevant for Retailer's operations. What mattered instead, he said, were cash and margins. But with the brand tarnished, sales went into free fall, and the distressed founders and their board soon pushed their new CEO out the door. An arduous rebuilding of consumer trust was now required, its cost an avoidable result of the poor fit that the directors had allowed between the CEO's capabilities and the company's needs.

Directors and executives are subject to the same misjudgments and misfires as the rest of us, and sometimes those stem from the most personal of considerations. Consider the situation at one of the five largest utilities in the United States as the board was deliberating over two internal CEO candidates in the mid-1990s.

Kenneth Ambler (again, pseudonyms are used), the chief financial officer, was a veteran company executive widely respected on Wall Street. Operating executive Robert Graves had been with the company for only five years but had successfully turned around a money-bleeding business unit, a restructuring during which he displayed an exceptional talent for strategic thinking and execution. One other notable difference between the two candidates: Ambler played golf every other week with one of the longest-serving and most influential directors of the company. Graves did not.

A five-person board committee devoted six months to resolving which of the two should succeed the utility's chief executive. In the end, two directors favored CFO Ambler and three preferred operating executive Graves. With succession seemingly settled, the CEO, who also served on the special committee, presented the two candidates to the board for final review and decision, with flip charts to lay out the pros and cons of the two finalists. Since both candidates were considered very strong, the boardroom presentation and dialogue dwelled mainly on the merits of each.

As soon as the chief executive informed the board that the search committee had voted 3–2 in favor of Graves over Ambler, the dominant director—the CFO's golfing partner—intervened. He asked, surprisingly, that the CEO step out of the room for a few minutes so the directors could deliberate without him. With just ten minutes of executive session, the board reversed the committee's recommendation and elected Ambler as chief executive, the brute force of one personality stacking the cards and overturning a committee's reasoned recommendation.

Ambler, now the CEO, soon pushed Graves out of the company and sold the business that Graves had brought back to health. The longer epilogue, however, was even less pretty. Within three years, the sold business had tripled in value under new ownership, while the utility itself succumbed to an unwanted takeover.

Many factors feed into a board's failure to create the right fit. The selection process may be hijacked by just one or two motivated directors, or left to the outgoing chief executive, or become overly dependent upon headhunters who are a step removed. Reference checks may be inadequate; interviews, not sufficiently exhaustive. Sometimes, directors simply balk at thinking ahead; they look for a CEO that fits past challenges rather than imminent changes. Whatever the source, the result is much the same: good person, good position—but a lousy fit.

Requirements First, Then Capabilities

Perhaps it is only natural, but boards too often focus on candidate capabilities first, and leadership requirements second, when what is needed is the reverse: leadership requirements first, *then* candidate capabilities.

Consider an early IBM's recruitment of a new chief executive when the company was in deep trouble with declining sales and drying credit. In response, long-serving chief executive John Akers—he had been president and then CEO for the past decade—announced a breakup.

To get on top of the growing crisis, directors created a special committee that included two highly experienced executives—Thomas

Murphy, chairman and CEO of Capital Cities/ABC, and James Burke, retired chairman and CEO of Johnson & Johnson. Special committee members spent a month visiting scores of people around the world to gain a view of their company looking from the outside in.

The board also retained two premier executive-search firms that had placed scores of CEOs in a wide variety of industries. Management pundits, security analysts, and business journalists offered a host of unsolicited recommendations as well. Most outsiders came to believe that the new CEO must have IT experience.

Directors Murphy and Burke, however, finally focused on several quite different criteria, which they came to see as required. In addition to the usual leadership "givens," including impeccable personal character and a business track record, they specified three other requirements: (1) customer orientation; (2) business savvy, including a capacity to accurately diagnose what ailed IBM; and (3) an ability to execute the necessary changes to reverse the decline. Not required: a technology background.

With the new leadership requirements now clearly articulated, IBM directors turned to Louis V. Gerstner Jr., who at the time was running the highly leveraged food and tobacco giant RJR Nabisco, controlled by investment firm Kohlberg Kravis Roberts. Gerstner had previously held senior roles at American Express and McKinsey & Company, but none in technology.

The board's criteria for the kind of CEO it needed proved prescient. Gerstner diagnosed two causes of IBM's main ailments within weeks. Its mainframe computer business suffered a bloated cost structure and its products were being priced by the wrong people. Rather than breaking up the enterprise, he concluded that a better redirection of the firm was to transform it from hardware to software and services. IBM did not need a new vision, he concluded, just worthy execution, and he engineered that in the years ahead, restructuring the company from a faltering behemoth into a formidable competitor.[2]

Nonnegotiable Strategic Criteria

Getting strategic fit right is inherently challenging, since the requirements of the CEO position are so diverse and complex and the capabilities of the candidates are so multifaceted and complex. Much data plus little time points to the importance of a defined process for ensuring a close fit around the most important criteria.

As a case in point on mastering the right strategic fit despite great complexity in the data, we turn to WorldCom, the large telecommunications company that had gone bankrupt in 2002 as a result of criminal malfeasance at the top. It sought to emerge a year later from Chapter 11 under the name of MCI (the name of a company it had earlier acquired)—and the leadership of a new chief executive. To that end, the board looked for a CEO who would be able to reinvigorate a demoralized sixty-thousand-person workforce, retain twenty million disaffected customers, foresee the emerging technologies that would carry the company in a fast-changing industry, and restore a shattered credibility on Wall Street.

WorldCom added to that all-purpose CEO description another dozen specific criteria, ranging from having a proven track record running a multibillion-dollar company to turning around languishing operations and developing and executing complex strategies. One of us sourced four finalists for the position, and for each candidate we prepared a several-page summary that detailed a broad array of that contender's capabilities. One candidate, for instance, was deemed to be a tough-minded and intense operating and financial expert. A second had held leadership positions at four global information services companies. A third brought three decades of experience in the telecommunications industry. And a fourth had already led turnarounds and was well versed in motivating large-scale workforces.[3]

Identifying the two or three position requirements and the two or three candidate capabilities around which the strategic fit would be tightest was vital but also inherently challenging because of the complexity on both sides of the equation. The documents outlining the WorldCom requirements and describing the four finalists' capabilities contained extensive information, and yet in the end the directors had to reduce all the data bearing on the strategic fit down to a simple binary decision of which of the four candidates to hire. Creating a process to pick through the vast array of information on the top position and top people was thus essential. And it evidently paid off: the candidate that the directors finally picked—Michael D. Capellas, former CEO of Compaq Computer Corporation and president of Hewlett-Packard—successfully restructured the company for sale to Verizon Communications in 2006 for $8.5 billion.

A Leadership Committee

We have witnessed a host of models for optimizing strategic fit, with no single best practice certain among them, but the essence of most is to seek convergence on the several criteria that best define a strategic match-up in a given case. We saw earlier how private equity giant Blackstone vets board members of the companies it acquires. The same care now goes into weighing the executive leadership of portfolio candidates. Too often in the past, Blackstone had found that chief executives of its portfolio companies departed or were replaced long before the five-year mark. A fifth of its portfolio CEOs had exited within a year of its investment, and another third was gone within the two following years. By the five-year point, more than half of the original CEOs had turned over.

Blackstone accordingly created a Leadership Committee in 2012 to provide more discerning assessments of the fit of the top team and governing board with the company's central idea and strategy before reaching a final decision to invest. Blackstone placed its top executives on the committee, including Steven A. Schwarzman, the cofounder and CEO; Hamilton E. James, chief operating officer; Joseph Baratta, global head of private equity; Sandy Ogg (whom we met earlier in the book), operating partner in the firm's private equity group; the head of the regional office where the prospective portfolio company is located; and several of Blackstone's executive advisers.

Building on the premise that, in the words of Blackstone's Ogg, the difference between a "good" deal and a "great" deal often came down to the quality of management, the Leadership Committee's task has been to reach discerning judgments regarding the quality of the company's top people and organizational architecture. Though Blackstone engages outside firms to conduct independent appraisals of the executives of the prospective companies, Ogg contends that the Leadership Committee's own sourcing and judgment on whether the CEO has the right talent to lead the enterprise is more predictive of performance than any other factor.

In truth, there never is a perfect fit between leadership requirements and candidate capabilities. What is more, the requirements for a good strategic match can change over time as the market evolves. But a better fit will come when director attention is explicitly focused on both requirements and capabilities, in that order. In cases where there is too little fit, incoming CEOs may be great performers elsewhere but doomed from the start, poorly suited for the new position in the first place.

Paraphrasing Peter Drucker, it is not whether a candidate is good, but good for what? If directors can preestablish two or three nonnegotiable criteria unique to the company's central idea and strategic challenges, they can start with Drucker's fundamental question resolved and then turn to which candidate's two or three most distinctive capabilities best match the several criteria. As directors increasingly join executives at the leadership table, getting that fit right—ensuring it is *strategic*—will increasingly serve as a defining measure of a board's leadership.

However good a match may have looked when directors anointed a new chief executive, mistakes are made. And then, as we will see in the next chapter, it becomes a question for directors whether to retain, revive, or relieve a faltering chief executive.

DIRECTOR'S CHECKLIST FOR A CEO CANDIDATE'S STRATEGIC FIT

✓ What are the two or three most critical requirements for executive leadership, given the company's expected competitors and future opportunities?

✓ What are the two or three most distinctive leadership talents required of the candidates, given that most finalists come with a proven leadership record?

✓ Is there convergence between the several criteria that best define a strategic match between the company's leadership requirements and a candidate's capabilities at a given moment?

8.

Spotting, Catching, or Exiting a Falling CEO

Like neutrinos and Higgs bosons, early signs of a faltering chief executive are often hard to detect. Most chief executives are constitutionally optimistic, and since by definition their role is to surmount challenges, the tenor they bring into the boardroom is likely to be relentlessly upbeat. Taking executive overassurance into account will aid directors in detecting nascent troubles ahead, but it is only one piece of a very complicated puzzle.

Spotting a Falling Chief Executive

From our several decades of witnessing more than fourscore fumbling CEOs, we have noted that, in virtually every case, warning signals were noticed early by at least one or two directors but were commonly not shared with fellow directors. We learned of the indications in real time because alarmed board members privately disclosed their rising qualms about the CEO in the course of our work with them. The concerned directors were nonetheless hesitant—no surprise—to get the ball rolling. After all, they had helped pick the top executive, and they realized that a forced exit could be not only a career-ender for the executive but also a reputation-killer for themselves. Perhaps most inhibiting of all, they knew that the CEO often retained avid defenders among the other directors.[1]

As a result, boardrooms frequently lack the time, heart, or resolve to act. They fail to listen openly for one another's reservations. Even when private apprehensions are discreetly aired, directors can still find it nearly impossible to agree on how—or even when—to intervene, until calamity strikes. In Warren Buffett's words, already noted at the beginning of this book, in the tight community of corporate directors, comity too often prevails. Few want to be known as the director who threw the first stone.

In our view, leadership at the top requires just the opposite mind-set, with directors acting quickly on troubling news even if their concerns ultimately prove to be false warnings. Just as for company executives, embracing a candid, data-seeking, and truth-telling role is critical for the board to meet its own leadership responsibilities, not only its monitoring functions.[2]

An unflinching focus on a CEO's perceived shortcomings, however, first requires a readiness to *recognize* the emergent facts. This is particularly important during a period of prosperity when it is harder for directors to spot, or even want to detect, signs of a CEO's decline. If earnings are up, stock is rising, and analysts are praising, nascent executive shortcomings can be conveniently—and predictably—overlooked.[3]

To ensure that potential problems are identified as early as possible, regardless of the company's current performance—and thus to strengthen the partnership between a well-functioning board and a well-performing management—it is useful for directors to keep a weather eye on early signs of executive deficits. Assuming that the company's central idea has been well formulated in the boardroom, three embryonic indicators, if ignored too long, often mushroom into far more: lack of clear strategy, failure to execute, and wrong people calls.

Lack of Clear Strategy

Chief executives frequently say that they have explicitly laid out a com-pelling strategy for the firm. Yet directors just as frequently report that they have received everything they need *except* the strategy in a form that is coherent, compact, memorable, and with a tangible sense for how it will enable the company to generate value in the immediate years ahead. That is bad enough, but when directors have failed to gain an appreciation for the company's strategy, they also have little to go on when executives bring tactical proposals to them for review and ap-proval, and thus little on which to base a board's response.

A telling incident: One of the four largest companies in the fast-mov-ing software industry faced top-line growth that lagged far behind its direct competitors. The chief executive had done a great job stabilizing the company by cutting costs, streamlining product lines, and focusing on customer segments. The bottom line improved, but increasingly worried about the top line as well, the board asked the CEO for ac-tions to bolster company growth. Directors patiently waited for many months, but by the time they regrouped around the still-unresolved issue, the firm had fallen even further behind in the race for profitable top-line growth.[4]

Market and technological changes, particularly when they cut across industries, ought to put directors on special notice. Existing strategies can be marginalized by a new bend in the road, and if the CEO does not see the turn coming, management may not have time to work in concert with the board to formulate a new strategy. The inability of the leadership of bookseller Borders and photography giant Kodak to anticipate such shifts helped bankrupt both in 2011 and 2012.

Chief executives who do not return straight answers to the board when questioned on strategic direction—or who release bad news only at the eleventh hour—are among the more telling signs of strategic ambiguity. One symptomatic complaint came to us from a lead direc-tor of the world's largest enterprise in its field. Obtaining information from his chief executive had become like pulling teeth, he said, re-quiring much exertion and inflicting great pain. The chief executive was playing almost everything close to his chest, and only as the company neared a precipice did the lead director and other board members finally extract the information they required to fully appreciate the scope of the strategic misdirection.

Failure to Execute

Whether a strategy is not clearly expressed or clearly working, directors cannot wait long to act. Strategy and the central idea underpinning it are too fundamental to the enterprise for a chief executive to remain unclear or elusive on either. But in our experience, it is actually a failure to execute that is the most commonly encountered of the three early-warning indicators, and the reason most failing CEOs lose their jobs. We have found that a leader's failure to execute is typically some combination of several troublesome habits, all early signals of peril ahead:[5]

1. Lack of clear focus on a few dominant priorities.

Instead of clearly focusing on what really matters to the company, some chief executives opt for the idea du jour or a long menu of initiatives—carrying out dozens of endeavors in the name of letting a thousand flowers bloom. Yet in doing so, they lose focus and allocate resources chaotically, starving the core. Others choose to execute what they had achieved in their past rather than what is needed ahead.

2. Dislike of follow-through.

Sometimes executives fail to follow through because it can seem tactical and demeaning, other times because it would imply that the chief executive did not trust his or her direct reports. The absence of effective follow-through by a CEO can seem mundane and not worthy of director attention, but it is almost never inconsequential. In the case of one company buffeted by incessant commodity price increases, for instance, the chief executive did not press the right executives to change their pricing decisions in response to market movements. When company margins collapsed, the directors finally recognized the chief executive's weak follow-through and belatedly gave the CEO a year to master the problem, an executive probation.

3. Underanticipation of unintended consequences.

Rarely does implementation of plans go smoothly, but a readiness to anticipate and adjust to setbacks is sometimes in short supply. In one $10 billion firm that built its success on product innovation, a new CEO aggressively introduced a quality-control program. From his previous leadership at another company, he was familiar with the program's ability to streamline processes and eliminate defects, and he insisted that quality-control precepts be adopted by all of his firm's major divisions, including research and development. As intended, the quality-control initiative did slash costs and cut errors, generating much-needed cash. But the program also generated unexpected side effects: the R&D function languished, and within four years the company's margins had plummeted as customers migrated elsewhere for more cutting-edge products.

Wrong People Calls

Decisions on senior management appointments, reassignments, and replacements are at the heart of executive life, but they are also notoriously difficult to make. Executives consistently report that the toughest decisions they face are personnel actions. Top managers can lead only through others, and if others prove unfit, an executive's leadership can be fatally impaired. Several early signs of a shortcoming in this arena deserve special attention.[6]

1. A chief executive becomes overly reliant on the decision making of a senior officer.

Consider the case of a long-serving chief operating officer at one major firm, a ten-year veteran.[7] She had developed deep personal relationships with major customers and negotiated well with its key suppliers, both of enormous value to the company's operations. At the same time, she tended to overpower other managers with her exceptional grasp of business details. Allergic to emergent technologies for running the business, she also thwarted attempts to introduce new digital systems necessary to modernize the enterprise.

Several directors concluded that the chief operating officer had become more of a liability than an asset, but despite their prodding, the chief executive proved unwilling to rein her in or replace her. Yes, he could see the shortcomings the directors pointed out, but he had come to depend on her for daily direction of the firm. Even after a majority of directors came to a consensus that her departure was overdue, the board remained reluctant to force a change. And without its direction, the chief executive officer repeatedly opted to postpone a messy reshuffling for another day.

2. A chief executive becomes captive to one or more special advisers who filter or choke off the upward flow of diverse views.

This scenario played out at a technology company that the founding chief executive had built, with great fanfare, into one of the world's four largest computer makers at the time.[8] After having come from nowhere just twelve years earlier, the computer firm and its chief executive were savoring their roaring success. The CEO's glittering reputation catapulted him onto the boards of several of the largest companies in their respective industries, and he began to devote great energy to his role as a director as well as to a host of philanthropic causes. Now with less time for his own enterprise, he opted to limit communication and information inside the company to just two executives, the chief financial officer and the chief human resource officer (CHRO).

While they performed well in their functional roles, the CFO and CHRO were not line executives, had never managed a business, and thus had no direct P&L experience. As a result, decisions at the top were delayed and unresolved conflicts spread through the matrix. This paralysis proved perilous for a company with only a 3 percent net margin and a massive inventory always on the verge of technological obsolescence. Senior managers divided into factions, while line managers increasingly kowtowed to the CFO and CHRO. Absorbed by his external obligations, the celebrity CEO still believed he could run the company through his two trusted associates, even as he drifted out of touch with the business. In effect, he had allowed himself to become his associates' captive.

3. A chief executive opts to elevate a functional executive with little line experience into a line position.

Consider one chief executive's decision to move a twenty-year veteran staff manager into one such operating role.[9] The veteran had performed brilliantly in strategic planning and a range of functional assignments. By finally giving him major P&L responsibility, the chief executive theorized, the staff manager would gain the line experience necessary to prospectively follow as the CEO's successor.

It was a promising gesture, but ultimately a costly one. Since the company was among the five largest consumer goods firms in the world, a major line position entailed oversight of an operation with several billion dollars in annual sales. It was in fact the largest freestanding operation in a company that was a century-old icon of American business. For the executive, it would be a very challenging assignment. The division was lumbering along, guzzling cash, and barely profitable. But that, of course, was the idea: what could offer a better baptism in line leadership than taking charge of a large and struggling operation? Who better to master the challenges than a manager with two decades of brilliant performance in staff functions? His analytic talents just needed the complementary line skills to round out the complete executive package.

In fact, the transition from function to line in a massive corporation—or even in a modest enterprise for that matter—is fraught with learning obstacles that might have been surmounted by proper mentoring from the chief executive. But the CEO in this case had no penchant and scant time for the careful coaching that was required. He was too absorbed by his own leadership trials, including labor negotiations and federal regulations. He failed to hold the functional executive accountable when the latter's performance soon fell short, nor was he willing to provide much genuine feedback to the executive on his faltering performance. In under twenty-four months, the division under the guardianship of the former staff executive nose-dived, cash drained, and the company staggered.

Lack of a clear strategy and a failure to execute are expressed in varied quantitative ways, among them:

- Three consecutive and significant misses in quarterly earnings. Falling short of company guidance on earnings per share for one quarter is not enough to draw a line, but after two or more consecutive quarters, directors will want to invest time and energy to identify the root causes and how the CEO plans to address them. If nothing else, directors may want to say "Enough," since investors may well be saying "Enough!" When Coca-Cola CEO Douglas Ivester fell short of targeted earnings without adequate explanation for several quarters in a row, the board forced him out after just two years in office.[10]

- A precipitous drop in stock price relative to peers and the market. When Hewlett-Packard CEO Léo Apotheker announced in August 2011 that the company planned to sell its personal computer division, HP's share price declined by 20 percent— $12 billion in value—over the next several trading days. (The new CEO who soon replaced him, Meg Whitman, rescinded the intended sale just three months later).

- Wrong people calls can explode in dramatic directions as well—for example, a surprise decision by the chief executive to fire the executive next in line on the succession chart, with little tangible evidence of misdeeds or coherent reasoning for the dismissal. Research confirms that when companies are in decline, entrenched CEOs resort to a well-worn tactic of blaming their subordinates and firing them instead of exiting themselves.[11]

Problem Spotted—Now What?

There are usually warning signs, early and late, that might enable vigilant directors to detect a faltering chief executive. What is sometimes less in evidence is a board's willingness to recognize and act on those intimations of trouble ahead. Rocking a boat that seems to be sailing smoothly can invite more criticism of the complaining director than the faltering CEO. Whatever the understandable reluctance in the boardroom, the directors' calling is to transcend it. Acting swiftly on problematic developments—whether evidenced by the lack of a clear strategy, failure to execute, or wrong people calls—can be essential for spotting a falling CEO before it is too late. Then the board can turn to the thorny issue of whether to catch and redirect the underperformer, or simply let the CEO go.

Directors will want to be confident that they can translate their concerns about a faltering CEO into specific steps, especially if they believe they are watching the CEO inch the company toward a precipice. Yet even for the most seasoned board members, this is not an uncomplicated task. Most know that even privately expressed criticism will make its way to the corner office, undermining whatever working relationship remains with the CEO and possibly resulting in the ouster of the doubting director instead of the stumbling executive.

When evidence of such indicators accumulates, directors will want to exercise their company leadership by considering three questions before deciding on a specific course of action:

1. Are the CEO missteps just an aberration that might well be rectified with some close-in coaching by the board leader?

2. If the missteps are more than an aberration, do they signal that the chief executive is indeed faltering, and if so, what director actions on top of coaching might help reverse the decline?

3. Either way, is the chief executive ultimately capable of strengthening the leadership capacities for the turnaround that is expected by directors and investors?

Keep the Lines Open

Individual directors whose suspicions have been aroused by negative responses to the above questions often wonder if they are the only board member harboring such doubts. Directors appreciate that they have only limited information on the CEO's behavior and that the chief executive knows far more about the business and industry than the board.

Sometimes, directors have simply been left in the dark until a pending action has become a fait accompli, as was the case in 2012 when Facebook CEO Mark Zuckerberg negotiated a $1 billion acquisition of photo-sharing start-up Instagram, informing his directors only after the deal was all but consummated. Directors also understand that their role within the company is a very part-time responsibility and that they are short of bandwidth for raising thorny issues that are likely to require time-intensive resolution. What is more, directors are unlikely to have any ready-made solutions at hand. As a result, it is important for a director with doubts to test concerns—cautiously—with others in the boardroom. From our experience, the tests can come in several ways with relatively low risk for the inquiring director.[12]

One avenue is to request information or analysis on what may be causing the company's decline. This helps separate unforced CEO errors from what any company executive might have been compelled by the market to do. We have heard a range of innocent-sounding questions posed in the boardroom to this end, including, "I would love to have a third-party view for the next meeting regarding the precipitous loss of our brand position" and, speaking directly to the CEO, "It would be nice to know your plan of action to get back to our preeminent position." The key, however, is discretion. One of us observed a veteran director walk over to a company's chief human resources officer with just six months at the company and bluntly ask, "What do you think of the CEO?" The HR executive predictably reported the director's offline but still indiscreet query to the CEO before the evening was out.

A second avenue is to test the waters with fellow directors during breaks in a board meeting. An innocent query about what seems to be causing the company's problems may well elicit shared concerns about the firm's top talent. The usefulness of this technique is one reason that chief executives who are in trouble with their board are known to minimize opportunities for directors to talk among themselves without the CEO present.

Working against any information sharing among the directors is the episodic cycle of board meetings and their jam-packed agendas. Directors typically assemble for no more than a day or two every other month, and when on site, devote much of their time to committee matters and the board's formal agenda. In between their crammed meetings, directors rarely communicate with one another. As a result, they may begin to sense that the CEO is faltering months before they are finally able to confirm their early intuition with others. Even then, unless there is evidence of a specific ethical transgression, directors may stall before summoning the courage to raise the issue in the boardroom. But by then the problems may be irreparable, leaving little choice but to replace the CEO. If there is still time for a fix, however, directors are wise to swiftly inform the CEO that the leash is short and a credible turnaround plan soon required.

Practices for Early Detection and Intervention

Several years or more might pass between the early warning signals of a potential CEO failure and the completion of a turnaround. Yet in fast-paced industries, that can be too long; prolonged remakes can push companies perilously close to the edge. Even in slow-moving industries, a several-month delay can prove serious.

Drawing on what we have witnessed at multiple companies, here are four practices that can make for early detection—and thus for early intervention—in any industry.

1. Ensure that executive sessions of the board include candid discussion of CEO behavior and performance.

The board leader can draw out unspoken director concerns in a private session with no executives present—provided that the board leader frames the commentary around problem solving and steers the exchange away from piling on the CEO. Making such reviews annually, semiannually, or even quarterly improves their odds of success. An ability to early detect a CEO's stumbles or a subtle shortcoming is one of those distinctive boardroom IQs.

After the board completes the candid discussion of the chief executive's style and performance, the lead director can offer concrete guidance to the CEO, following up with sustained coaching to overcome the evident shortcomings. The chief executive can facilitate the process by asking the board leader after every executive session of the board for feedback on how he or she can alter behavior or improve performance.

In one illustrative case, an early board intervention not only caught a chief executive well before the failure point, but also turned him into a superstar.[13] The CEO in question presided over a company in a languishing industry, one in which most major players had not even been able to earn back the cost of capital over the previous decade. The company's lead director had additional insight into these problems from his outside service as chief executive of a large customer of the company. At first, the lead director's suggestions on how to reinvigorate the company were not appreciated by the faltering CEO. After a year of little improvement, the lead director detected a rising restlessness among fellow directors. Several had even sought out the lead director to privately but forcefully voice their unhappiness with both the company's results and the chief executive's stewardship.

In a preemptive strike, the lead director asked each director privately to identify one step or action that the chief executive ought to take in the next twelve months to best set the company up for recovery and then success. After compiling the directors' proposals on a single sheet of paper and appending his own suggestions, the lead director circulated the draft among all the directors for comment or change. Once the document was finalized, the lead director then met the chief executive in a neutral city to present the directors' specific ideas for action. The director explained to the CEO that the board's idea list was intended to help him succeed, not to pester him with gratuitous criticism or demand tactical changes. The lead director added that his personal intervention came with the blessing of every member of the board, and he asked the CEO to report his progress in meeting the directors' recommendations to all board meetings during the coming year.

With the lead director's early intervention and specific direction, the CEO reinvigorated the company. Earnings began to exceed the cost of capital, an accomplishment that eluded his still-floundering peer companies. Simultaneously, he brought innovations to a tired industry. Soon, investors were applauding with stronger multiples for the company's stock than for its primary competitors. Even more impressive, this turnaround occurred during the very difficult environment following the 2008 financial crisis. Directors managed not only to catch a falling chief executive but also to reverse his fortunes—and those of the company—during one of the economy's most challenging periods.

2. Make the chief executive's annual evaluation and feedback more tangibly useful.

The chief executive's annual performance review is often focused primarily on financial metrics. Usually driven by the compensation committee, the board's appraisal sends a vital if limited signal to the CEO when it sets the CEO's annual bonus and long-term stock compensation based on the company's results made public in the yearly 10-K report.

While this obviously makes good sense, given the board's obligation to serve as a monitor on behalf of shareholders, it does little to provide the substantive guidance required by the board's role as a leader on behalf of shareholders. In primarily focusing on last year's financial results, directors ignore strategic thinking, incisive decision making, and other leadership capacities that the CEO may need to strengthen in the months ahead. When limited to an annual cycle, as such appraisals often are, the board is also missing an opportunity to provide midyear guidance and correction to the CEO, the very essence of what it means to exercise ongoing collaboration at the top.

Concentrating on just several priorities for the year has advantages, a point we have previously stressed in advocating better execution. The board leader provides the chief executive with just a few areas that require special attention and then requests that the two follow up on those specific priorities in the months ahead.[14]

Consider the chief executive of a major company that had been performing well.[15] Indeed, he had already managed to pull the company out of a downward spiral and, in the view of the directors, was exceptionally strong in execution. But directors also found it hard to decipher his strategy. His presentations to the board were filled with operating details, but the driving conception behind them remained implicit, leaving too much guesswork for most directors.

The lead director decided to spend half a day with the CEO to informally draw out the strategy that the CEO had in mind but had been unable to effectively articulate. The board leader kept copious notes on their discussion, and by the end of the evening's dinner together, he became convinced that the chief executive was indeed a strategic thinker, if not perfectly so. The lead director's prescription for the CEO was to work on several blind spots, communicate his thinking more clearly, and recruit an executive experienced in strategic planning and business development to work under him.

Coaching the CEO back from the edge proved providential. With the lead director's guidance, the chief executive brought in a new director for company strategy, sharpened his strategy story for both directors and investors, worked on the gaps in his thinking, and ultimately carried the company to the commanding heights of the industry. The company's initial public offering proved attractive, its stock price soared, and directors succeeded in recruiting two major shareholders onto the board.

This turnaround was a near-textbook illustration of the power of a productive collaboration at the top. The lead director first consulted his fellow directors, then coached the CEO, and finally reported the CEO's evolution back to the board. More generally, a board leader can usefully start with an open and candid dialogue in the boardroom. He or she asks what the CEO already does well and where the skill set requires strengthening. The process is nonlinear, with the board leader working back and forth with the CEO, drawing all the while on fellow directors' instincts, hypotheses, and sometime even misguided perceptions. Likewise, a tone of constructive dialogue that avoids peripheral issues and personal blame is usefully maintained. Then, with feedback from both inside and outside the boardroom, the board leader coaches the chief executive in constructive ways that reach and change the CEO. Of course, all of this is conducted with utmost discretion, since anything but complete confidentiality is likely to undermine the CEO's willingness to hear or learn anything.

3. Learn about the top management team.

From research and experience, we know that corporate leadership is more than a single layer deep. The top management team's leadership is as vital as that of the top executive alone—if not more so. For that reason, wise directors increasingly devote time not only to meeting and appraising the CEO's direct reports but even those one or two echelons below.[16]

Robert E. Weissman, a former chief executive at Dun and Bradstreet who has also served on the board of several major companies, including State Street Corporation, Pitney Bowes, and Cognizant Technology Solutions Corporation, devised one technique that appears exceptionally useful. At several of his companies, he arranged for each director to meet privately with one of the senior company managers for an hour before every board meeting. The senior managers were selected at random from the three top tiers below the CEO. At the start of the board meeting, Weissman then asked his fellow directors to share what they had each gleaned from the personal dialogue with a senior manager just prior to the board meeting.

4. Exercise caution and engage all the directors in any decision to relieve or revive a faltering CEO.

A rush to judgment on a failing CEO during a challenging period carries the same risks as aborting a takeoff when an aircraft is already halfway down a runway. Scrubbing a liftoff too late can be far more disastrous than gunning the engines, and yanking out a struggling chief executive in the middle of a mess can be more damaging than staying with the imperfect performer. Reviving the chief executive's leadership is normally a preferred alternative to showing him or her the door.

As a case in point, consider a financial institution fighting for traction in an era defined by slow growth, new regulations from the Dodd–Frank Wall Street Reform and Consumer Protection Act of 2010, uncertainty about the future of the Eurozone, and public hostility toward banking.[17] Its chief executive had a deep-rooted understanding of the industry, an essential foundation for any financial executive, but he came up short on the full repertoire of contemporary leadership skills. While he was winning battles against daily attacks from varied directions, he was also hoping that he would not have to fend off rearguard assaults from directors unhappy with his less-than-complete leadership bearing. Mindful of this concern, the lead director worked to ensure that all of the directors lent support to the chief executive's efforts, at least for the moment.

Replacing the CEO at Motorola

Finally, directors must be steeled to pull the plug when all else fails, and to do so before the damage spreads irreversibly through the enterprise. Being active is no guarantee, however, that a board will create value and not destroy it. A board that uses poor judgment in removing a CEO too soon is just as much of a value destroyer as one that passively allows a nonperforming CEO to overstay. Take the case of Motorola, an eighty-three-year-old company that for decades contributed mightily to the US economy through technology development and employment and has now been reduced to a shadow of its former self.[18]

After losing over $4 billion between 2007 and 2009, Motorola in 2011 split into two pieces—Motorola Solutions and Motorola Mobility Holdings, the latter since sold to Google. First listed on the NYSE in 1948, Motorola's stock market symbol MOT is no longer even traded. The destruction of value at Motorola—arguably the destruction of the company itself—began in 2003 when the board lost patience and removed CEO Christopher Galvin at the tail end of a turnaround and replaced him with the wrong CEO, but the underlying problem goes back a decade earlier.

Christopher Galvin was the third generation of Galvins to lead Motorola. His grandfather, Paul Galvin, had founded the company in 1928, and his father, Robert, had been its leader from 1958 to 1990. Throughout those decades, the company developed one new technology after another, attracted top engineering talent, created employment opportunities for vast numbers of people, and became an American icon. Motorola was a pioneer in car radios, two-way radios, pagers, cell phones, computer chips, and even Six Sigma, for which it received the first Malcolm Baldrige National Quality Award in 1989.

When Robert Galvin gave up his CEO post in 1986, the board promoted George M. C. Fisher to the job. Then in 1993, Fisher left abruptly to head Eastman Kodak, and Galvin, still chairman of the board, urged the directors to consider naming his son, Christopher, as CEO. The board, however, felt Christopher was still too inexperienced and instead chose Gary Tooker.

The mid-1990s was a critical time for the mobile phone business. Technology was changing quickly, and Motorola, under Tooker, stuck too long with its old technology, investing millions of dollars in a new analog-based handset while the rest of the world was moving to digital. The cell-phone carriers made it clear that they wanted to move to digital and, trusting Motorola's reputation for quality, asked the company to provide handsets for them. When Motorola stalled, new players gained traction.

Making matters worse were Motorola's choices among the three competing standards when it did move into the digital field. It focused on GSM phones first, which were popular in Europe but less so in the United States, and was late to the game with CDMA-based phones. Consequently, the company's 60 percent share of the wireless telephone market in 1995 plummeted to just 26 percent a year later.

The market misses tarnished the company's reputation and hit the bottom line hard. Predictably, the stock market was punishing. In 1997, directors concluded that they needed a new CEO and this time chose Christopher Galvin, who was then senior executive vice president, having come up through sales and marketing to head semiconductors and then paging systems.

Galvin's tenure was hardly smooth sailing. He had to take a huge write-off when Iridium, an expensive space-based satellite system, went online but failed to live up to its commercial promise. He also had to navigate the Asian currency crisis, which hit Motorola hard because a significant percentage of revenues came from that region. But Galvin was driven to rebuild the corporate culture he had seen unravel. He remembered the Motorola where great engineers worked as a tight-knit group to conquer the toughest technology challenges with a clear focus on satisfying customers. Hoping to end the myopic internal bickering that had become commonplace, he reorganized the company into larger divisions and gave people throughout the business greater decision-making authority. Meanwhile, the company was catching up in digital wireless phones and building a business around cable modems.

The stock price lifted, but the company's problems ran deep. Costs were too high, and poor decisions were wasting time and money. The stock price rose to $134 in spring 2000 but dropped to $86 one month later as investors lost confidence in Motorola's future. A turnaround was in order, and beginning in 2000, Galvin took it on.

The medicine was hard to swallow: $12 billion in pretax write-offs, a workforce reduction of 55,000 out of 150,000 people globally, the closing of nearly half of Motorola's facilities worldwide, the implementation of a GE-type ranking system, and the replacement of seventy of the top one hundred leaders. It was not all cuts, though. Intent on keeping Motorola true to its roots as a diversified technology company that takes risks and continually renews itself, Galvin instituted a new product development process and preserved $3.8 billion for R&D spending. He also rejected suggestions to narrow the company's focus by selling some divisions, such as semiconductors.

Galvin was convinced that he was doing the right things, but investors were not. Two years into the turnaround, the stock price had dropped to $11.98. What the market did not see was that the seeds were being sown for the Razr, which was to become the best-selling wireless phone of its time. Directors did not see it either, although they should have. What the board saw instead, with laser-like clarity, was a restless shareholder base that wanted quarterly earnings *now*. Given the public scrutiny boards were under at that time in the wake of Enron and other fiascos, the board was intent on representing its shareholders well. Consequently, directors pressured Galvin to deliver better numbers, regardless of the dot-com bust, 9/11, and the 2003 SARS epidemic that cut sales in China nearly to zero.

One director who seemed especially sensitive to shareholders' concerns was B. Kenneth West. He had been on the Motorola board since the mid-1970s, held the special title of senior director, and was very influential among his peers, who tended to give his opinions extra weight. West had never been enamored of the cell-phone business, suggesting at several junctures that Motorola get rid of that business before it became commoditized. West also was TIAA-CREF's corporate governance expert and longtime chairman of the National Association of Corporate Directors. In both capacities, he had been paying considerable attention to business judgment rulings and had become acutely concerned about the Motorola's board liability as shareholder and bondholder suits against other companies mounted.

As Christopher Galvin recalls events, West called him one day to insist he sell a piece of the business—any piece, according to Galvin. Galvin stuck to his own conviction not to sell, since he believed that technologies were going to collide, that companies were going to be getting into each other's businesses, and that having more pieces on the chessboard improved the odds of winning. Disagreement about the benefits of a diverse portfolio never got resolved.

Other directors, including two new members, hammered on the numbers, and Galvin walked the directors through the development efforts that were under way. It sounded like the same old saw—improvement is just around the corner—but at that very moment many insiders and customers were energized about a breakthrough product that was ready to launch in a matter of months. The CEO and the engineers showed directors the sleek new wireless Razr phone and explained its technical merits, but the board was unimpressed. One director confessed that he was not technology-savvy and said bluntly that he did not want to delve into the technology issues. The CEO extended an invitation for directors to meet with customers, but they did not.

In 2003, West and lead director John Pepper asked Galvin to step down. Some would argue that the board was governing well by responding to shareholders' impatience. But was it an act of sound judgment and leadership on the part of the board? Did that decision create or destroy value? Consider what happened next.

Galvin knew that the hard work of transforming the company had been done and that the Razr was on track for a huge market success.

Order bookings were zooming. He urged the board to reconsider its decision. But the board set about wooing Edward J. Zander, an outsider who had headed operations at Sun Microsystems and was currently working at Silver Lake Partners in Silicon Valley.

Galvin protested until the bitter end, suggesting that the board members delay making the change until they saw the quarterly results. Face-to-face with West, Galvin also made a prediction that if the board went ahead and hired a new CEO, that person would be viewed as a hero for groundwork that had already been laid.

The board nonetheless forced Galvin to exit in January of 2004. Eight weeks later, West visited with chief operating officer, Mike S. Zafirovski, who gave him a preview of the results for the first quarter of 2004. As he looked at the numbers, West kept shaking his head, saying, "Oh my God, Chris will say he told me so." Still, there were no second thoughts, and the board handed the reins to Zander in March 2004 as planned. Ten days later the quarterly results were released:

- A 42 percent jump in revenue

- Operating earnings just shy of 10 percent

- More cash on the balance sheet than debt for the first time in Motorola history

Virtually every key financial metric was at a record high, and that was *before* Razr sales. The Razr went on sale later that year and was a big hit. For the next three years, the mobile-phone business grew sales, earnings, and market share, and gross margins doubled.

Investors and other outsiders lauded Zander for overseeing such remarkable financial results—and to his credit, he pushed to market the phone aggressively—but insiders had a different take. They understood that technology development has a lag time as well as a short shelf life. A leader can soon become a laggard. While Motorola reaped the fruits of the Razr, it was not working on its replacement. To the contrary, the organization that had produced it was crumbling.

The Razr's positive impact on sales, margins, market share, and cash flow lasted into 2006, but Motorola missed the shift to 3G, and Samsung and Nokia sped ahead. By 2007, the mobile-devices business swung to a loss, overall profits went negative—the beginning of that $4 billion-plus loss—and the stock price took a nosedive. Carl Icahn smelled opportunity and bought a stake in the distressed company. Soon after, he pressed for a change in management. With that, the board asked Zander to leave and gave the reins to Gregory Brown, who had joined the company in 2003.

Having lost momentum, the mobile business failed to bounce back. Icahn pushed to break up the company, and Brown made plans to split the company into two parts. In 2010, the board of directors approved a plan to spin off Motorola Mobility Holdings, Inc., and rename the remaining business Motorola Solutions, Inc., which would begin trading on the NYSE in 2011 under the symbol MSI. In August 2011, Google purchased Motorola Mobility and its seventeen thousand patents for $12.5 billion—a bargain, according to many observers.

Obviously, the Motorola board—an evolving set of people, as some directors left and were replaced over time—did not set out to destroy value. Yet directors picked an inappropriate CEO in the early 1990s, then removed his successor after he had managed to set the company on course for its best performance ever. For an encore, the board then chose a new CEO who did not lay the groundwork for continued success and it seemed to have given him the wrong mandate: to fix something that might not have been broken. The company lost time and momentum and accelerated the company's demise.

Compare the Motorola of 2003 when the board pushed Galvin out to the Motorola of 2010 after Zander had been shown the door and Brown's mop-up operation was under way: revenues were 16 percent smaller, earnings were 21 percent lower, and its market value had declined 40 percent. By the time the company was split and its stock symbol retired in 2011, its product portfolio was much like it had been in 1936 while its research labs no longer existed.

Why did it take so long for the board to see that the changes Galvin had made were losing steam under Zander's watch and that the company was neglecting to reinvest in technology—the heart and soul of Motorola? To be sure, the waters were choppy, even turbulent. But waiting until results were in before backing a bet on technology or strategy was not a model of leadership. Nor was a reflexive response to the demands of investors, some of whom were short-term traders. Board leadership means digging deep, thinking and debating hard, and sometimes holding firm when outsiders are clamoring for change.

The directors' dismissal of a chief executive is rarely pretty, if occasionally necessary. It helps to have had unambiguous metrics for performance—or termination—already in place. The same is true for severance packages when necessary. The executive in question should feel satisfied, but key stakeholders need to view the exit as properly golden, not wrongly gilded. And director discretion remains large in defining those exit terms. Although hiring packages can be well-informed by comparable numbers from other companies, firing packages tend to be all over the map, offering far less guidance. Constructing the right package depends very much on the directors' leadership of the moment.

Companies compete intensely around products, but equally around talent. That makes quality at the top a prime responsibility of the board—one of its callings—and the center point is the board's decision on retaining, reviving, or relieving the chief executive. Directors carry enormous responsibility for ensuring that they find and retain the right CEO, catch a falling star before it is too late, or let one go before the damage spreads and becomes ingrained. The business tempo in many industries can punish board indecision in this realm with a vengeance.

Once boards have the right directors in the boardroom and the proper managers in the executive suite, they can turn to the fundamental task of creating value. Drawing on the experience of General

Electric, Procter & Gamble, Rohm & Haas, and India's GMR Group, we examine in the following chapter how directors bring value to enterprise risk management.

DIRECTOR'S CHECKLIST FOR SPOTTING A FALLING CEO

✓ Absence of clear strategy

✓ Lack of focus on a few dominant priorities

✓ Dislike of follow-through

✓ Underanticipation of unintended consequences

✓ Overreliance on the decision making of a senior executive

✓ Captive of special advisers

✓ Functional executive appointed to line position without line experience

DIRECTOR'S CHECKLIST FOR RETAINING, REVIVING, OR RELIEVING THE CHIEF EXECUTIVE

✓ Are CEO missteps an aberration that coaching by the board leader can overcome?

✓ If missteps are more than an aberration, what additional corrective actions are warranted?

✓ Is the CEO capable of strengthening the leadership capacities required for full revival?

✓ Does the board have information about the root cause of a company's decline?

✓ Do most of the directors believe that the CEO is faltering?

✓ Is the board's annual evaluation of the CEO focused on leadership indicators, not just financial metrics?

✓ Have directors and the CEO coached other executives on how to work with the board?

✓ Does the board learn directly from and about executives who report to the CEO?

✓ If moving toward relieving the CEO, are most or all of the directors of common mind?

✓ Are performance metrics and severance terms well in place before advancing toward dismissal?

PART THREE

VALUE CREATION

9.

Turning Risk into Opportunity

The need for directors to lead risk management has become more vital in a threatening era that requires an unrelenting focus on downside risks and upside opportunities. As a result, boards are increasingly working directly with top executives to institute enterprise risk management (ERM) systems. Yes, leading a company's leaders—assuring the right CEO is in place, with the right strategic fit—remains a director's primary duty, but in an era of heightened risks of all sorts, assuring the company is prepared for the unexpected runs a close second. If the ship sinks in a storm under an excellent captain's watch, shareholder value is destroyed as surely as if it sank with an incompetent skipper at the helm.

The dramatic catastrophes that have already dotted the twenty-first century—the financial crisis of 2008–2009, the 2010 BP *Deepwater Horizon* oil spill, the Japanese tsunami of 2011, and the cyberhacking of 2013, to cite the more prominent examples—are unlikely to be repeated in any exact detail. But the raw number of natural and human-caused disasters has been rising steadily on an annual basis for at least

the last forty years as globalism spreads enterprise into sometimes po-
litically—and even geologically—unstable regions of the world.

The year 1970 tallied slightly more than 50 natural catastrophes and
40 unnatural disasters, according to the global reinsurer giant Swiss
Re. By 2010, those numbers had swollen to over 160 natural and about
140 unnatural events, totaling $218 billion in economic losses and
$43 billion in insured losses. And 2011 blew away virtually all exist-
ing records, with $370 billion in total losses, $116 in insured losses, the
highest insured earthquake losses ever ($49 billion), and the highest
insured losses ever for a single flood event ($12 billion, in Thailand).

Trend lines like that—in frequency and cost—cannot be ignored.
Little wonder, then, that executives and directors are now devoting
substantial board time to both appraising potential hazards and devis-
ing practices that will protect the firm from catastrophic risk as well
as help it recover swiftly from disaster. At the same time, they are also
giving time to identifying uncertainties that present fresh opportunities for advantage. Managing risk is a matter of both seizing upside
possibilities and dodging downside consequences.[1] To appreciate how
that partnership is being constructed, we look at the risk management
initiatives of one of America's flagship enterprises.

Balancing Risk and Reward at General Electric

Founded in 1892, General Electric is known globally for its managerial strength, marketing brand, and operating discipline.[2] One of the
world's largest companies, GE operated within more than 150 countries
in 2013, employing some 300,000 people. A year earlier, *Fortune* listed
GE as one of the top global companies for leadership development.[3] The
magazine also regularly includes GE among its globally "Most Admired
Companies." Others have heaped praise on the company for its innovative services and product diversity, with good cause: GE's $145 billion
in revenue for 2012 came from a broad portfolio of businesses in infrastructure, financial services, health care, and industrial products.

General Electric has also been exceptionally mindful of risk, not content to assume that its decentralized approach is sufficient for mitigation. Some years back, the board and CEO asked a number of consultants for guidance on its risk management practices. The conclusions of both insiders and outsiders were very similar: risk was still best managed within the individual business units, such as GE Aviation or GE Energy, and by corporate functions, such as legal or finance, since each faced dramatically different risks. Nonetheless, senior management still included an explicit focus on companywide threats during its annual strategy review process, and in 2008, at the depth of the financial crisis, that threat arrived in full roar, greater than even the worst pessimist had anticipated.

The financial crisis did not bring down GE, but it did impel executives and board members to significantly bolster the company's enterprise risk management. With encouragement from the directors, chief executive Jeff Immelt and his lieutenants moved to create an enduring framework for tracking and managing risk. In 2009, they appointed a veteran GE manager, Mark Krakowiak, as the company's first chief risk officer. Krakowiak had worked in or closely with all of GE's businesses over his twenty-seven-year career in financial management. At the time of his appointment, Krakowiak already had a huge array of responsibilities, including company insurance, cash management, and capital allocation, as well as overseeing the corporate treasury function and managing GE's relationship with credit rating agencies.

Mark Krakowiak was, in short, already a very engaged executive, but in addition to his nearly three decades of experience within GE, the board had also found risk management value in his close ties with senior managers throughout the firm. Krakowiak soon enlisted the help of another GE veteran, Michael Eshoo, to serve as director of enterprise risk management. Eshoo had worked for six years on GE's internal audit team, completing assignments across the company's industrial and financial businesses. Together, Krakowiak and Eshoo set out to heighten risk awareness across the company, strengthen frameworks for identifying and managing risk within each business, and expand director and executive engagement in the oversight of both.

Their objective was not to avoid risks at General Electric. The purpose was instead to understand the risks that the company was already taking, whether they were managed well, and if they were generating enough gains given the uncertainties. "We realize we have very high returns relative to others, and one reason for those high returns is because we're willing to take on certain things that have risk, and we can manage that risk better than others," Krakowiak explained. "If you manage the risk better, you should be able to deliver better shareholder value than companies that are strictly defensive about risk."

At the core of risk management is balancing options—a decision-making process often made agonizingly difficult because it takes place in a grey area. General Electric's governing board and top management directed each business unit to make its willingness to accept risk explicit and, in doing so, help define the boundaries of its strategy. If the business's boundaries were set too narrowly, it would miss opportunities to expand. If fixed too broadly, the business would take on an excessive level of uncertainty.

Individual units were tasked with assessing where they could or could not grow, and many had to struggle with these issues before reporting to the board. But others had already instituted relatively straightforward paths. GE's medical business, for instance, had historically defined its boundaries with a simple statement: "We're not going to go into anything that goes inside the body." If the medical business had a compelling rationale for crossing that line—for example, moving into pharmaceuticals—it would have to demonstrate to the board and CEO that doing so not only made strategic sense but also that the added risks would be both manageable and profitable.

Similarly, the GE energy business had created quarterly risk reviews several years earlier, focusing on averting compliance shortfalls or technology failures. Potential risks here were hardly minor, given the terrain: gas explosions, power outages, reactor meltdowns.

What Krakowiak and Eshoo decidedly did not want to do was create another control function. They were looking for a delicate balance, a way to bring a stronger central touch into what should still remain a largely decentralized operation. "We wanted to steer clear of creating bureaucracy," Krakowiak explained. "In a company like ours that operates in almost every country in the world, there's no way you're going to know what is going on in all those different places. There's only so much you can do from a central office before it becomes superficial. We wanted people in those businesses and functions to continue to own the risk." Yet they needed to ensure that risk management was in fact in place and that they would have a way to detect how discrete risks might combine or interact to impact the company as a whole.

Once the company's individual units had presented their risk management preparations, a committee chaired by the chief risk officer and populated by the company CEO, vice chairs, general counsel, and audit head reviewed them. The Corporate Risk Committee, as it became known, convened quarterly to review each business's appetite for risk, the risks to which it was exposed, and how well the risks were managed. Like Krakowiak and Eshoo, the Risk Committee appreciated that institutional investors looked to GE to allocate its capital in superior ways and that doing so required substantial risk taking.

To that end, the Risk Committee worked closely with directors, reporting twice annually to the board's Audit Committee on risks across the business and how they might combine to create systemic threats. To further strengthen their mastery of enterprise risk management, GE directors created a separate Risk Committee of their own, requiring that it review the company's risk assessment and management with the CEO and confer separately with the chief risk officer.

GE's risk management team won commendation from the board for moving so fast during its first year, but Krakowiak and Eshoo thought important steps remained. They had created a preliminary dashboard of metrics for identifying and measuring risk by business and function, but questioned whether it was sufficient. Many financial measurements were required by regulators or raters, so those were straightforward.

But other risks required their own metrics, the creation of which may not necessarily make the business safer.

"I firmly believe that people spend too much time on quantification," warned Krakowiak. "They want that to be the answer because it is simple. But I'm not sure that quantification is the sign of a robust ERM system. It is a false crutch."

Other issues remained for the executive team and governing board to resolve. How many indicators should the risk dashboard focus on? At what granular level? And how should the board best be informed? In financial services, regulators demanded a host of specific metrics, but how are those multiple data points best reported to the board? "There's value in cutting through to the ten or fifteen things the board should be watching," Eshoo told us.

One particularly dangerous blind spot in risk assessment that the board, CEO, and chief risk officer had to be wary of was the low-probability but high-consequence event. "It is the one-in-a-hundred event that can kill you," said Krakowiak. "To not figure out how to mitigate it, or how you're going to react if it does happen, is unacceptable. It could be that a plane goes down, or you could wake up one day to learn that the Federal Aviation Administration says a single part in an entire installed base is defective and grounds the entire fleet of 737s. Those are things you have to look for."

Not only do these possibilities pack potentially devastating impact, but managers tend to ignore them. "Too often people just dismiss that kind of risk for a variety of reasons," Krakowiak told us. "One, it scares the hell out of them—they don't know what to do about it—and two, because it is low probability, they think it is okay to work on other things. That is a failure of leadership."

Board Leadership in a Transformative Acquisition at Procter & Gamble

Few company decisions entail greater downside risks and greater upside potential than a major acquisition. The statistical track record of acquisitions is dreary, with well over half destroying instead of creating value. But for those that do yield value, the gains can be enormous, as seen in companies like Cisco Systems that significantly enhanced their growth through repeated acquisitions over many years. Here the board can play a vital role in guarding against downside risk and seizing upside opportunity.

As a case in point, consider Procter & Gamble's decision to acquire Gillette in 2005.[4] With a heritage dating to 1837, P&G had become America's largest consumer products company. With a founding year of 1901, Gillette had emerged as a preeminent consumer player as well, not only for its signature razor division but also for its Oral-B dental care products and Duracell batteries. It would be P&G's largest-ever acquisition by far. To get it wrong could badly hurt the buyer; to get it right could be transformative.

The drama began with a confidential telephone call from Gillette CEO James Kilts to his Procter & Gamble counterpart, CEO A.G. Lafley. The offer: rather than shopping the firm around, Gillette wanted P&G in particular to acquire it, assuming of course that they could agree on price. Lafley instantly appreciated that it was an offer of a lifetime, a strategic "no-brainer" in his own words, broadening and strengthening P&G's portfolio of leading global consumer businesses. Like many major firms, P&G routinely tracked prospective acquisition targets, and it had been watching Gillette for some time.

Still, with a workforce of more than twenty-nine thousand and revenue of $9.3 billion, Gillette was sure to demand a high price, and if anticipated synergies did not materialize, the deal could prove extremely costly and even a career-ender for the deciders. P&G was already well familiar with acquisition strategy and integration, having executed some ten to fifteen acquisitions annually, and it had studied the buying experience in detail at well-known serial acquirers outside its own industry, including GE. Still, the sheer size of a Gillette deal would take P&G into unexplored territory. The price was likely to be ten times greater than that of any of its prior purchases.

Facing a unique opportunity that he concluded could not be ignored, Lafley moved his executives, advisers, and directors into campaign mode, all sworn to secrecy. He set up a control room for the acquisition SWAT team in the basement of P&G's Cincinnati's headquarters to work out the details of due diligence. He sought strategic counsel from McKinsey and other consulting firms, and investment advice from Merrill Lynch. He along with his CFO, CHRO, and global R&D officer met repeatedly with Kilts and a few top executives at Gillette to understand the business, study its performance, and appraise the talent. Since Goldman Sachs had already been retained by Gillette, P&G could not engage its longtime investment banking partner directly, but Lafley did informally contact its chief executive, Henry Paulson, who was not involved in the transaction. Lafley talked with Paulson about the longer-term strategic implications and likely short- and long-term market reactions to a P&G acquisition of this magnitude.

But even the emerging best understandings and numbers would not be enough to affirm and then close the deal. Lafley knew it would require detailed vetting and ultimate approval by the board, and he appreciated that his experienced directors would require comprehensive data and persuasive explanation. A number had themselves served as CEOs of other large companies that had undergone the rigors of major takeovers of their own. The boardroom included nine sitting or former CEOs of major enterprises (see table 9–1).

Norman Augustine had overseen the integration of Martin Marietta into Lockheed Martin; Scott Cook had acquired several software firms, including Chipsoft; and Charles Lee had merged GTE into Verizon. So when Lafley first took the prospect of a Gillette acquisition to the boardroom, he was not surprised by a barrage of experience-informed, hard-hitting questions:

1. Since P&G's business is strong and growing, why does it need to acquire Gillette?

2. Could we simply build positions in oral care, women's hair removal products, and men's personal care rather than having to buy them?

TABLE 9-1

Procter & Gamble board members with CEO experience, 2004

Director	Current or former CEO of . . .
Norman R. Augustine	Lockheed Martin
Scott D. Cook	Intuit
Domeneco De Sole	Gucci Group
Joseph T. Gorman	TRW Inc.
Charles R. Lee	Verizon Communications
W. James McNerney, Jr.	3M
Johnathan A. Rodgers	TV One, LLC
John F. Smith, Jr.	General Motors
Margaret C. "Meg" Whitman	eBay

Source: Procter & Gamble, *Annual Report, 2004.*

3. How much value should be placed on each of Gillette's major business lines? Would the value of the shaving business and Oral-B alone be sufficient to justify the final acquisition price?

4. Were the business strategies and business models of the two companies compatible? Were their cultures compatible?

5. Gillette CEO James Kilts stood to receive some $200 million by the terms of his publicly known employment contract. Would P&G directors be comfortable with that payout—and be prepared to withstand a public uproar over it? How long would Kilts be expected to stay with an acquired Gillette? What kind of a retention incentive would be required? And, at a minimum, would he be willing to join the P&G board to help assist the multiyear integration of the two companies?

6. Was there reliable and compelling data to demonstrate that the anticipated synergies between the two firms could substantially reduce operating costs and bolster product sales?

7. Assuming that P&G's stock price would fall off in the wake of the acquisition announcement—as some investors were expected to be hostile to the idea—how many quarters or even years would be required until the stock rebounded?

In taking it to the board, Lafley opted for a neutral stance. Since he was trying to remain as objective as possible, he sought the board's independent counsel. It was a matter, he said, of "leading an inquiry process rather than an advocacy process." He knew there would be a time for advocacy at the end of the due diligence process when a "go/no-go" decision would have to be made on whether to make an offer for Gillette. Since becoming CEO in 2000, Lafley had adopted a practice of transparency with his directors, taking information up and accepting guidance down. He worked to ensure directors were well informed and that questions were raised and issues discussed before asking them to reach decisions. He arranged for a prominent investment analyst to meet with the directors to walk them through the impact of a Gillette acquisition on P&G's stock price and its credibility with institutional investors. The directors hit the analyst with a barrage of questions: Was P&G's valuation of Gillette fair? Was the strategy behind the acquisition sound? How much damage to P&G's market value could be expected?

Other sources of data were compiled for the board by the executive team. A study of Gillette's brand worldwide, for instance, found that males in most major geographies recognized and preferred the Gillette brand not only for shaving products but also for a wide range of men's personal care products—many of which Gillette did not then sell. Another study detailed how the two companies could go to market together, product by product and country by country. Lafley took such analyses to the board as they came in, and the board began meeting weekly through early 2005.

"The directors were incredibly important" for the deal's vetting and for putting together the final offer, Lafley recalled. "Every director played an active role. There were no 'wallflowers.'" The extensive acquisition experience of Norman Augustine, Scott Cook, Charles Lee, James McNerney, and others, and the extensive CEO experience of nine of the board's sixteen directors made for tough but productive grilling. The directors adopted a "trust but verify" posture toward Lafley and his team, confident that they were proceeding in good faith but repeatedly demanding the rationale and the data to evaluate the Gillette prospect.

The two CEOs negotiated a final price—arriving at $54 billion, a point midway between what P&G had first offered and Gillette had first sought. Following the premise that the board's decision should be one informed by but not advocated by management, the chief executive and the lead director, Norman Augustine, asked directors to individually comment on whether they favored or opposed the acquisition. The final vote was unanimous.

Lafley from the outset had taken the view that a Gillette deal was certainly strategic and could be transformative if the price, terms, and all-important "soft factors"—the culture and the leadership teams of the two companies—could be made to work. But he had to be convinced it would work, and here the board as an experienced collaborator played a vital role in resolving whether to go forward and, later, *how* to go forward.

With the board's sustained vetting and final approval, P&G announced the $54 billion acquisition on January 28, 2005. Gillette CEO Kilts converted his Gillette holdings into P&G shares, and he agreed to hold them and to join the P&G board for a year to colead the initial integration effort with P&G's CFO. P&G stock during the first year after the acquisition was up by 8 percent (while the Dow Jones Industrial average grew by 4 percent and consumer product company peers by 2 percent). Five years later, its stock was up by 12 percent, compared with a declining S&P 500 index over the same period. P&G's share of the domestic razor and blade market rose over the next several years, and with Oral-B, P&G moved back into oral-care leadership in the United States.[5]

Board Leadership at Rohm and Haas in Its Sale to Dow Chemical

On the other side of an acquisition, the seller's board has a vital role in risk management as well. In deciding on a buyer, a price, terms, and timing, directors in our view can and should be at the leadership table. For a case in point, we turn to a decision by the family owners of special product maker Rohm and Haas.[6] Though publicly traded, family trusts held approximately 30 percent of the stock, and their representatives approached company chief executive Raj L. Gupta in late 2007 to ask for a way to liquidate their stake to diversify their portfolio. With annual revenue of $9 billion and relatively steady growth in sales and dividends, the company was valued at $13 billion at the time. The family trusts wanted a full, fair, and fast exit for their share. Their request, especially its timing, came as a bolt from the blue.

CEO Gupta immediately called his lead director, Sandra O. Moose, a senior adviser with The Boston Consulting Group. She asked that the board retain top-flight counsel, and it brought in Goldman Sachs and the law firm of Wachtell, Lipton, Rosen & Katz, well known for its takeover and governance services. The board decided that two family representatives who served on the board—David W. Haas and Thomas W. Haas—would have to recuse themselves, and it also concluded that the issue was so significant that all directors—not just a special committee—would have to be directly involved in the decision.

The board turned to the company's valuation. Shares had been trading in the $50–$55 range, and with the counsel of its advisers, the board initially concluded that any sale would have to fetch a minimum of $75 per share. And then the directors focused on the three options of monetizing the family's stake to a buyer, such as a strategic investor or sovereign wealth fund; breaking up and selling the company in pieces to several buyers; or selling the company as a whole to a global chemical company such as DuPont, Dow Chemical Company, or German chemical giant BASF.

Analytic, methodical, and demanding, the directors instructed Gupta to test the waters with prospective strategic partners. Mukesh Ambani, CEO of Reliance Industries, India's largest energy and materials producer, and several others proved very interested in a strategic stake for a minority share. The board then asked Gupta to talk with DuPont, Dow, and BASF, and just thirty minutes in secret meetings with the chief executives of each garnered explicit interest from all three, but only Dow and BASF persisted when it became known that Rohm and Haas would require the acquirer to pay cash, pay a significant premium, and guarantee a closing of the deal within six months, subject only to regulatory approval by the United States and European Union.

Through it all, directors were at the table, meeting in person or by call twenty-six times over the several months required for finalizing a deal. The lead director and the CEO worked to ensure that the board grasped the strategic and financial stakes, understood what shareholders would require, and appreciated the disastrous downside if a deal derailed after public announcement. Shareholders, customers, and employees would all question the company's strategy and leadership at a time when the firm required their unwavering confidence amidst a deteriorating economy. It was left to the CEO and lead director to keep the Haas family and trust representatives informed.

The directors pressed the executive team to explain again why the company could not remain independent. They wondered if an announced acquirer would be able to fully follow through in case the economy faltered. And they asked how the directors could best play their collaborative leadership role through what would indeed become a wrenching process. Gupta, in turn, sought daily counsel from individual directors. He turned, for instance, to Ronaldo H. Schmitz, who had served on the managing board of BASF before joining the managing board of Deutsche Bank, for insight into the how large chemical companies like Dow operated.

In the end, Dow committed to the acquisition at $78 per share in July 2008. As the economy sputtered later that year in the wake of Lehman Brothers' failure and the financial meltdown, Dow sought to renegotiate its commitment, but the terms set forward by the Rohm and Haas directors and executives proved airtight. The deal finally closed in April 2009 at the price originally negotiated. Through it all, the board had steadily shaped the contours of the deal, helping the firm avoid a catastrophic downdraft that would have resulted had Dow been able to pull out so late in the game.[7]

The Advisory Board

Still another way to support a company's leadership: the advisory board. With enterprises expanding rapidly and globally, with entrepreneurs trying to break into emerging markets, with complexities and uncertainties on all sides—both executives and directors can benefit from an even more expanded base of knowledge and experience. Since advisory boards are by definition constituted for strategic advice but not for shareholder oversight, they can serve as a pure, unambiguous leadership collaborator with management. Well composed, they can regularly provide diverse thinking and fresh perspectives on a company's changing landscape. Used with consistency, they can also furnish executives with a steady source of tested knowledge, timely intelligence, and risk appraisal.

Advisory boards are still largely the province of Western multinational companies—they have been used by Citigroup, Deutsche Bank, GE, and PepsiCo—though increasingly they are found in emerging markets as well. They are usually comprised of individuals well informed about and well connected with a region's commercial and political worlds. And they are more often found among family-controlled enterprises.

The leadership of Mars, Incorporated offers a case in point. A US-based privately held food and confectionary company—the producer of M&M's—Mars boasts $30 billion in annual sales, sixty-five thousand employees, and revenue from sales in more than one hundred countries. Company executives receive regular guidance from five disparately located and diversely experienced "Mars Global Advisors":

Gurcharan Das, former CEO of Procter & Gamble for India; David Kessler, former commissioner of the U.S. Food and Drug Administration; Alan Milburn, former UK Secretary of State for Health; Moisés Naím, a writer with the Carnegie Endowment for International Peace; and Rosanna Wong, director of the Hong Kong Federation of Youth Groups.[8]

GMR Group, a large family-controlled Indian firm, has made equally effective use of an advisory board of its own. Grandhi Mallikarjuna Rao established the firm in 1978 and then rode a wave of growth following India's liberalization of its economy in the early 1990s. His company emerged as a major infrastructure player in aviation, energy, highways, and agriculture. International travelers unknowingly appreciate GMR's handiwork as they pass smoothly through sleek new terminals in freshly constructed airports at Hyderabad, New Delhi, and even Istanbul, Turkey.[9]

Flourishing success, though, came with a lurking downside. Given the unfamiliar markets that the company was serially entering, GMR's executive for Emerging Businesses and Governance, Prasad M. Kumar, concluded that the company would also benefit from an advisory board in ways well beyond what its governing board was capable of providing, especially since it was family dominated like many Indian enterprises.

Already a devotee of drawing on strategic guidance from others, Kumar had created dedicated teams in the company for strategic planning, workplace safety, regulatory compliance, product pricing, project management, and leadership development. An advisory board, he reasoned, could furnish the kind of overarching guidance that the firm as a whole still required. In 2007, he began pressing for the formation of such a board, arguing to the founder and the family that it must have real influence on company strategy and that top management should listen carefully to its guidance, criticisms, and recommendations. Kumar noted that some advisory boards were valued primarily for their members' networks, but he insisted that GMR's have substantive impact on company practices and plans.

The company finally created its Group Performance Advisory Council (GPAC) in 2009 to "provide an outside-in perspective on evaluating group performance." It populated the council with luminaries of the Indian landscape and required that they provide tough and candid feedback to the governing board and top management. The company also asked council members to rate company performance yearly on a scale of 1 to 10 in three areas—business performance, process improvement, and values practice—and to provide an overall score of the company's achievement compared to a pre-agreed annual target and last year's performance. Their collective assessment would even figure into a significant portion of the annual compensation of company executives.

A GPAC meeting that one of us attended captures the value of the advisory board. Following opening pleasantries, the chairman asked a spokesperson from the advisory board to lead the session. After describing advisory board activities over the past year and complimenting the staff for its support, the speaker displayed the pièce de résistance—a summary slide. The speaker pointed out that the company had measured in several vital areas at only the 4 or 5 level on the 10-point scale. He further reported that the company's overall score for the year stood between 6 and 7, a modest metric that was one peg lower than the previous year. Discomfort in the room palpably increased, but not for the chairman.

Rao, an inveterate learner in his company leadership, immediately broke the tension. "Now we are getting somewhere!" he declared. "We need to look at ourselves in the mirror." For the next two hours, he pressed the advisory board members to candidly explain each of the modest ratings, to identify the root causes for the subpar performance, and finally to advise what the company should do the coming year to make up for the shortfalls.

Consider the dialogue on just one of the criteria for which the advisers gave the company poor marks. When asked to justify the rating, a member of the advisory board explained that the company's executives had not delegated sufficient authority to the professional, nonfamily managers who carried responsibility for several complex, fast-growing, and capital-intensive business lines. Those top executives, their start-up instincts still in evidence, had insisted on staying directly involved in managing the several business lines' day-to-day operations. This adviser said that instead, the successful development and growth of the firm's senior talent required a longer leash and less micromanagement. He finished by saying that the board would return a year later to review whether the executive team had indeed backed away from its down-the-neck-breathing style.

Rao could almost certainly have garnered the same advice elsewhere. But with the volatility of the global financial system and with the challenges of working with governments that can be competitors, partners, and regulators all at the same time, a dedicated group with exceptional contacts, experience, and wisdom can provide more informed and strategic moves in a risky and fast-changing context. And in this case, it delivered the advice personally, perhaps the most valuable element of all.

Advisory boards bring others pluses not necessarily available from a governing board alone. Qualified individuals wary about financial or reputational liabilities of a governing board may be more ready to step forward. Advisory boards can focus on specific regions—Latin America for instance—or on a specific issue, such as race or gender. And they may drill further into the details of execution than governing boards would normally countenance. In the experience of consultant Roger Kenny, who has helped companies create more than a half dozen such bodies, advisory boards are "like the Marines: They get you on the beach."

Leadership of company risk taking provides an excellent opportunity for directors to test their mettle—by pressing executives to better appraise, mitigate, and capitalize on risk and prepare for extreme circumstances. Some of that work entails setting out clear rules and controls, but much of it requires strategic insight and informed judgment, a forte of both directors and executives, and all the stronger if combined together. In doing so, directors and executives help forge better led and more valuable enterprises.[10]

While engaged directors add value to a company's risk management capabilities, they can also overstep themselves if they stray into operations that are the prerogative of management. The next chapter shows how directors and executives can work to draw a line between where directors should lead and partner with management—or just stay out of the way.

DIRECTOR'S CHECKLIST FOR LEADING RISK

✓ Is the company's risk appetite well defined by directors and disciplined by executives?

✓ Is the board well informed and accepting of the company's risk management strategies?

✓ Are directors regularly updated on company risks via the board's audit or risk committee?

✓ Does the board include directors with prior executive experience in managing risks?

✓ Are the company's risk management practices preemptive rather than reactive?

✓ Does the company properly balance downside risks and business opportunities?

✓ Is excessive risk well defined and properly avoided?

✓ Is risk management embedded in operating practices and in the mind-set of managers throughout the ranks?

✓ Has the company prepared for low-probability but high-consequence events?

✓ Does the board lead with management in conducting due diligence and deciding on major acquisitions and other highly risky
  transactions?

✓ Has the board considered creating an advisory body?

10.

Staying Out of the Way

For all the advantage it brings, the increasing leadership by the governing board in major company decisions can create seriously adverse repercussions. Directors who wander too far into day-to-day operations where they have little expertise but strong opinions do an enterprise little good and can cause real damage.

Yet as boards have evolved from rubber-stamping to monitoring and now to leading, so the boundary between directing and managing is shifting too. Yes, a too-nosy board can gum up the works, but directors who bring to the table relevant expertise and prudent judgment on issues of strategy, market, risk, and beyond can provide vital insight that the executive team would not otherwise readily obtain. Finding the right line between leading and staying out of the way is a challenging but critical task.

Minding Without Meddling

By way of illustration, the chief executive of Universal Investments, Mary Cantrell (both pseudonyms), faced a risky decision when she focused on whether to close an investment vehicle—a fund that placed bets on diamond-mining companies—to new monies coming in.[1] Although the fund's overall assets constituted a tiny fraction of the firm's assets under management, she asked the board to review her tentative recommendation to limit the size of the fund. Cantrell's reasoning for going to the board: this was a tough call, the directors' collective wisdom had historically been invaluable in similar situations, and the decision would touch on the company's core value of customer service.[2]

Universal's diamonds-fund manager, John Shore, was a well-established professional, having advised the fund since the early 1990s and run it since 1995. Shore had assembled a portfolio that increased an investor's initial holdings of $10,000 in 1995 to more than $17,000 by the end of 2003, a period during which the S&P 500 index had barely budged. Clients and prospective clients alike noticed this exceptional performance and began pouring cash into the fund, but rather than celebrate his success, Shore feared that the astonishing growth in assets contained the seeds of the fund's destruction.

In the diamond-mining industry, publicly traded companies are small in number and tend to be large in size. Shore concluded that the growing dollars under his management were quickly making the fund a major player in a minor market, forcing him to make riskier investments at the margins of the industry. The problem was exacerbated by consolidation in the industry, which was reducing the number of players in which to invest. Believing he could no longer prudently allocate all of his fast-growing assets, Shore recommended to CEO Cantrell that the fund be closed to investors.

Cantrell's first reaction was, "Sure, let's close the fund. There's too much money coming in, and we want to save the existing customers from becoming disadvantaged." But then second thoughts intruded. Cantrell had inherited from her predecessor a company culture that stressed reliable returns at reasonable costs and, above all, customer care ahead of company welfare. To limit the fund would be to deny Universal's current and future clients an opportunity to invest where they wanted. Uncertain of which way to go, but certain that the issue had become strategic, since it was testing one of the company's primary values, Cantrell decided that the board should weigh in. Although she chaired it, the board was a model of independence, with seven strong-willed non-executive directors.

"I don't know what the answer is," she candidly admitted to the board. "I'm here to roll ideas around with you." After intense discussion, the directors decided that they should move beyond batting ideas back and forth and help resolve the issue. Were there alternatives to closing the fund? What about creating a diamonds index fund that would simply mirror the market? If the fund were closed, would it be reopened when the demand to invest in it cooled down? The directors soon concluded that they required more information on fund customers and diamond producers to reach an informed decision. They directed company staff to conduct a far-reaching analysis of client needs and diamond trends.

After several months of study, the staff reported to the board that consolidation had left the diamond industry without the capacity to absorb the sharply rising investment flows. With this analysis in front of them, the directors decided to keep the diamonds fund open but expand its boundaries to include companies that mined other precious stones, metals, or even coal. Customers, the directors concluded, generally would want to invest in a range of valuable rocks, not just diamonds, and they instructed the fund manager to find good investment opportunities in this larger domain. The directors had moved from discussion to data to decision, and they voted unanimously to expand the fund's charter.

John Shore, for his part, welcomed the board's decision. As his fund's assets grew—to $1 billion by 2005—he spread his investments across a host of mining companies, including Rio Tinto, a firm that extracted virtually anything of value from the ground. Before Cantrell took the question to the board, the diamond fund had invested in fewer than twenty companies; now it spread its holdings among more than forty. Consistent with client interests, the newly titled Precious Stones Fund outperformed most benchmark indexes. Indeed, the fund's first one-year return was four times greater than an S&P/Citigroup benchmark index for precious metals and mining.

Even after this success, Cantrell was still wary of too much director involvement. In her words, "You don't want the board running every aspect of the company." What is more, the diamond fund constituted little more than 0.2 percent of Universal's dollars under management. Still, the strategic and symbolic implications of the decision for customer service made board involvement both attractive and imperative. With the aid of staff analysis, the directors reached a decision that was different from what Cantrell and Shore had originally proposed. As the ultimate defenders of the company's mission, they chose a course that reflected both customer concerns and company objectives. "It is a great example," Cantrell says, "of the board doing the right thing," since it came up with "a better solution for customers than it began with."

Universal's experience highlights a useful governance principle that might become part of a company's informal decision-making norms when uncertainty is significant: complex decisions entailing even relatively modest resources can usefully be taken to the board if they are of strategic significance because they touch on the firm's central idea, business strategy, or core values. Minding that store does not necessarily bring meddling. Universal offers evidence that when directors have the opportunity and resources to carefully vet the underlying issues, the board can bring invaluable insight and analysis to bear. The result: more options and better decisions on risky courses than management might have reached on its own.

Lines in the Sand

To encourage director involvement in critical issues but not beyond, many companies explicitly identify which decisions should be made by directors, either alone or in concert with executives, and which should be reserved for executives alone. They typically do so through several devices.[3]

Annual Calendars

In recent years, many corporations have created yearly schedules for major topics the board must consider. The company strategy might be set for the January meeting, the business plan for February, the capital budget for March, and so on, through executive compensation for November and succession planning for December. Similar schedules have been established for the audit, governance, and compensation committees. As rudimentary a process as these calendars represent, they help ensure that directors participate in key decisions. Table 10–1 shows the

TABLE 10-1

Annual governance calendars of HealthSouth

Board of directors

February	Review annual plan and quarterly results; evaluate board and committee performance
March	Conduct annual review of executives and equity awards
April	Review committees' reports and quarterly results
June	Conduct annual review of quality of care
July	Review committees' reports and quarterly results
September	Review compliance procedures and internal audit
October	Review committees' reports and quarterly results
December	Review annual budget

Audit committee

January	Review draft of SEC Form 10-K and annual audited financial statement
February	Evaluate performance of committee; review quarterly results
March	Review financial risk exposure and performance of independent auditor
April	Review quarterly results
May	Review management reports

(continued)

TABLE 10-1   *(continued)*

June	Review prior year's quarterly reports
July	Review earnings release, guidance for investors, and quarterly results
August	Review management reports
September	Review internal audit function
October	Review compliance procedures and quarterly results

Governance committee

February	Evaluate performance of committee; review governance guidelines
April	Review management reports
July	Review management reports
October	Assess director nominees

Compensation committee

February	Evaluate performance of committee; review director and executive compensation plans
March	Review executive performance and compensation
April	Review trends in compensation; authorize equity plan
July	Review benefits program for coming year
October	Review executive compensation philosophy and policy
December	Review performance goals of CEO and other executives

decision calendars for the board of health-care provider HealthSouth and its three main committees.

Committee Charters

Most companies have also developed charters to define the decisions for which board committees are responsible. Often, committee recommendations must be ratified by the full board, but the actual decisions are largely made within the committee rooms. At HealthSouth, for instance, the charter of its compensation committee requires that directors choose independent compensation consultants and review all compensation plans, equity awards, and executive employment agreements.

Decision Protocols

Many large companies explicitly identify which decisions should be made by directors and which should be left to executives. Although these protocols are typically confidential, HBOS, a large financial services company in the United Kingdom, has made its "matters reserved to the board" public; these include dozens of items under the directors' purview, such as financial statements, annual dividends, executive remuneration, significant changes in internal controls, and new business that would represent more than 1 percent of a division's gross income.

Another company follows a highly detailed, thirty-page "delegation of authority" that specifies a host of decisions that must be brought to the directors for final resolution:

Decisions Reserved for the Board of Directors

- Annual business plan

- Officer hiring and compensation

- Stock options

- Capital structure and indebtedness

- Dividends

- Risk management and insurance policies

- Acquisitions, divestitures, and capital expenditures above $30 million

- Litigation settlements above $30 million

- Fines and penalties above $30 million

- Restructurings that exceed $60 million

- Tax settlements that exceed $125 million

- Contingent liabilities above $275 million

- Pension contributions that exceed $275 million

A third corporation uses a protocol for director decisions on financial reporting, risk management, human resources, competitive strategy, acquisitions and divestitures, technology, and governance and compliance. After reviewing a decade's worth of board minutes, the chief executive instituted this process to bring order to what he saw as a dangerously ad hoc approach to determining which decisions the directors would make and which ones would fall to the executives. Some items that had previously belonged to the board, such as substantial borrowing decisions, went to management, and vice versa.[4]

The No-Fly Zone

A host of other decisions should remain purely the province of management. Here, the chief executive and lead director often evolve together an unwritten understanding on what should stay out of the boardroom.

A chief financial officer of a large company employing more than 150,000 spoke for many in describing a working concept for a fine line dividing what directors want to decide or should decide. "I think as if I were a board member, what would I want to know, what's important for me to know." But, he added, even though "I want to be forthcoming, I also would not take details to the directors, such as data on consumer segments. The challenge is not to push the board into managing the company . . . Even we who run the company, spending all of our time doing this, have enough of a problem knowing how it really operates, and it's absurd to think that directors with the little time they have can really make intelligent decisions."

Directors and executives learn from accumulated experience the criteria for decisions directors should face or stay out of the way of. An executive for another major company summed up his approach: "We continually are going back to the board and asking, 'What do you want to know more about?'" He followed an iterative agenda-setting process, calling and e-mailing directors for their ideas on what issues should be on the agenda and then sending a draft agenda for directors to review before the meeting. The executive confided, as a result, that he lost "no sleep about what should go up to directors since it is an active and demanding board" and one that is "explicit about what should come to its attention."

Similarly, the CEO of a large non-financial services company said his obligation was to "find ways to channel" his board's "discussion into the high-leverage activities where the board can really have an impact and where I can leverage their engagement and their candor to advance the interests of the shareholder." Another CEO was working to streamline his board meetings and process to ensure that it stayed out of the weeds. "I've been spending too much time with the board," he reported. "Simplification of process has to evolve so that we can figure out what's important and what's not and really be focused on high-leverage activities."

By contrast, in the case of a major retail chain, executives reported that they learned the hard way not to take quarter-by-quarter, store-by-store sales trends to their directors. Most of the directors resisted a natural, though undisciplined, impulse to dive into the data, but several could not help themselves, demanding to know why sales at specific stores had dropped more than others, a terrain for which not even the executive team had time.

For boards to be engaged but not veer into a no-fly zone, executives and directors of well-led boards point toward the importance of the board's confidence in the judgment of the chief executive and board leader for knowing what to bring up to the board—or not. Governance policies, delegation rules, and formal measures are all important for cordoning off the area of avoidance, but the single most critical factor is the directors' earned trust in the CEO's and board leader's capacity to bring informed, strategic, and timely decisions to the directors—but not operational issues or lower.[5]

Directors are also poorly prepared to directly represent the company to regulators, raters, or reporters, another no-fly zone. Consider the wave of criticism, for instance, that swept over BP non-executive chairman Carl-Henric Svanberg after the 2010 explosion on BP's *Deepwater Horizon* in the Gulf of Mexico. At first, critics jumped on his seeming invisibility as more than fifty thousand barrels of crude oil gushed daily into the Gulf. Then, when he finally spoke out, they pounced on his unfortunate expression of empathy, "We care about the small people" (a mistranslation from Swedish of what should have come across as "the common man").

There is one exception to the prohibition against directors' venturing beyond the walls of the firm on behalf of the firm, and that is a well-orchestrated, face-to-face engagement of directors along with executives in direct dialogue with investors. Virtually no director understands a company's financials as well as its chief executive and chief financial officers, and end-running executives to meet privately with institutional holders or equity analysts is sure to be a fool's errand. Still, companies are wise, in our view, to heed the call of then Vanguard Group chair John J. Brennan, who urged directors to "establish an 'owners' relations committee' through which directors engage serious stockholders on 'a regular, meaningful, and candid basis.'"[6]

One variant is for the board's lead director to selectively accompany the CEO to private meetings with dissident shareholders. Another is for the board to designate one or two directors to work closely with the CEO in communicating with major investors. A third is for the board leader to connect directly with investors, in consort with the CEO, but limit content exclusively to issues of company governance. If activist investors make their way onto the board—in effect bringing a voice of the equity market inside the boardroom—ensuring that the activists transcend their parochial concerns is yet another job for the board leader. Whatever the particular device, a carefully tailored director outreach to the company's major investors in direct collaboration with the executive team would thus not violate the no-go canons of effective board leadership.

When well orchestrated, such contact can be important for vigilant investors since it raises a curtain on how a board really operates. Institutional shareholders prefer directors who are independent, informed, and thoughtful, and then they want reassurance that the directors work well with one another and with top executives. Otherwise the directors' independent and informed thoughtfulness may be completely wasted.

When it comes to specific concerns, such as board decisions on governance matters or succession planning, investors value direct contact not only with the CEO but also with the lead director; or in the case of executive pay, contact with the chair of the compensation committee rather than an executive on the payroll. Yet too few boards have one or two directors who are "camera-ready," in the estimation of Abe M. Friedman, formerly head of corporate governance at investment manager BlackRock, a founding partner at governance firm Glass Lewis, and now a managing partner of CamberView Partners, which advises companies on working with investors. But more directors are likely to become better informed as shareholders increasingly seek to hear directly from them about the inner workings of the boardroom.

Looking in the Mirror

While it is the responsibility of directors to define when to take charge, when to partner, or when to stay away, chief executives can help sharpen the dividing lines as well. As tensions arise over where the lines should be drawn—and they inevitably do—chief executives should consider how their own actions might have contributed. As one *Fortune* 500 Top-20 chief executive advised, when ambiguities arise over what is or is not board business, the first thing a CEO should do is look in the mirror. In his own experience, after a director probed too far for details, this CEO began to furnish the board with that area's particulars so that directors would not waste board time in the future.

Kevin Sharer, a chief executive of Amgen and long-serving director of Chevron, Northrop, Unocal, and 3M, is of that school. As CEO, he explained, "I developed what you might call a mature relationship with my board," and as a result "the board was as much my partner as my boss."[7] The directors were supportive, but still, "not every meeting was a lovefest." From "time to time," he said, "the board or individual board members would develop operational points of view that made me feel like they were crossing the line on decision rights." It was not often nor directive when it came, but when it did, Sharer reported, it made him uncomfortable.

The chief executive's occasional annoyance was not surprising given the fact that he was on the job every day while the directors convened only several times a year. "But the tension was always constructive," Sharer found, "and often they were right." He had opposed, for instance, Amgen's entry into producing "bio-similar" drugs, generic drugs that are akin to patented biologics. The company's culture, he believed, would not support such an initiative, but the directors believed that it would help sustain the company when existing patents expired. "I was wrong on that," Sharer later confessed, "and they eventually convinced me." Fortunately, "they had their hands on the wheel" even though at the time it felt like backseat driving.

With a glance in the mirror and working under the premise that it's more productive to act than to complain, Sharer developed a mental checklist of four conditions for defining the dividing lines, conditions for which he would take prime responsibility along with the lead directors:

Shared reality: Directors and executives agree on where the company is going and the market threats and opportunities ahead.

Mutual respect: Directors and executives have confidence and trust in one another.

Performance: Directors and executives concur on the company's financial, operational, and compliance targets.

Alignment: Directors and executives are in accord on company strategy, capital budget, and their respective decision rights.

Sustaining those four conditions came to guide Sharer's work with the board. "Whenever things started to go wrong," he recalled, "I'd pause and think, 'Why is the board getting out of control?'" He would ask himself, "Was it something I did or didn't do? Maybe we don't have alignment, or share the same reality. Maybe we're losing trust and respect."

To establish the four conditions, Sharer had taken several tangible actions. First, he penned a message to his directors before every board meeting that identified new developments in the company and the market, an approach he had learned while working for then senior manager at General Electric, Larry Bossidy. He would single out a dozen developments with just a sentence on each—"the kind you would have underlined"—and when combined, they created a brief but "comprehensive view of the business" for the directors. Looking at it from the other side was vital as well: "I tried to be sensitive to having the right level of detail and context," he explained, "so it was easy for them to see my reality."

Second, Sharer created a handout with basic facts about the company for distribution to the directors at every meeting, including obvious particulars such as the company's product names and the diseases they combated. Third, after each board meeting, he summarized the directors' deliberations and what he himself had taken away from the meeting, in effect asking, "Did I get this right?" And fourth, he intervened when he perceived that the dividing lines on decision rights were blurring, meeting privately with individual directors to sharpen them.

Finding the right dividers for when directors should exercise authority over management, collaborate with management, or stay clear of management is the work of directors—but also of executives. "If, in their heart of hearts, CEOs see the board as a bunch of meddlers who don't know anything about the company and just get in the way," Sharer warned, "they'll never become true partners."

Creating a Decision Culture

While the decision protocol defines many of the areas in which directors retain explicit decision-making control, other board-worthy issues—such as regulatory changes, competitor moves, and natural disasters—can arise unexpectedly. When they do, choices have to be made on the fly concerning when (and when not) to seek a board decision. The chief executive and board leader usually make that judgment call together, drawing on informal understandings that have evolved over time. While such norms vary from company to company, most revolve around the idea that boards should have a say whenever a question touches on the central idea or company strategy or risk appetite. Even then, demarcation will remain hazy unless the two parties work to articulate and hone the lines.

The chief executive of one firm, for instance, reported that his board should be involved in "large-impact decisions" and those that "will change the future." The board chair of another firm sought to ensure that the board was well informed about any decisions that had "a big outcome for the company." The CEO of a third firm reported that her board needed to be in the picture on "any issue that could have material impact on the company, from either a financial or a public perspective."

Chief executives have a role to play in coaching their own executives to work with directors without inviting micromanagement. The head of a large biotechnology firm, for instance, instructed his executives to stay focused in the boardroom on answering specific director questions without inviting extraneous additional questions. He would tell his executives that although they wanted to build credibility in the boardroom, a presentation to the directors was not their "time to shine" with topical digressions or unnecessary depth. "The board will eat anything you feed it," he warned, and he actively guided his executives on what information to provide the board—"a learned art" that he explicitly sought to foster.

Before executives presented information to the board, for instance, the chief executive asked them to scrub the data to focus precisely on the issues at hand so as not to sidetrack boardroom discussion. The chief executive also believed that directors required their own coaching on the right level of attention, and he asked newly elected board members to undergo an orientation that included guidance on the altitude of dialogue expected in the boardroom.

Whatever the directors' micromanaging motives or methods, some board leaders and chief executives make conscious efforts to help their directors know when to lead and when to stay out of the way. "Execution is where management starts and the board stops," offered the chief executive of a health services company. Among the tools the board leader and chief executive can use to ensure their directors lead without meddling: providing the right information; sustaining an elevated level of discussion; focusing on the central idea, company strategy, and succession plans—but not the details of execution; and reinforcing a no-micromanagement norm.

These broadly defined standards can, if nothing else, force a chief executive and board leader to think about how major decisions should be divvied up. Meanwhile, directors would do well to continually ask themselves a set of basic questions:

- What do I need to know so that good decisions about the central idea, strategy, risk, and talent will move my enterprise to the next performance level?

- What do I need to know to ensure that decisions do not put the company at risk?

- What do I need to know so that my leadership at the top can be generative and productive without at the same time becoming intrusive?

- What do I need to know to create value for the company and for the shareholders whose interests I am sworn to uphold?

These questions go to the very heart of how a board can help the enterprise by defining its role as a leader with management in reaching key decisions. This is one way for directors to help build and sustain a culture that invisibly guides what and when they decide—and how to decide what not to decide. When directors bring experience and judgment to bear on important company decisions where the course ahead is complex, unsure, and risky, they play a vital leadership role. To ensure they address the right decisions but avoid veering over the edge, annual calendars, board charters, decision protocols, and informal norms help. With the right decisions reaching the boardroom with the right mix of information and counsel, companies and their owners can be more confident that the firm's course will be well guided by not only executive intelligence but also director IQ.

When directors appropriately—and necessarily—engage with executives in leadership of the enterprise, their contributions can be far-reaching, as we will witness in two contrasting experiences in the following chapter. In one, the board had failed to define the company's limits for risk, and in doing so allowed the firm to topple over a cliff. In the other, the board had intervened to bring the company back from the cliff, and in doing so revived a failing giant.

DIRECTOR'S CHECKLIST FOR STAYING OUT OF THE WAY

✓ Are complex operating decisions taken to the board for counsel?

✓ Are the lines between leading, collaborating, and staying out of the way clearly drawn through annual calendars, committee charters, and decision protocols?

✓ Have directors and executives evolved a mutual understanding of which decisions go to the board for direction, collaboration, or not at all?

11.

The Leadership Difference

A board can be a destroyer or a creator of value—a difference starkly evident in the two cases that follow. The names and incidents are well known, but the outcomes could not have been more dissimilar. Here we see the difference that a board's leadership can make for recovery of a damaged company, or the absence of a board's leadership can make for destruction of a faltering company.

In one case, a board failed in its basic obligations of company leadership, and its irresponsibility contributed to a financial calamity. It was as if the board had embraced Will Rogers's famous dictum, "If stupidity got us into this mess, then why can't it get us out?" In the other case, directors took a company shocked to its core and teetering on bankruptcy, partnered with the new executive team in critical ways, brought their expertise to bear where most useful, and saved an enterprise that went on to prosper.

In the first instance, shareholder value was nearly destroyed; in the second, it was rescued, preserved, and enhanced. The critical difference: leadership in the boardroom and executive suite, or its near complete absence.

Asleep at the Helm of AIG

As Lehman Brothers was tumbling into oblivion on September 15, 2008, attention suddenly turned to global insurance giant AIG. Would it go, too? And could AIG be the domino that would bring the world financial community to its knees, even causing the world's main economy to collapse? Claims on its insured financial instruments were mounting by the minute. Liquidity had dried up. Near-panic had set in with the secretary of the Treasury and the chair of the Federal Reserve. Enormous stakes hung in the balance, yet AIG leadership—both executives and directors—proved woefully ill-prepared to avert its own collapse.[1]

Remarkably, neither the board, the chief executive, nor the managing director for AIG's Financial Products division (AIGFP) appears to have anticipated such a meltdown. According to AIG employees, AIGFP president Joseph Cassano led the financial products division, while the chief executive gave scant attention to the division's outsized risks. Cassano exercised an autocratic hand and had little tolerance for challenges on the inside, including questions regarding these enormous risks. In hindsight it is apparent that neither the then chief executive nor his predecessors or their boards had ever defined the firm's risk appetite, nor did they seem to have monitored it. AIGFP may have carried the largest concentration of private risk on earth, but AIG directors were evidently not sufficiently engaged in risk management to have detected its alarming rise. They had lost sight of the central idea that AIG was making money by marketing and managing risk, focusing instead on only the selling side of the equation.[2]

The board, it seems, was more ceremonial than substantive—despite visible warning signs that its leadership was required. One agency that rated corporate governance on an A-to-F scale, for instance, had given the AIG board a grade of D, barely passing. AIG's board had been repeatedly warned by regulators and its auditor about the extraordinary risks that the company was taking on through its AIGFP subsidiary. As early as 2005, the Office of Thrift Supervision, which

served as AIGFP's primary regulator, began reporting to AIG directors what it had found to be "weaknesses in AIGFP's documentation of
complex structures transactions, in policies and procedures regarding
accounting, in stress testing, in communication of risk tolerances, and
in the company's outline of lines of authority, credit risk management
and measurement." In mid-2007, on the eve of the deluge, the federal
regulator warned AIG of the risks associated with subprime mortgages
and demanded that directors improve AIGFP's organizational controls
and risk management. In mid-2008, AIG's outside auditor, Pricewater-
houseCoopers, further warned the board of accounting weaknesses.[3]

Collectively, these warnings should have been more than enough
for executives and directors to closely scrutinize the financial products
division and the risks it was taking. But AIGFP had enjoyed a period
of spectacular business growth over nearly two decades, and executives
and directors current and past were evidently loath to look hard at the
goose that had been laying the golden eggs. Division president Cassano
was not inclined to look either. He had grown wealthy off AIGFP and
viewed much of his division's success as a product of his own making.
Similarly, a succession of AIG chairs and CEOs had themselves experienced extraordinary success as the company emerged as the world's
largest insurer, and they had basked in its inclusion in the Dow Jones
Industrial Average and other blue-chip rosters of the nation's most
prominent and successful companies.

It gets worse. When Cassano was finally fired in February 2008,
directors allowed him to keep $34 million in bonuses and monthly
stipends of $1 million through the spring and much of the summer,
only to be castigated by New York State attorney general Andrew M.
Cuomo, who ordered AIG directors to desist from further such "fraud-
ulent conveyances."

By then, AIG was living on the taxpayer's tab. When a credit-rating
agency downgraded AIG from AAA to A−, collateral calls began
pouring in from AIG's customers. By the close of 2008, AIG had lost
$61 billion, the largest annual shortfall in American business history. In
the end, the United States injected more than $180 billion to save the

company from complete collapse and seized control of it. Had Congress not acted to legislate the Troubled Asset Relief Program (TARP) in time, AIG alone would have been the pivot for what Federal Reserve chairman Benjamin Bernanke warned could have been worse than the 1929 market crash. AIG's failure directly contributed to the abrupt shrinkage of the US economy, resulting in widespread unemployment and distress. And at the very heart of the problem was a board that failed to understand what concentrated risk can do to a company—or even the world economy. After the debacle, a new set of directors and two new chief executives—Edward M. Liddy in 2008–2009 and then Robert H. Benmosche—led the company back to health, repaying the government by 2013.

Partnering to Save Tyco

Six years before AIG's near collapse, a new management team at Tyco International also inherited a mess for the ages. Directors had replaced Dennis Kozlowski in mid-2002 after he was indicted for sales tax evasion and resigned as chair and chief executive. In the months that followed, the company began digging through massive accounting irregularities, repaid a huge debt, and replaced 290 of its top 300 executives. By spring 2003, the entire board resigned in the wake of an estimated $600 million in fraud, for which Kozlowski and his chief financial officer would later be convicted.[4]

With a fresh board in place, new chief executive Edward D. Breen set out to undo the damage of the Kozlowski era. Uppermost was restoring a culture of integrity, and for this he worked hand in hand with new lead director John A. Krol (whose role in the remake of Delphi was described in chapter 3). They early separated the company's finance function from operating management to ensure that the former could serve its controllership role. They did the same for general counsel, requiring operating unit counsels to report directly to the corporate general counsel. They required the audit function to report directly to the board's audit based on rather than the chief financial officer. They enlarged promotion based on results to results plus values. And they worked to strengthen the ethical climate, issuing a new "Guide to Ethical Conduct" with illustrative vignettes and scheduling personal visits by top management to dozens of Tyco's operating locations.[5]

Kozlowski had built Tyco from a $3 billion company in 1992, when he took the helm, to a $36 billion conglomerate with nearly 260,000 employees at the time of his resignation. Much of the growth had come from acquisition after acquisition, but in Kozlowski's buying binge—some nine hundred companies at a total cost of $63 billion—he had taken on multiple operations that fit poorly or performed weakly. While Kozlowski had focused on acquiring rather than consolidating, Breen vowed to do the opposite. He imposed a moratorium on acquisitions and made plans to shed whatever remained a mismatch. Tyco's revival, the new CEO concluded, would depend on its swift conversion from a buying engine to an operating machine.

Representing the board, lead director Krol was already in agreement on the need to discard weak assets. A highly respected company executive who had recently retired as chairman and chief executive of DuPont, Krol had been recruited to the board just after Breen's appointment as new CEO. Krol had been sought in part because of his impeccable reputation for tested leadership on other boards as well as his business performance and professional wisdom—values that had seemingly withered at the top during the Kozlowski era and ones that Tyco directors were now intent on restoring.[6]

As lead director, Krol was determined that enterprise risk—including executive fraud—would never again go undetected and unmanaged. Neither regulators nor directors had spotted the ransacking of the company that had brought the firm close to indictment and bankruptcy. Krol drove an effort to create a systematic approach to evaluating not just financial risk, which the audit function was already charged with monitoring, but also operational risks of the kind that the board had unfortunately missed, including the risks inherent in a sprawling enterprise with little synergy among its many parts.[7]

Breen's first months in office were consumed with the tasks of stabilizing operations, restoring confidence, and compiling cash. With the worst behind him, he turned in mid-2003 to the company's

restructuring. His first step was to make certain he and the lead director were still of the same mind. Krol was, and the two agreed that the
time had come to get rid of the underperformers. They also concurred
that the board should have a direct hand in deciding which divisions
would stay and which would go. The mass disposal would so remake
the firm that the directors, Krol and Breen felt, had no choice but to
be heavily involved.

After the new directors received a crash course in Tyco's operations, Breen and Krol asked them to authorize management review of
Tyco's hundreds of business units, one by one. The board unanimously
endorsed the plan, adding that management should not waste its time
trying to fix anything of marginal value.

Breen assigned Tyco's new treasurer, Martina Hund-Mejean, the
task of appraising those units. With the board's blessing, she set out the
disposal criteria. Did an operating unit generate enough value to justify the capital invested in it? If not, did it support other units, display
turnaround potential, or hold the promise of rapid growth? In short
order, Hund-Mejean compiled a list of 130 units that did not meet
these standards. Some were tiny, with assets of as little as several hundred thousand dollars; others were hefty, with assets running into the
hundreds of millions.

One unit—TyCom, which laid undersea cable—was hemorrhaging
so much cash (some $300 million annually) that Breen and Krol rec-
ommended to the board that it be sold immediately. Breen then turned
to the remainder of the disposal list and, in discussions with the directors, whittled it down to sixty units. Breen and Krol presented the
candidates to the board for review at its annual off-site strategy meeting
in September 2003.

The directors pressed Breen's team to explain the financial and strategic pros and cons of disposing of each unit. They questioned timing:
would putting all sixty units on the block at the same moment depress
the prices Tyco might fetch? They asked about each unit's management: could not its team, or a better one, resurrect the unit? And they
asked about the strategic plan of each: why exactly would it not work?

In six instances, the directors decided that the case for divestiture was not yet conclusive or that the timing was not right. Otherwise, the directors gave the go-ahead. Breen publicly announced the disposal of units generating, at that time, 6 percent of Tyco's revenue.

Hund-Mejean then began the process of shedding some four dozen of those units. Over a period of months, she kept the directors abreast of the divestiture progress in meeting after meeting, typically highlighting in detail the six largest deals under way at a given moment. She later reported to the directors that several units were better liquidated than sold. Upon further study, she also determined that several others were in fact too good to let go. Brought into the loop on management's rationale for these changes in the plan, the board backed their retention. The transformation of Tyco from aggressive buyer to lean operator took two years, with the last units on the disposal list finally sold in 2005.

Reflecting on the directors' decisions during the divestiture process, Krol characterized the board's approach as one of granting approval, but with a discerning eye. Instead of rubber-stamping management's disposal plan, the board reviewed each of the proposed divestitures and ultimately approved a modified list. "The board's 'value-add,'" Krol concluded, was "in the questions it asked."

Critically, too, the collaborative leadership did not stop after Tyco was brought back from the brink. Under Krol's direction, the new Tyco board continued working closely with management to establish a risk-assessment process. The process relied heavily on analysis by individual business units on the premise that those closest to an operation would bring the best insight into the nature of the risks each faced. But the board insisted on active engagement by arranging for its members to visit the major business units annually for review of their assessment and management of risk.

Typically, Krol led the visit with one or two other directors. He rotated directors among the various visits so that they would learn about each of the business lines. The leadership team of the local business unit prepared well ahead of time (and in fact had been directing a risk management process within its ranks throughout the year), and the board members spent a full day asking detailed questions. The business managers reported that they learned from the directors' own experience and knowledge on how to address their risks.

"It is key to establish an all-inclusive process to be sure the businesses touch all the important bases," Krol explained. "It starts with teaching the management. Once they do it, they find it very useful for the entire board to really understand their business." Visiting directors would then summarize for the entire board at its next meeting the risks that the operating unit faced, what mitigation steps were under way in response to the greatest of those risks, and what the unit had done to reduce the gravest risks identified during the directors' visit a year earlier.

The site visits brought a second advantage as well: directors not only acquired an in-depth view of enterprise risks; they also came to know the leaders of each of the business units, including their president, chief financial officer, and managers of human resources, information technology, and manufacturing. Directors could directly appraise their leadership effectiveness and promotion prospects. So informative were the site visits for director understanding of both enterprise risk and executive talent that the board instituted them as part of its annual cycle.

Enterprise risk emerged as a major topic on the directors' agenda. Breen and his team furnished regular updates, and risk management entered frequently into director discussions of strategy and operations. Directors asked: What risks do you anticipate? What are the top two or three risks that keep you up at night? And what specifically are you doing to mitigate those risks?

When Tyco International spun off one of its business lines in 2007 to form Tyco Electronics, the risk management system that Breen and Krol had jointly crafted furnished a blueprint for the new enterprise. Given the parent company's near brush with disaster in 2002, spin-off executives and directors were highly sensitive to the issue of risk and sought to build on what the parent had already established.

Part of Tyco Electronics' central idea is to have manufacturing engineering facilities spread all over the world, with some of those facilities supplying their outputs as inputs to other facilities. If one such facility is closed, it can wreak havoc in the company's flow of manufacturing across the globe and throughout its customers' supply chains. In one incident, the Mexican government urged businesses to temporarily shut down to stem the spread of swine flu. Suspending operations at Tyco's Mexican plant might have exposed the company to a bevy of lawsuits from its customers and its customers' customers for breach of contract. Fortunately, by the end of a planned holiday, the situation had eased. But it is these kinds of operating risks that the committee dwelt on and for which they had management design and execute the response systems.[8]

The AIG board never did define or limit the firm's appetite for risk, one of six areas where directors should want to lead collaboratively with management. At Tyco, a new set of directors put themselves out front in both risk leadership and the allocation of vital resources to help steady a listing behemoth. In one case, we saw a laxity in the boardroom bordering on negligence; in the other, a well-led board restoring a company's potential after a prior board had allowed the executive team to run roughshod over its ethical values and even criminal statutes.

One company, with no board leadership, failed—or would have if taxpayers had not stepped into the breach. At the other, ample board leadership helped a floundering corporate giant to revive. Directors of the first stood aloof, while those of the second stepped forward, embracing the duty of leadership that boards are increasingly called to take. They partnered with executives, made tough calls on personnel and assets, and devoted extensive time outside formal board gatherings.

Drawing on the experience of companies ranging from AIG and Lenovo to Apple and Tyco, we offer a revised definition of corporate governance in the following chapter. We suggest that regulators, raters, shareholders, and directors expand the concept of governance to include leading, not just monitoring of, the company. We offer one final illustration of a board that made the leadership difference—placing a team on top of the world.

12.

A Revised Definition of Corporate Governance

Discussions about who leads a company typically focus on the chief executive and the executive team. That is understandable: the CEO gets the ink and, when things go badly, most of the heat. But we have discovered that the defining conception of leadership has been expanding at many companies to include the firm's directors as well.

Boards must still monitor management, of course, but in addition they are also more often leading with management. "It's great to have a partnership with our directors," offered the chief executive of a *Fortune* 20 company. And for that to come to life, he and his board have come to review and revisit company strategy and its risks and opportunities at every board meeting. "The partnership allows us to know where we are going," he reported, and that partnership served in turn not only to "hold management accountable" but also to "make directors accountable." At the same time, he worked conscientiously to keep his directors out of the weeds, deeming transgressions into the no-fly zone a product of his own failure, not just that of the board leader.

This is the essence of our argument, and it is a case that anticipates a very different role for governing boards than has been prescribed or observed in the past. The board certainly does not run the company—that of course remains the job of the chief executive and top team—but directors at many firms are now very much a part of the leadership team.

In light of the far-reaching and irreversible developments in company leadership that we have seen in these chapters, this is a good moment to redefine our working concepts to more accurately characterize the emergent reality of board leadership. While companies have long worked with an ambiguous and often inconsistent combination of chief executive, president, board chair, lead director, and presiding director, for instance, we would suggest simply designating the senior executive as *chair and CEO*, and the top director as *board leader*. We believe that these titles are likely to better reflect how leadership now works at many firms—and more in the future—than titles created in an earlier era when executives led and directors monitored.

It is also a good moment to redefine the very concept of corporate governance. Rarely do traditional definitions of governance make much reference to company leadership. "The board of directors has the important role of overseeing management performance on behalf of shareholders," declared the Business Roundtable, adding that "corporate directors are diligent monitors, but not managers, of business operations."[1] By extension, directors should not become directly involved in their company's leadership. Yet, given the emerging leadership practices by the board that we have chronicled here, a revised definition would wisely incorporate the new reality that boards are now in fact leading directly and in partnership at many enterprises—and should, in our view, be doing so at all companies.

These developments also point to moving beyond a decades-old debate over how best to regulate, rate, and require a board to align and discipline management around shareholder value. Such issues as "say on pay" and separation of chair and CEO have been much deliberated. An even more important debate now, in our opinion, is how best to create and design a board that can lead with management to create more shareholder value. For starters, this would point to a redefinition of the role of one of the three key committees of the governing board.

The audit committee has long been of great importance for effective monitoring of management, and the compensation committee has acquired special significance in recent years as executive pay and its proper alignment with shareholder value has become of special interest to not only investors but also regulators and the public. The governance committee, by contrast, has been less central to the monitoring function, but it is now becoming seminal for the exercise of leadership at the top.

The governance committee carries special responsibility for ensuring that the right directors are in the room, dysfunctional directors are out of the room, director evaluations are consequential, board committees are headed by those who can lead, and the board leader is indeed a director who can both lead the board and partner with management to lead the company. In recognition of this new reality at many enterprises—and in the interest of catalyzing that reality at other firms where it has yet to take hold—we suggest reconstituting the governance committee as the board's *leadership and governance committee*, with a charter and budget to reflect its greater leadership obligations.

It will also be important for those who are the most experienced and adept in leading companies and boardrooms to be among the prime candidates for the leadership and governance committee, and for the board leader to serve as its chair. We would go even further, urging that the committee apply a new set of yardsticks for appraising director candidates and director performance, stressing their ability to fashion a central idea, map out a company strategy, select the right chief executive, and otherwise contribute to the real work of the enterprise. The compensation committee will also want to ensure that the board leader is properly compensated for the special responsibilities now thrust on that person.

By way of summary, boards will want to identify where they will lead, partner, or stay out of the way; create protocols for selecting and assessing the chief executive and the board leader; heighten compensation for the board leader; establish a board leadership and government committee; recruit new directors who substantively contribute to the central idea and ease out those who do not; institute a coaching system to ensure that a faltering CEO is either mentored or removed; and open a channel for directors to connect with investors. Shareholders, as a result, may want to expand their attention. We have outlined areas for investor attention in a memo:

Memo to Shareholders

Shareholders have long been concerned with the structure of the governing board, and what is needed now is also a focus on a well-led board with a:

- *Compelling central idea*

- *Board leader who organizes and directs the board*

- *Board leadership and governance committee*

- *Working partnership with top management*

- *Set of active directors with leadership experience*

- *Absence of dysfunctional directors*

- *Regular evaluation of directors and the board*

- *Set of protocols for making or delegating decisions*

- *Commitment to lead, not just monitor, the company*

The Board Leads a Team to the Top of the World

Everybody has heard the story of how Mount Everest was won. More than half a century ago, Edmund Hillary and Tenzing Norgay confronted the mountain, braved its dangers, and made it to the top through sheer talent and will. It is an inspiring tale, yet it obscures a deeper one. The hidden story is less classically heroic—it involves an unassuming manager and a board of directors—but it reveals heaps more about the nature of great achievement.[2]

Hillary and Norgay were not supposed to be the first atop Everest. England's leading climber, Eric Shipton, seemed destined for that honor. A gentleman-adventurer in the romantic mold of Robert Scott and George Mallory, Shipton had been central to four of England's seven Everest expeditions and knew the mountain better than anyone. No one was surprised when the worthies and scientists of the Himalayan Committee, a board-like affiliate of the Royal Geographical Society, chose him to lead England's 1953 attempt.

Almost immediately, though, board members had second thoughts. Shipton's lightly equipped, improvisational climbs had shown entrepreneurial flair. But his inattention to detail and planning was notorious; on one trip, he even forgot his backpack. And now the board had a new worry: foreign competition. Just the year before, a Swiss team had come within a few hundred feet of Everest's 29,035-foot summit. Should the British fail this time out, both the Germans and the French would have a crack at reaching the summit next.

The Himalayan Committee, led by its chair Claude Elliott, president of the Alpine Club and provost of Eton College, did not want another romantic failure—something gentleman-adventurers excelled at. So just six weeks after choosing Shipton, it did the unthinkable: it turned around and fired him. In the ensuing uproar, one climber withdrew. The committee's subsequent decision to replace Shipton with John Hunt, a career military man whose very name conveyed lack of dash, roiled the controversy still further.

Yet the board had done something more profound than replace one chief executive with another. It had replaced an old central idea with a new one. This new idea was reshaping British industry, where the ideal of the gentleman-capitalist—an untutored amateur who relied on character and talent to get the job done—was running up against reality. The modern corporation was simply too big and complex for one man to run. Everest was big, too. It required a new method—what some were calling the art of organization.

Colonel John Hunt was the very picture of the modern professional manager. A demon for logistics, he specified that each box of rations contain twenty-nine tins of sardines. His strategy—soon to become standard in mountaineering—called for an army of climbers, Sherpas, porters, and yaks that would methodically move up the mountain, shuttling supplies to ever-higher camps. Hunt gave the human element systematic attention as well. Everest demands an "unusual degree of selflessness and patience," he later wrote. "Failure—moral or physical—by even one or two [people] would add immensely to its difficulties." The desire to reach the top, he added, "must be both individual and collective." That last point was important: the goal of this huge effort was to deliver just two climbers to the summit.

Who would they be? Had Shipton been in charge, one may well have been Eric Shipton. In the event, no fewer than ten climbers—including a thirty-three-year-old New Zealand beekeeper's son, Ed Hillary—were in the running. The final choice, Hunt declared, would hinge on impersonal factors: who was climbing well and who was in high camp when the weather broke. On May 26, 1953, two men were selected for immortality.

They came within three hundred vertical feet of it.

Tom Bourdillon and Charles Evans would have been household names had the limits of stamina, oxygen, and daylight not turned them back. Yet in retreat they laid a platform: leaving behind a stash of oxygen canisters and bringing down a trove of useful intelligence. Hunt—who had placed the platform's final plank by ferrying supplies himself to within two thousand vertical feet of the summit—had a second team ready to go.

Tenzing Norgay and Ed Hillary moved out swiftly on the morning of May 28, reaching Hunt's supply cache, which made a miserable night at least survivable. At 4 a.m., they arose, five miles in the sky. The frozen air had turned Hillary's boots to steel. But there was a stove on hand to thaw them. There was breakfast as well: crackers, lemonade, and, most satisfying of all, the final tin of Hunt's sardines. It was enough nourishment to give them one shot at bringing thirty years of frustration to an end.

At 11:30 a.m., Hillary snapped the photo: Norgay, ice ax raised aloft in victory, left foot planted atop the highest point on the planet.

It was an extraordinary feat of mountaineering that rightly made them instant legends. Still, to say that they "conquered" Mount Everest is a bit like saying that Neil Armstrong and Buzz Aldrin conquered the moon. For when they stood atop the stone pyramid of Everest, Hillary and Norgay were also standing atop a pyramid of people.

Is the lesson here that the world needs more John Hunts—diligent organization builders content to dwell in the shadows of others? (He was, at least, knighted.) Actually, the world has plenty of John Hunts—great CEO candidates. The problem is that boards and their leaders do not always pick them. Starstruck with charisma and style, they sometimes go for the Eric Shiptons. That is why the unsung hero of Everest is not an individual at all, but a well-led board of directors with a better central idea and CEO to make it happen. By redefining the expedition as a corporate effort—and having the backbone to take the criticism that followed—the Himalayan Committee built the ultimate platform for success, a final illustration of how boards can lead and the difference they can make when they do.

In a final summary that follows, we gather what we have learned from company experience in the United States and abroad into a set of director's checklists. These are the mission-critical principles that are the foundation for directors to lead a company and for owners and others to recognize when a firm's directors have indeed stepped forward to do so.

The Complete
Director's Checklists

Satirist Ambrose Bierce noted, upon finishing a fulsome work, that "the covers of this book are too far apart." For those drawn to brevity, we have distilled eighteen checklist principles and questions, broken into several phases, for directors to review just as pilots refer to separate checklists for takeoffs and landings, or as physicians turn to separate checklists for surgeries or emergencies. Treat the principles and questions as a starting foundation around which additional principles and questions are added to focus on special concerns that directors may have at their specific enterprise. If you are about to join a governing board, walk into a board meeting, or become a board leader, explicitly checking these principles and questions can give you a leg up. Review is also useful if you are about to appraise a company, invest in a company, or acquire a company.[1]

From Ceremonial to Monitor to Leader

Governing boards delegate almost all operating decisions to top management, but they will want to retain a guiding voice in eleven areas—directly in the case of five decisions areas and in partnership with the chief executive in six others, leaving all else to management. Directors' proactive leadership of the eleven is essential, but like approaching a cliff, knowing when to stop is vital if directors are to guide the enterprise without micromanaging, to colead the enterprise where necessary without strangling it.

DIRECTOR'S CHECKLIST 1: BOARD LEADERSHIP DECISIONS

When to Take Charge

- ✓ Central idea
- ✓ Selection of chief executive officer
- ✓ Board competence, architecture, and modus operandi
- ✓ Ethics and integrity
- ✓ Compensation architecture

When to Partner

- ✓ Strategy, capital allocation
- ✓ Financial goals, shareholder value, stakeholder balance
- ✓ Risk appetite
- ✓ Resource allocation
- ✓ Talent development
- ✓ Culture of decisiveness

When to Stay Out of the Way

✓ Execution

✓ Operations

✓ Delegated executive authority

✓ Nonstrategic decisions

✓ Excluded by board charter

Define the Central Idea

The central idea is a foundation for any company, and a strategy derived from it and a plan for executing it are equally essential. Here are eight questions, along with several subsidiary questions under each, for directors to check in concert with company executives for assessing whether the firm's central idea is sound, a driver of strategy, and capable of execution:

DIRECTOR'S CHECKLIST 2: DEFINE THE CENTRAL IDEA

✓ Is the central idea clear and compelling?

- What are the underlying assumptions, risks, and advantages?

- What can be expected from competitors and regulators?

- Is the central idea in sync with management's understandings of customer needs, market segments, emerging technologies, and economic trends?

- Are some parts still missing, to be evolved and shaped by management?

- How well do the parts fit together? Does their cohesiveness create momentum as a sustainable advantage? Is the central idea expressed in everyday language that everybody can understand and remember?

✓ What is distinctive and compelling about the central idea?

- Is it a game creator, opening a new need or a new market that has not yet been recognized by others?

- Or is it a game changer, giving the company a defensible lead over others?

- Or is it a game ender, nominally appealing but destined to fail?

✓ How sound is the central idea's value-creating proposition?

- On what underlying value drivers is the central idea premised?

- Will top management be able to fashion a strategy around those drivers, and is management ready to execute around them as well?

✓ What is the company's advantage over each of its primary competitors?

- How is the central ideal distinctive from the competitors' central ideas?

- What hurdles might other firms erect, including government regulations and legal rulings, that could blunt or even eliminate the central idea's advantages?

✓ What are the risks, and how will they be mitigated?

- Will the firm be able to cope with low-probability but high-consequence events that could weaken or undermine the central idea?

- Whether routine or catastrophic, could the risks undercut the company's strategy for and execution of the central idea?

- Are there not only financial and operational risks but also human capital risks that should be anticipated?

✓ Has the chief executive considered all the viable alternatives?

- Are directors aware of the full range of realistic alternatives?

- Is the top management team reluctant to consider a bold but uncomfortable move into one of those alternative directions?

✓ How good is the strategic fit between company and leadership?

- How strong is the correspondence between the central idea, company strategy, and execution steps, on one side, and the leadership capacities of the chief executive and top lieutenants on the other side?

- If there is a significant gap, how can directors best mentor the CEO and direct reports to close the gap?

- Are underqualified executives in positions that could sabotage the best-intended strategy and plan of execution?

✓ Is the central idea tracked and measured?

- What metrics should be used to monitor company strategy and execution stemming from the central idea?

- How can directors best track whether their executives are indeed consistently strategizing and executing around the central idea?

Judging a central idea in a diversified or conglomerate enterprise requires a distinctive approach. Most diversified corporations define their overarching goals in broad comparative measures of financial performance, such as outshining the Standard & Poor's 500 index in the United States or its equivalent elsewhere. Earnings per share or total shareholder return are useful as well, as are less tangible indicators such as debt rating, "most admired" status, and inclusion in "best place to work" lists.

Regarding portfolio mix, conglomerates have sometimes reached for whatever market opportunities are available—think Berkshire Hathaway's diversified holdings in a range of industries from media and airlines to banking and insurance. Other diversified firms have opted for adjacent products that current customers need—think American Express's effort to build a tightly integrated financial supermarket. Whatever the blend, here are six questions for directors to consider in concert with company executives:

DIRECTOR'S CHECKLIST 3: THE CENTRAL IDEA IN A DIVERSIFIED ENTERPRISE

✓ Is this the right mix of businesses in the portfolio?

- Is *each* business driven by its own, unique central idea, and are all the businesses tied to the firm's overarching idea?

- And is each business outperforming its major competitors, including those that are stand-alone in the industry?

✓ How well is the company syncing its portfolio mix with changing markets and a forward outlook?

- Should the mix be more focused or more diverse?

- Should a business be divested because it might be of greater value to other owners or perhaps because it is close to peaking?

- Is the company missing new market opportunities that a conglomerate should consider entering?

✓ If a further diversifying acquisition is proposed, does it come with its own central idea?

- Does a target enterprise fit well with the conglomerate's overarching idea?

- And might resources be too drained from existing performers to fund a risky newcomer?

✓ Are sufficient routine systems in place to measure and manage diverse operations?

   – Does the executive team effectively drive portfolio strategy reviews, capital budgeting cycles, and compensation schemes that appraise and reward both business and overall results?

✓ What is the vulnerability on the balance sheet to operational or uncontrollable risks?

   – Could weakness in one division threaten the strengths of others?

   – Have periodic stress tests been conducted to ensure resilience of each of the businesses in a volatile environment?

✓ Are the chief executive and possible successors up to the special demands of leading a range of operating units in a varied set of markets?

   – A great chief executive for a highly focused company is not necessarily an ideal leader for a diversified firm. Is the talent pipeline preparing the next generation for not only divisional but also parental leadership?

✓ Does the board include directors who bring experience and understanding of the diverse markets in which the conglomerate operates?

   – The directors need not be familiar with all of the segments, but some directors with deep understanding of at least the most important markets can be vital.

Recruit Directors Who Build Value

DIRECTOR'S CHECKLIST 4: RECRUIT DIRECTORS WHO BUILD VALUE

✓ Does a prospective director have the capacity to think strategically about the firm's competitive position and thus contribute to the ongoing evolution of its central idea?

✓ Is the board candidate familiar with and experienced in the specific strategic and execution issues derived from the central idea?

✓ Does the would-be director have a proven record of working collaboratively with executives at other companies in developing and implementing business practices stemming from the central idea?

✓ Will the prospect add intellectual and experiential diversity to the board, plugging weak spots and adding bench strength for guiding the central idea, strategy, and execution?

✓ Will the candidate be ready to stand tall when vital issues are on the line, the stakes and stress are high, and direct leadership of the company becomes essential?

✓ Does the prospective director generally add real value not only to the boardroom but also to the executive suite?

Root Out Dysfunction

Though directors vary in their contributions to the company's leadership, some boards have one or two directors whose disruptive behavior verges on the anti-leadership end of the spectrum. Should they gain seats on the board's governance committee, they can also effectively block efforts to change or remove them. Here are nine questions for directors to ask of themselves and their fellow directors about the one or two board members who appear to be taking more out of the boardroom than bringing into it:

DIRECTOR'S CHECKLIST 5: DEALING WITH NONPERFORMING DIRECTORS

✓ Does the director bring few useful skills and a lack of relevant experience to the boardroom?

✓ Is the director often unprepared for board meetings?

✓ Does the director fail to grasp the firm's central idea and business strategy?

✓ Are the director's questions distracting or inappropriate?

✓ Does the director bring few ideas or leads on business development?

✓ Has the board established norms on what is expected of directors in the boardroom?

✓ Has the line between leading and staying out of the way been made clear by the lead director and chief executive?

✓ Have directors and executives been asked for confidential feedback on a dysfunctional director?

✓ Has the lead director privately coached a director whose behavior has been disruptive?

Wanted: A Leader of the Board

As boards assume an ever-greater governance role in the life of the corporation, the job of board leader takes on ever-greater significance. Next to getting the central idea and CEO right, choosing the right board leader is the most important decision directors are called to make. Several personal and professional qualities have become important for identifying who among the directors on the board would be most qualified for elevation to leader of the board.

DIRECTOR'S CHECKLIST 6: PERSONAL QUALITIES IN SELECTING A BOARD LEADER

✓ Extensive business leadership experience, including crisis leadership

✓ Respect and confidence of other directors

✓ Collaborative and restrained in style

✓ Personally bonded with other directors

✓ Comfortable in own skin and station in life

✓ Resilient, with a drive to confront and surmount setbacks

✓ Complete candor and expectation of the same in others

DIRECTOR'S CHECKLIST 7: PROFESSIONAL QUALITIES IN SELECTING A BOARD LEADER

✓ An experienced mentor of business leadership in others

✓ Shows mastery of the company's central idea, strategy, and operating issues, and applies seasoned and judicious judgment

✓ Downplays self-interest and serves as a trusted counselor and partner of the CEO

✓ Displays a passion for corporate governance, including both monitoring and leadership

✓ Brings the personal time and emotional energy to devote to board leadership

✓ Listens well and draws out ideas, learns what other directors have on their minds, crystallizes directors' diverse views, facilitates expression of underlying concerns, and focuses deliberations

✓ Displays effective influence, corporate diplomacy, and constructive guidance

✓ Embodies integrity and expects it in all directors and executives

---

An additional set of specifications can help guide the board leader once in office.

DIRECTOR'S CHECKLIST 8: BOARD LEADER OBLIGATIONS

✓ Works with the board to guide management on the central idea, strategic issues, and long-term planning

✓ Serves as liaison between directors and executives

✓ Presides over regular and special board sessions without executives present

✓ Determines who attends board meetings, including members of management and outside advisers

✓ Consults with executives and directors on meeting schedule, agenda, and materials

✓ Responds in alliance with the CEO to shareholder inquiries and approves company responses to investor communication

✓ Works with the chair of the compensation committee on CEO performance evaluation and compensation

✓ Works with the chair of the governance committee on the selection of committee chairs and board members, and presides over an annual board and director evaluation

✓ Works with the chair of the audit committee to ensure compliance with laws and regulations and appropriate risk management

✓ Ensures that a succession plan is in place for both the CEO and the board leader and that a backup for the CEO is in place in case the CEO unexpectedly exits

---

CEO Succession

After ensuring that the company is focused on the right central idea, the directors' next most critical task is ensuring that they have the right executive in the corner office.

DIRECTOR'S CHECKLIST 9: CHIEF EXECUTIVE SUCCESSION

✓ Are company strategy and executive succession explicitly linked?

✓ Is a board process in place for evaluating the CEO and potential successors?

✓ Does the board explicitly assess the CEO's management of a succession plan for the next generation of company leaders?

✓ Is the board leader driving the succession process for the CEO and direct reports?

✓ Is the board working to retain a high-performing chief executive—but also to keep capable successors?

✓ Does the board have a member who could serve as CEO in the wake of an unexpected exit if no insider is yet ready for succession?

✓ Has the board compiled comparative data on the inside CEO candidates from those who had worked with all of them?

✓ Have directors had direct contact with both the CEO candidates and information sources to verify information about them?

✓ If executive search consultants are retained, have they been vetted to ensure that there are no conflicts of interest?

✓ Does the board ensure candidate confidentiality?

✓ Has the board gathered independent references on the outside candidates?

✓ Is succession planning embedded in the company's culture?

A Question of Fit

DIRECTOR'S CHECKLIST 10: A CEO CANDIDATE'S STRATEGIC FIT

- ✓ What are the two or three most critical requirements for executive leadership, given the company's expected competitors and future opportunities?

- ✓ What are the two or three most distinctive leadership talents required of the candidates, given that most finalists come with a proven leadership record?

- ✓ Is there convergence between the several criteria that best define a strategic match between the company's leadership requirements and a candidate's capabilities at a given moment?

Spotting, Catching, or Exiting a Failing CEO

If the chief executive shows signs of faltering, here are specific indicators of their shortfall that can trigger director intervention, followed by director questions in resolving whether to retain, revive, or relieve the chief executive:

DIRECTOR'S CHECKLIST 11: SPOTTING A FALLING CEO

- ✓ Absence of clear strategy

- ✓ Lack of focus on a few dominant priorities

- ✓ Dislike of follow-through

- ✓ Underanticipation of unintended consequences

- ✓ Overreliance on the decision making of a senior executive

✓ Captive of special advisers

✓ Functional executive appointed to line position without line experience

---

DIRECTOR'S CHECKLIST 12: RETAINING, REVIVING, OR RELIEVING THE CHIEF EXECUTIVE

✓ Are CEO missteps an aberration that coaching by the board leader can overcome?

✓ If missteps are more than an aberration, what additional corrective actions are warranted?

✓ Is the CEO capable of strengthening the leadership capacities required for full revival?

✓ Does the board have information about the root cause of a company's decline?

✓ Do most of the directors believe that the CEO is faltering?

✓ Is the board's annual evaluation of the CEO focused on leadership indicators, not just financial metrics?

✓ Have directors and the CEO coached other executives on how to work with the board?

✓ Does the board learn directly from and about executives who report to the CEO?

✓ If moving toward relieving the CEO, are most or all of the directors of common mind?

✓ Are performance metrics and severance terms well in place before advancing toward dismissal?

Turning Risk into Opportunity

DIRECTOR'S CHECKLIST 13: LEADING RISK

- ✓ Is the company's risk appetite well defined by directors and disciplined by executives?

- ✓ Is the board well informed and accepting of the company's risk management strategies?

- ✓ Are directors regularly updated on company risks via the board's audit or risk committee?

- ✓ Does the board include directors with prior executive experience in managing risks?

- ✓ Are the company's risk management practices preemptive rather than reactive?

- ✓ Does the company properly balance risks and business opportunities?

- ✓ Is excessive risk well defined and properly avoided?

- ✓ Is risk management embedded in the operating practices and mind-set of managers throughout the ranks?

- ✓ Has the company prepared for low-probability but high-consequences events?

- ✓ Does the board lead with management in conducting due diligence and deciding on major acquisitions and other highly risky transactions?

- ✓ Has the board considered creating an advisory body?

Staying Out of the Way

DIRECTOR'S CHECKLIST 14: STAYING OUT OF THE WAY

✓ Are complex operating decisions taken to the board for counsel?

✓ Are the lines between leading, collaborating, and staying out of the way clearly drawn through annual calendars, committee charters, and decision protocols?

✓ Have directors and executives evolved a mutual understanding of which decisions go to the board for direction, collaboration, or not at all?

A Revised Definition of Corporate Governance

As boardroom leadership further strengthens in years ahead—and we believe it will—here are boardroom checklist questions that insiders and outsiders can usefully raise. We invite you to post additional questions from your own experience on our website, BoardRoom IQ, at http://www.boardroomiq.com.

DIRECTOR'S CHECKLIST 15: CURRENT DIRECTORS AND EXECUTIVES

✓ Do all directors understand and back the company's central idea, competitive strategy, and execution plan?

✓ Does the board have the right board leader, committee chairs, and chief executive in place?

✓ Does the board have an established procedure for selecting the next board leader, committee chairs, and chief executive?

✓ Are directors and executives in regular formal and informal dialogue on the eleven key areas of decision making?

✓ If the board was built from scratch, are the current directors and board leader those you would want in place?

DIRECTOR'S CHECKLIST 16: WOULD-BE DIRECTORS AND EXECUTIVES

✓ Have you held substantial responsibility for P&L operations in business?

✓ Do you have a proven record of understanding central ideas, company strategies, execution plans, and the drivers of shareholder value?

✓ Are you comfortable leading laterally in concert with executives and other directors?

✓ Does the board that you are considering help lead the company, not just monitor management?

✓ Would you add value to the boardroom not already provided by other directors?

DIRECTOR'S CHECKLIST 17: EQUITY ANALYSTS, INSTITUTIONAL INVESTORS, PUBLIC REGULATORS, AND GOVERNANCE RATERS

✓ Is the company built on the right central idea, pursuing the right strategy, and capable of executing?

✓ Does the board leader have a reputation and record for adding shareholder value, providing guidance on the central idea and competitive strategy, and working closely with company executives?

✓ Does the board have a meaningful process for selecting its leader and committee chairs and, conversely, for evaluating directors and weeding out dysfunctional members?

✓ Has the board established a procedure for preparing chief executive candidates, and has it readied a replacement in case the CEO is unexpectedly sidelined?

✓ How regularly is the board leader in contact with the chief executive and other top executives regarding financial performance, strategic direction, enterprise risk, talent management, executive compensation, and company culture?

DIRECTOR'S CHECKLIST 18: IS THE BOARD READY TO LEAD, NOT JUST MONITOR, THE COMPANY?

✓ Does the board include the needed experience and diversity at the table?

- Engaged boards concentrate on where the company is headed and when to alter course to stay competitive. For that to work, directors with requisite variety in both experience and views will be essential for formulating the central idea and executing strategy in collaboration with the executive team.

✓ Does the board ensure careful selection and assessment of the board leader?

- As a leader of leaders, the board leader plays a pivotal role in bringing to life the board's monitoring of management and its leadership with management. The board leader's duties range widely from identifying committee chairs to coaching top executives. Appointing a board leader with the right capabilities is essential at the outset, and periodic review of the board leader's performance is essential once in office.

✓ Does the board ensure the right executives are in place?

- The board has among its most vital duties the selection of the right chief executive, grooming of the next CEO, and guidance of the sitting CEO. For that to work well, continuous vigilance is essential in the boardroom, as is swift intervention if the chief executive shows signs of faltering. These matters increasingly extend as well to the chief executive's direct reports, including the chief financial officer, chief human resource officer, and general counsel.

✓ Does the board ensure rapport among executives and directors?

- Directors and executives have much to achieve together, ranging from designing strategy to preventing catastrophe, and little time together to achieve it. For a partnership at the top to work, a personal chemistry between the boardroom and the executive suite requires active construction by both sides.

✓ Does the board directly engage directors in business opportunities and enterprise risk?

- The directors' leadership role calls for their direct engagement in strategic planning, business cultivation, brand protection, fraud prevention, risk mitigation, and other issues vital to firm performance.

✓ Does the board ensure the right tenor at the top?

- Decisions of the directors and executives are shaped at a deeper level by the unspoken norms and values of the boardroom. For major decisions to be properly grounded and guided, directors will want to set a principled tone at the top.

If directors can affirmatively answer these final self-evaluation questions or if their initially negative appraisals are reversed through active intervention, they should finally be ready to deliver the company leadership potential that many boards are now coming to embrace. Demanding investors and rising complexity require no less. After years of fits and starts, directors and executives are finally building the joint leadership at the top that companies need and their shareholders deserve.

Appendix A

Trends in Director Monitoring and Leading

Directors as Monitors of Management

In 1950, a small fraction of the shares of publicly traded companies were in the hands of professional investors, but during the decades that followed, institutional investors gradually acquired a far greater portion, and in doing so also attained a substantial degree of influence on these companies. The percentage of US corporate equity held by institutional investors rose tenfold from 6.1 in 1950 to 61.2 in 2005.[1]

The growing concentration of shares in the hands of professional money managers is even greater among large firms. Drawing on the thousand largest enterprises by market capitalization as of May 1 each year, institutional investors held 46 percent of their shares in 1987 but 73 percent in 2009, the latest year for which comparable data is available (figure A-1). Similar trends are evident in most other national equity markets, ranging from Japan to Korea and Germany to the United Kingdom.[2]

With the strengthening of institutional investors and their ability to apply greater pressure on directors to serve as their elected agents for monitoring management, we see a corresponding rise in board practices for stronger director oversight of the company on behalf of

FIGURE A-1

Percentage of shares of largest 1,000 US companies held by institutional investors, 1987–2009

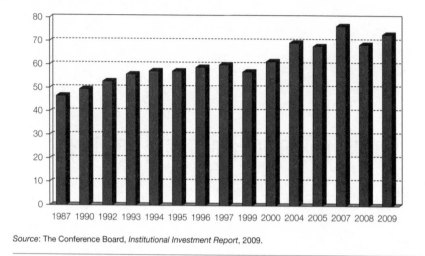

Source: The Conference Board, *Institutional Investment Report*, 2009.

shareholders. Focusing on the Standard & Poor's 500 largest companies as ranked by market value (the S&P 500), we find that the fraction of company boards with only a single non-independent director, the chief executive, rose from 23 percent in 1998 to 59 percent in 2012 (table A-1); separation of the CEO from board chair increased from 16 to 43 percent; and the proportion of boards with a lead or presiding director climbed from 36 percent in 2003 (data was not collected in prior years, since virtually no companies had instituted such a position) to 92 percent in 2012. Similarly, 67 percent of the companies included an independent governance or nomination committee in 1998, but 100 percent did so by 2012; and the fraction of companies compensating directors with both retainer and equity rose from 38 to 76 percent.[3]

The rise of institutional investor influence has also led to a decline in the prevalence of anti-shareholder devices such as poison pills (also known as shareholder rights plans, intended to deter hostile acquisitions) and classified boards (directors are elected for multiyear rather than single-year terms) that are generally deemed to help shield managers

TABLE A-1

Percentage of S&P 500 companies with shareholder monitoring devices, 1998–2012

Monitoring device	1998	1999	2001	2002	2003	2004	2005	2006	2007	2008	2009	2010	2011	2012	Percentage point change
CEO is the only non-independent director	23	21	27	31	35	39	30	39	43	44	50	53	57	59	36
CEO is not chair of the board	16	20	26	25	23	26	29	33	35	39	37	40	39	43	27
Boards with lead or presiding director	n/a	n/a	n/a	n/a	36	85	94	96	94	95	95	92	92	92	n/a
Independent governance or nominations committee	67	69	70	75	91	98	100	99	100	100	100	99	100	100	33
One-year term length for directors	39	38	41	40	40	55	50	56	62	66	68	72	>75	>80	41
Directors receive equity in addition to retainer	38	46	42	42	47	50	60	64	72	74	79	79	77	76	38

Source: Spencer Stuart, *Board Index*, 2012 and earlier years (New York: Spencer Stuart, 1998–2012).

from shareholder pressure. The 2000s, indeed, saw a substantial retreat among large publicly traded companies from such devices.[4]

Focusing again on S&P 500 companies, table A-2 confirms that between 1998 and 2012 the proportion of firms with a poison pill declined from 59 percent to 8 percent, and the fraction with classified boards declined from 61 to 17 percent. Trends in other anti-shareholder devices for the period 2002–2012 are also displayed in table A-2, and though their trend lines are more modest in slope, they are downward over the decade as well.

With the greater alignment of directors with shareholders as a result of these changes, we also find executive pay trending away from fixed salary and benefits and toward compensation contingent on financial results that directly benefit shareholders. As seen in table A-2, total pay for the top seven managers of forty-five large US manufacturing firms has indeed sharply shifted between 1982 and 2012 from primarily fixed to predominantly variable. Since directors exercise a direct hand in setting executive compensation through the board's compensation committee, the trend line points to greater board monitoring of executives on behalf of shareholders.

Directors as Leaders with Management

The rising institutional investor demands on directors for vigilant shareholder monitoring has been paralleled by an equally important, externally fostered call for directors to work collaboratively with executives for direct or joint leadership of the company's central idea, strategy, and beyond. We believe that a major driver behind the willingness of directors and executives to enter into shared leadership of the company has been the increasing market complexity of company decisions. Annual metrics for trends in complexity are not as readily available as for institutional holdings, making its impetus more difficult to document, yet many data traces point in that direction, and informed observers suggest the same.[5]

One source of complexity is the increasing movement of enterprise operations or sales across national boundaries. Company managers as

TABLE A-2

Percentage of S&P 500 companies with anti-shareholder devices

1998–2012

Anti-shareholder device	1998	1999	2000	2001	2002	2003	2004	2005	2006	2007	2008	2009	2010	2011	2012	Percentage point change
Poison pill	58.8	57.2	59.8	60.2	60.0	57.0	53.2	45.4	34.2	28.8	21.4	16.8	13.2	10.2	7.6	−51.2
Classified board	60.6	60.6	60.0	58.8	61.2	57.2	53.3	47.4	41.5	36.1	34.2	32.5	28.9	24.4	16.9	−43.7

2002–2012

Anti-shareholder device	2002	2003	2004	2005	2006	2007	2008	2009	2010	2011	2012	Percentage point change
Directors removed only for cause	52.2	51.8	48.8	45.0	42.5	39.6	39.6	38.8	37.5	35.5	33.6	−18.6
Shareholders cannot call special meetings	59.1	59.0	59.6	58.1	57.7	56.9	55.1	52.9	51.1	49.7	46.8	−12.3
Fair price provision	32.9	32.2	31.2	30.0	26.5	24.1	23.4	22.2	20.4	19.1	18.2	−14.7
Supermajority vote for mergers	31.0	29.3	29.9	29.0	28.1	26.0	24.4	24.0	23.4	22.0	20.9	−10.1
Supermajority vote to remove directors	32.9	32.8	32.4	31.0	30.0	28.7	28.5	28.1	25.5	23.6	23.4	−9.5

Source: FactSet Research Systems Inc., 2012 and earlier years.

FIGURE A-2

Compensation of top seven executives at forty-five US manufacturing firms, 1982–2012

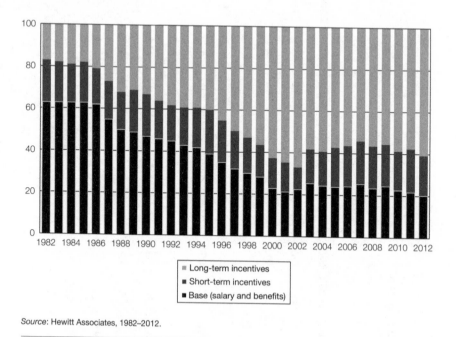

Source: Hewitt Associates, 1982–2012.

a result are obliged to be more conversant in the challenges of facing markets diverse in regulatory regimes, consumer preferences, and cultural traditions. Consider the source of revenue for the S&P 500. The fraction of their sales from abroad, as displayed in table A-3, increased from 32 percent in 2001 to 48 percent by 2008, though it declined after that year's financial crisis and by 2010 stood at 46 percent.[6]

Consistent with this framing, surveys of company executives regarding their boards point to an increasing emphasis on the role of directors in formulating company strategy. An annual survey of corporate secretaries and general counsels of S&P 500 firms beginning in the mid-2000s reported that company strategy had increasingly come to occupy boardroom concerns. The report based on its 2006 survey, for instance, indicated that company boards "will be even more focused on regularly reviewing and tuning strategy over the long term," and that companies are increasingly focusing on company strategy at most

TABLE A-3

Percentage of sales outside the United States by S&P 500 companies, 2001–2011

	2001	2003	2004	2005	2006	2007	2008	2009	2010	2011	Percentage point change
Foreign sales as percentage of total sales	32.3	41.8	43.8	43.3	43.6	45.8	47.9	46.6	46.3	46.1	12.8

Source: Standard and Poor's, various years.

FIGURE A-3

Governance topics requiring greatest attention by S&P 500 boards of directors, 2008–2012

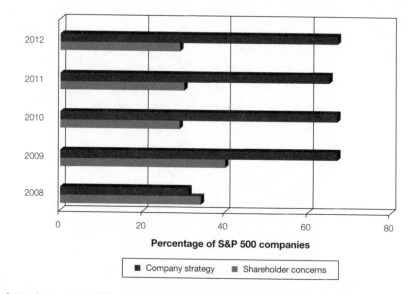

Percentage of S&P 500 companies

■ Company strategy   ■ Shareholder concerns

Source: Spencer Stuart, 2012 and earlier years; survey of corporate secretaries and general counsels of S&P 500 companies (N = 101 in 2012; 102 in 2011; 92 in 2010; 123 in 2009; 127 in 2008).

board meetings. Corporate secretaries and general counsels annually surveyed from 2008 to 2012 cited company strategy as a top concern among some two-thirds of the companies, while shareholder value was a primary focus at two-fifths or less, symptomatic of the separate importance of the dual roles that directors have now been pressed to embrace by both investors and executives (figure A-3).[7]

Strengthening Board Committees

As board leadership has gained traction, companies rely more on three board committees that are now required by regulators or exchanges, and companies more often compensate committee members and chairs for their service (table A-4). Those companies that did recompense committee service in 2012 provided committee members with an average stipend of $8,189, and committee chairs with $13,035.

Percentage of S&P 500 companies with board committees and committee practices, 2001–2012

	2001	2006	2011	2012	Percentage point change
Board committee					
Independent audit committee	93	100	100	100	7
Independent compensation committee	70	100	100	100	30
Independent governance committee	94	99	100	100	6
Committee practice					
Audit committee chair is financial expert	4	19	32	33	29
Committee chairs receive extra retainer	57	84	91	92	35
Committee members receive extra retainer	13	29	37	38	25

Source: Spencer Stuart, *Board Index,* 2012 (New York: Spencer Stuart, 2012).

Evaluating Directors

The intensification of both the monitoring and the leadership functions of the governing board has moved directors beyond the more passive role they played in earlier decades at many American companies. Among the consequences anticipated by the rise of both roles is a greater emphasis on evaluating the performance of the board and its members.

To examine this, we turn to The Conference Board, an independent business–sponsored research organization, for its annual profile of the boards of a large number of publicly traded American companies. As expected from the strengthening of both director roles, the fraction of the boards that evaluated board performance rose from 25 percent in 2000 to 86 to 97 percent (depending upon the sector) in 2011. The portion that evaluated the performance of individual directors grew from 11 percent in 2000 to 34 to 38 percent in 2011 (table A-5).

TABLE A-5

Percentage of large companies conducting evaluations of their board and individual directors, 2000–2011

Performance evaluation	2000	2001	2002	2003	2004	2005	2006	2009	2010	2011
Board evaluation	25	24	29	48	69	83	85	94 to 97	86 to 96	93 to 97
Director evaluation	11	11	13	23	28	35	41	28 to 36	25 to 35	34 to 38

Source: The Conference Board, U.S. Directors' Compensation and Board Practices Report, 2011 and earlier years.

Appendix B

Director Evaluation

A form used by the board of a publicly traded US technology company in 2012 for directors to evaluate the service of each of the other directors on their board—and themselves—appears in this section.

Evaluation criteria	Director										
	1	2	3	4	5	6	7	8	9	10	11

Attendance, participation, and responsiveness

1. Attends board meetings regularly

2. Prepares adequately for board meetings

3. Participates in board meetings attended

4. Available for consultation with management between meetings

5. Returns calls/signs documents in a timely manner, and makes time available as necessary for previously unscheduled time-sensitive calls/meetings

Substantive issues

6. Understands company's business and products

7. Makes quality contributions to board discussions

8. Is financially literate

9. Contributes new ideas/insights on business issues raised by management

10. Provides thoughtful and constructive feedback to management

11. Anticipates new issues that management and the board should consider

12. Provides valuable introductions to, or support with, business partners, government authorities, or outside advisers

13. Assists the company in employee recruiting (including interviewing)

14. Understands and actively exercises board governance responsibilities

15. Makes concise contributions without distracting discussions from the important issues

Qualitative issues

16. Brings a different and valuable perspective and experience to the board

17. Facilitates open and interactive discussion of issues

18. Participates in rigorous decision making

19. Takes ownership of an issue on behalf of the board

1 = Exceeds expectations; 2 = Meets expectations; 3 = Needs improvement; N = Not a sufficient opportunity to observe
Source: A publicly traded US technology company.

Appendix C

Division of Responsibilities Between the Board Leader and Chief Executive Officer

We include in this appendix a document setting forward the division of responsibilities between the board leaders and chief executive officer that Tyco board leader John Krol developed in collaboration with new CEO Edward Breen when both set out to rescue Tyco International in 2003.[1] It guided their joint leadership of the company in the years that followed. Recognizing that every enterprise has distinctive needs, we include the document verbatim as a useful illustration of the specific and tangible ways in which the identification and separation of their leadership duties can be explicitly expressed.

We also include a similar document from Select Comfort Corporation, a publicly traded manufacturing corporation with a market capitalization in mid-2012 of $1.6 billion.[2] Though the specific format and framing are different, here, too, we can see the value of an explicit inventory of the leadership that is expected of company executives and directors.

Leadership of the Chief Executive and Board Leader, Tyco International

Chief Executive Officer

Builds positive working relationship with the board; meets commitments

Strives for constructive, effective, value-added, focused meetings

Ensures focus on the right issues and provides useful information

Keeps board informed on a timely basis of significant positives/negatives; totally open and honest

Uses meetings and other contacts with board to tap knowledge and wisdom

Strives to make the board a competitive advantage

Provides board open access to senior management team

Board Leader

Chairs board meetings

Leads executive sessions of board and provides prompt and candid feedback to CEO

Communicates on an ongoing basis with CEO—messages from board (other board members also encouraged to do this)

Obtains board members' and management input and sets board agenda (with CEO)

Works with CEO to get right flow of information to the board on timely basis

Facilitates communication among directors

Partners with/coaches CEO (helps make CEO successful)

Stays current on major risks; focuses board on these

Molds a cohesive board to support success of CEO

Assists in recruiting effort for new board members (with Nominating and Governance Committee and CEO)

Ensures governance processes are leading edge (with Nominating and Governance Committee)

Discusses (with chairman of Compensation Committee) the CEO's personal development and compensation

Leadership of the Senior Management and Board of Directors of Select Comfort Corporation

Overview
[It] is critical for the Board and Senior Management to be aligned on the strategic focus of the company to ensure accelerated profitable growth to maximize shareholder and stakeholder value.

Objectives

- Where we are going: Clarity on the strategy, short and long-term

- How we will work: Sense of the Board, with management

- What we will work on: Building blocks of the strategy, 24-month Board calendar

Insights

- CEO/Board Chair leads versus facilitates

- Board and Management have clear expectations of each other—Norms

- Board and Management are aligned on the strategic focus and risk profile

- Board and Management have a high sense of confidence in each other and the ability to have open, honest, and productive dialogue

- Board and Management plan to review, recommit and/or revise Norms on an annual basis—in May

Board Norms—Rules of Engagement

- "Act with a sense of the Board"

  - Neither monopolize nor shy away from airtime

  - Value different judgments, express ideas, and be totally open

  - Let everyone speak before decision made

- Discuss and align on underlying assumptions of major decisions

  - Use facts and analysis to narrow field of judgment

  - Use external validation where appropriate

  - Be open to new information and learn from the past

Board Expectations of Each Other

- As a general rule, communication to Senior Management should go through Board Chair. Exceptions include ideas where no response or action from Management is expected.

- Chairman leads executive sessions, CEO is clear on business actions—focuses and crystallizes what is agreed upon

- Broad participation by every Director

- Assume each Director's positive intent and concern for long-term shareholder value

- Confidentiality and candid communication with one another; discretion with e-mail; strong bias to group discussion versus individual conversations

- Annual assessment/feedback process

Board Expectations of Senior Management

- Clearly communicate expectations of the Board: update, input, or decision

- Set Board agenda to govern (versus manage), and to effectively make decisions

  - 1–5 year view of the business

  - 24-month agenda

    - Strategic building block review

    - External discussion/speaker/bend-in-the-road exercise

    - Unfiltered customer feedback

    - Questions for input

    - Summarize meetings with 3 likes, dislikes, and suggestions

- Strategy for long-term, consumer-driven growth to maximize shareholder value

  - Advantaged, focused

  - Investments by year, milestones, and range of outcomes

  - Risk profile, SWOT

- Operating plan for profitable growth aligned with strategy—sales, earnings, contingencies, results

  - Goal-setting proposal

- Be clear on what the issues are and where we are making progress

• Talent management and development; succession plans for Senior Management

• Concise presentations and operating metric reviews

- Deliver commitments; open and credible style

Management Expectations of Board

• Knowledge of the business (industry, business model, etc.)— sufficient to evaluate strategy

• Understanding of target customer

• Provide direction on risk profile for the company

- Support the necessary changes and appropriate pace for the business to reach its potential

• Share external perspective and personal experience to improve long-term performance of the company

- Provide input and decisions as requested by Senior Management

- Anticipate bends in the road; early warning signs

- Challenge and add value to strategy

- Surface risks and opportunities, including external social changes

• Alignment on strategy, goal setting, and annual operating plan

• Confidence in and development of CEO, Senior Management and bench

- Seize opportunities to know and understand capabilities

• Be responsive to Senior Team request for involvement; be consultative, not directive

• "Act with a sense of the Board"

FURTHER READING ON
DIRECTOR AND EXECUTIVE LEADERSHIP

We believe the best way to learn how to lead at the top—whether in the board-room or the executive suite—is to engage directly in it. Nothing, in our esti-mation, is as effective a learning experience as taking personal responsibility for a company's performance and fate.

For those hoping to reach that apex but not quite yet there, additional learn-ing avenues can also be fruitful. One path is to seek out personal time with those who have so served. Mentoring by experienced executives and directors can provide development insights that are nuanced, personal, and indelible. Another path is to absorb what has been written by those who have observed, analyzed, or occupied the top of the pyramid. For the latter, we provide several suggestions for readily accessible books and articles on executive and director leadership:

Behan, Beverly. *Great Companies Deserve Great Boards: A CEO's Guide to the Boardroom.* New York: Palgrave Macmillan, 2011.

Bennis, Warren. *On Becoming a Leader.* New York: Perseus, 2003.

Bossidy, Larry, and Ram Charan. *Execution: The Discipline of Getting Things Done.* New York: Crown Business/Random House, 2002.

Bowen, William G. *The Board Book: An Insider's Guide for Directors and Trust-ees.* New York: Norton, 2008.

Cannella, Bert A., Jr., Sydney Finkelstein, and Donald C. Hambrick. *Strategic Leadership: Theory and Research on Executives, Top Management Teams, and Boards.* New York: Oxford University Press, 2008.

Cappelli, Peter, Harbir Singh, Jitendra Singh, and Michael Useem. *The India Way: How India's Top Business Leaders Are Revolutionizing Management.* Bos-ton: Harvard Business School Press, 2010.

Carey, Dennis. "Ensuring Great Non-Executive Board Leadership." *Director-ship Magazine,* September 1, 2010.

————."Don't Force Firms to Split CEO and Chair." *Wall Street Journal*, May 26, 2009.

Carey, Dennis, and John J. Keller. "How the Ford Board Recruited Alan Mulally." *Directors & Boards Magazine*, 4th Quarter, 2012.

Carey, Dennis, John J. Keller, and Michael Patsalos-Fox. "How to Choose the Right Non-Executive Board Leaders." *McKinsey Quarterly*, May 2010.

Carey, Dennis, Melanie Kusin, and Jane Stevenson. "How Companies Can Avoid CEO Hiring Failure." *Fortune.com*, May 10, 2012, http://management.fortune.cnn.com/2012/05/10/how-companies-can-avoid-ceo-hiring-failure.

Carey, Dennis, Dayton Ogden, and Judith A. Roland. *CEO Succession: A Window on How Boards Can Get It Right When Choosing a New Chief Executive*. New York: Oxford University Press, 2000.

Carey, Dennis, and Michael Patsalos-Fox. "Shaping Strategy from the Boardroom." *McKinsey Quarterly*, August 2006, http://mkqpreview1.qdweb.net/Governance/Boards/Shaping_strategy_from_the_boardroom_1813.

————. "Strategy Should Start in the Boardroom." *Financial Times*, August 20, 2006.

Carey, Dennis, Michael Patsalos-Fox, and Michael Useem. "Leadership Lessons for Hard Times." *McKinsey Quarterly*, July 2009.

Carey, Dennis, Daniel Phelan, and Michael Useem. "Picking the Right Insider for CEO Succession." *Harvard Business Review*, January–February, 2009.

Carter, Colin B., and Jay William Lorsch. *Back to the Drawing Board: Designing Corporate Boards for a Complex World*. Boston: Harvard Business School Press, 2004.

Chait, Richard P., William P. Ryan, and Barbara E. Taylor. *Governance as Leadership: Reframing the Work of Nonprofit Board*. Hoboken, NJ: Wiley, 2004.

Charan, Ram. *Boards That Deliver: Advancing Corporate Governance from Compliance to Competitive Advantage*. San Francisco: Jossey-Bass, 2005.

————. *Owning Up: The 14 Questions That Every Board Member Needs to Ask*. San Francisco: Jossey-Bass, 2009.

————. "Why Boards Fail to Choose the Right CEO." *Fortune*, August 8, 2012, http://management.fortune.cnn.com/2012/08/08/why-boards-fail-to-choose-the-right-ceo.

Charan, Ram, and Noel M. Tichy. *Every Business Is a Growth Business: How Your Company Can Prosper Year After Year*. New York: Times Books/Random House, 1998.

Clarke, Thomas, and Douglas Branson, eds. *The Sage Handbook on Corporate Governance*. Los Angeles: Sage Publications, 2012.

Collins, Jim. *Good to Great: Why Some Companies Make the Leap . . . and Others Don't*. New York: HarperBusiness, 2001.

Collins, Jim, and Morten T. Hansen. *Great by Choice: Uncertainty, Chaos, and Luck—Why Some Thrive Despite Them All*. New York: HarperBusiness, 2011.

Conger, Jay, ed., *Leading Corporate Boardrooms: The New Realities, the New Rules*. San Francisco: Jossey-Bass, 2009.

Gardner, Howard. *Leading Minds: An Anatomy of Leadership*. New York: Basic Books, 1995.

Gardner, John W. *On Leadership*. New York: Free Press, 1993.

Gandossy, Robert, and Jeffrey Sonnenfeld, eds. *Leadership and Governance from the Inside Out*. Hoboken, NJ: Wiley, 2004.

George, Bill. *Authentic Leadership: Rediscovering the Secrets to Creating Lasting Value*. San Francisco: Jossey-Bass, 2003.

Institute of Directors, ed., *The Handbook of International Corporate Governance: A Definitive Guide*. London: Kogan Page Ltd. and Institute of Directors, 2009.

Kakabadse, Andrew, and Nada Kakabadse, *Leading the Board: The Six Disciplines of World Class Chairmen*. New York: Palgrave Macmillan, 2008.

Kay, Ira T., ed., *Executive Pay at a Turning Point*. New York: Pay Governance, 2013.

Kallifatides, Markus, Sophie Nachemson-Ekwall, and Sven-Erik Sjöstrand. *Corporate Governance in Modern Financial Capitalism: Old Mutual's Hostile Takeover of Skandia*. Cheltenham, UK: Edward Elgar, 2010.

Kogut, Bruce, ed. *The Small World of Corporate Governance*. Cambridge, MA: MIT Press, 2012.

Larcker, David, and Brian Tayan. *Corporate Governance Matters: A Close Look at Organizational Choices and Their Consequences*. Upper Saddle River, NJ: Pearson, 2011.

Leblanc, Richard, and James Gillies. *Inside the Boardroom: How Boards Really Work and the Coming Revolution in Corporate Governance*. Mississauga, ON: Wiley, 2005.

Lorsch, Jay W., ed. *The Future of Boards: Meeting the Governance Challenges of the Twenty-First Century*. Boston: Harvard Business Review Press, 2012.

Lorsch, Jay W., with Elizabeth MacIver. *Pawns or Potentates: The Reality of America's Corporate Boards*. Boston: Harvard Business School Press, 1989.

Monks, Robert A. G., and Nell Minow. *Corporate Governance*, 5th ed. Chichester, UK: Wiley, 2011.

Nadler, David A., Beverly A. Behan, and Mark A. Nadler. *Building Better Boards: A Blueprint for Effective Governance*. San Francisco: Jossey-Bass/Wiley, 2006.

Roe, Mark J. *Strong Managers, Weak Owners: The Political Roots of American Corporate Finance*. Princeton, NJ: Princeton University Press, 1996.

Sherman, H. David, Dennis Carey, and Robert Brust. "The Audit Committee's New Agenda." *Harvard Business Review*, June 2009.

Sonnenfeld, Jeffrey A. "What Makes Great Boards Great." *Harvard Business Review*, September 2009.

Sonnenfeld, Jeffrey, Melanie Kusin, and Elise Walton, "What CEOs *Really* Think of Their Boards," *Harvard Business Review*, April 2013.

Tichy, Noel M. *The Leadership Engine: How Winning Companies Build Leaders at Every Level*. New York: HarperBusiness, 1997.

Tricker, Bob. *Corporate Governance: Principles, Policies, and Practices*. New York: Oxford University Press, 2009.

———. *Essentials for Board Directors: An A to Z Guide*, 2nd ed. New York: Bloomberg Press, 2009.

Useem, Michael. *The Leader's Checklist*. Philadelphia: Wharton Digital Press, 2011.

———. "How Well-Run Boards Make Decisions." *Harvard Business Review*, November 2006.

———. *The Leadership Moment: Nine True Stories of Triumph and Disaster and Their Lessons for Us All*. New York: Random House, 1998.

———. *Investor Capitalism: How Money Managers Are Changing the Face of Corporate America*. New York: Basic Books/HarperCollins, 1996.

———. *Executive Defense: Shareholder Power and Corporate Reorganization*. Cambridge, MA: Harvard University Press, 1993.

Also see articles appearing in the *Academy of Management Journal, Administrative Science Quarterly, California Management Review, Corporate Governance: An International Review, Directors and Boards, Harvard Business Review, Journal of Applied Corporate Finance, Journal of Corporate Finance, Journal of Governance and Management, Knowledge@Wharton, McKinsey Quarterly, MIT Sloan Management Review, Strategic Management Journal*, and other management publications and academic journals as well as reports and publications of BoardRoomIQ, Conference Board, Corporate Board Center, Corporate Secretary, Council of Institutional Investors, Harvard Law School Forum on Corporate Governance and Financial Regulation, International Finance Corporation's Global Corporate Governance Forum, National Association of Corporate Directors, National Investor Relations Institute, SSRN Corporate Governance Network, University of Delaware's Center for Corporate Governance, and Wachtell, Lipton, Rosen & Katz.

NOTES

Chapter 1

1. Warren Buffett, "Chairman's Letter," in Berkshire Hathaway Inc. Annual Report, 2002, http://www.berkshirehathaway.com/2002ar/2002ar.pdf.

2. Kevin Sharer, "Nine Lessons for CEOs," presentation, Prium CEO Academy, November 17, 2011.

3. Quotations from directors and executives that appear in the book are drawn from author interviews and observations, 2010 to 2013, unless otherwise noted.

4. Manda Salls, "Why Nonprofits Have a Board Problem," *Harvard Working Knowledge for Business Leaders*, April 4, 2005, http://hbswk.hbs.edu/archive/4735.html.

5. Patrick Jenkins, "New Barclays Chairman Sets out Challenges," *Financial Times*, September 12, 2012; Walker Review Secretariat, *A Review of Corporate Governance in UK Banks and Other Financial Industry Entities* (London: Walker Review Secretariat, 2009), http://webarchive.nationalarchives.gov.uk/+/http://www.hm-treasury.gov.uk/d/walker_review_consultation_160709.pdf.

6. Board decisions and actions are drawn from personal interviews or experiences with those in management or the boardroom. Additional information is drawn from Robert H. Rock and James Kristie, "Ed Woolard: A Life in Governance," *Directors and Boards*, Fall 2000; Adam Lashinsky, "Apple Brings Back Steve Jobs," part of a larger article by Brian Dumaine et al., "The Greatest Business Decisions of All Time," *Fortune*, October 8, 2012, adapted from the book by Verne Harnish and editors of *Fortune*, *The Greatest Business Decisions of All Time: How Apple, Ford, IBM, Zappos, and Others Made Radical Choices that Changed the Course of Business* (New York: Time Home Entertainment, 2012); Walter Isaacson, *Steve Jobs* (New York: Simon & Schuster, 2011), p. 319; Adam Lashinsky, *Inside Apple: How America's Most Admired—and Secretive—Company Really Works* (New York: Hachette, 2012).

7. Michael Dell later explained that he had not thought carefully about what it would take to turn around Apple; Mark Milian, "14 Years Later, Dell Founder Backtracks on Apple Attack," *CNN Tech*, October 18, 2011, http://articles.cnn.com/2011-10-18/tech/tech_web_michael-dell-apple_1_michael-dell-apple-employee-dell-first?_s=PM:TECH.

8. Adolf Augustus Berle and Gardiner C. Means, *The Modern Corporation and Private Property* (1932; Piscataway, NJ: Transaction Publishers, 1991).

9. Jay W. Lorsch with Elizabeth MacIver, *Pawns or Potentates: The Reality of America's Corporate Boards* (Boston: Harvard Business School Press, 1989.)

10. Carolyn Kay Brancato and Stephan Rabimov, *The 2007 Institutional Investor Report* (New York: The Conference Board Report R-1400-07-RR, February 2007); see also appendix A in this book.

11. Michael C. Jensen, "Eclipse of the Public Corporation," *Harvard Business Review*, September 1989, 61–74.

12. Michael Useem, *Investor Capitalism: How Money Managers Are Changing the Face of Corporate America* (New York: Basic Books/HarperCollins, 1996).

13. See appendix A.

14. New York Stock Exchange, "Final NYSE Corporate Governance Rules," November 4, 2003, http://www.nyse.com/pdfs/finalcorpgovrules.pdf.

15. Lucian A. Bebchuk and Michael S. Weisbach, "The State of Corporate Governance Research," *Review of Financial Studies* 23, no. 3 (2010): 939–961; Lawrence D. Brown and Marcus L. Caylor, "Corporate Governance and Firm Operating Performance," *Review of Quantitative Finance & Accounting* 32, no. 2 (2009): 129–144; Stijn Claessens and Joseph P.H. Fan, "Corporate Governance in Asia: A Survey," *International Review of Finance* 3, no. 2 (2002): 71–103; Henrik Cronqvist and Rüdiger Fahlenbrach, "Large Shareholders and Corporate Policies," *Review of Financial Studies* 22, no. 10 (2009): 3941–3976; David Finegold, Gordon S. Benson, and David Hecht, "Corporate Boards and Company Performance: Review of Research in Light of Recent Reforms," *Corporate Governance: An International Review* 15, no. 5 (2007): 865–878; Stuart L. Gillan, "Recent Developments in Corporate Governance: An Overview," *Journal of Corporate Finance* 12, no. 3 (2006): 381–402; Stuart L. Gillan and Laura T. Starks, "The Evolution of Shareholder Activism in the United States," *Journal of Applied Corporate Finance* 19, no. 1 (2007): 55–73; Paul A. Gompers, Joy L. Ishii, and Andrew Metrick, "Corporate Governance and Equity Prices," *Quarterly Journal of Economics* 118, no. 1 (2003): 107–156.; Eugene Kang and Asghar Zardkoohi, "Board Leadership Structure and Firm Performance," *Corporate Governance: An International Review* 13, no. 6 (2005): 785–799; David Larcker and Brian Tayan, *Corporate Governance Matters: A Closer Look at Organizational Choices and Their Consequences* (Upper Saddle River, NJ: Pearson Prentice Hall,

2011); Justin Fox and Jay W. Lorsch, "What Good Are Shareholders?" *Harvard Business Review*, July–August 2012, 48–57.

16. Spencer Stuart, *Spencer Stuart Board Index 2012* (New York: Spencer Stuart, 2012).

17. Additional information on the chief executives of the S&P 500 can be found in Jason D. Schloetzer, Matteo Tonello, and Melissa Aguilar, *CEO Succession Practices, 2012 Edition* (New York: The Conference Board Report R-1492–12-RR, April 2012); Harvard Law School Forum on Corporate Governance and Financial Regulation, September 2, 2011 (http://blogs.law.harvard.edu/corpgov/2011/09/02/good-monitoring-bad-monitoring); also see appendix A.

18. See appendix A.

19. David D. Court, Thomas D. French, and Trond Riiber Knudsen, "The Proliferation Challenge," in *Profiting from Proliferation*, ed. Allen P. Webb (New York: McKinsey & Company, 2006); Ian Austen, "A Boggle of BlackBerrys," *New York Times*, December 16, 2011, http://www.nytimes.com/2011/12/17/technology/rim-stock-hits-eight-year-low.html?pagewanted=all; J. Kevin Bright, Dieter Kiewell, and Andrew H. Kincheloe, "Pricing in a Proliferating World," in *Profiting from Proliferation*.

20. A. Edmunds and A. Morris, "The Problem of Information Overload in Business Organizations: A Review of the Literature, *International Journal of Information Management* 20, no. 1 (2000): 17–28; M. J. Eppler and J. Mengis, "The Concept of Information Overload: A Review of Literature from Organization Science, Accounting, Marketing, MIS, and Related Disciplines, *Information Society* 20, no. 5 (2004): 325–344.

21. See appendix A.

22. IBM, *Capitalizing on Complexity: Insights from the Global Chief Executive Officer Study*, 2010, http://www-935.ibm.com/services/us/ceo/ceostudy2010/index.html; IBM, *Leading Through Connections: Insights from the Global Chief Executive Officer Study*, 2012, http://www-935.ibm.com/services/us/en/c-suite/ceostudy2012.

23. See appendix A.

24. Deborah Ancona and Henrik Bresman, *X-Teams: How to Build Teams That Lead, Innovate, and Succeed* (Boston: Harvard Business School Press, 2007).

25. Michael Useem, *The Leader's Checklist: Fifteen Mission-Critical Principles* (Philadelphia: Wharton Digital Press, 2011).

26. Albert Einstein, "On the Method of Theoretical Physics," *Philosophy of Science* 1, no. 2 (1934): 163–169.

27. Dennis Carey, Michael Patsolos-Fox, and Michael Useem, "Leadership Lessons for Hard Times," *McKinsey Quarterly*, July 2009.

Chapter 2

1. The idea is akin to what Jim Collins and Jerry I. Porras have identified as the defining quality of companies that are built to last, or what Jim Stengel has identified as the essential core of brands that grow. See Jim Collins and Jerry I. Porras, *Built to Last: Successful Habits of Visionary Companies* (New York: HarperCollins, 1994); Jim Stengel, *Grow: How Ideals Power Growth and Profit at the World's Greatest Companies* (New York: Crown Business, 2011).

2. Board decisions and actions are drawn from personal interviews that we conducted with those in management and the boardroom, along with personal interviews conducted by three colleagues, Peter Cappelli, Harbir Singh, and Jitendra Singh, reported in Peter Cappelli, Harbir Singh, Jitendra Singh, and Michael Useem, *The India Way: How India's Top Business Leaders are Revolutionizing Management* (Boston: Harvard Business Press, 2010). See also Rebecca Buckman, "Outsourcing with a Twist: Indian Phone Giant Bharti Sends Jobs to Western Firms in a Multinational Role Switch," *Wall Street Journal*, January 18, 2005, http://online.wsj.com/article/SB110598769048027949.html.

3. This section is adapted from Cappelli et al., *The India Way*, 2010.

4. Clay Chandler, "Wireless Wonder: India's Sunil Mittal," *Fortune*, January 17, 2007, http://money.cnn.com/magazines/fortune/fortune_archive/2007/01/22/8397979/index.htm.

5. Board decisions and actions are drawn from personal interviews that we conducted with those in management and the boardroom.

Chapter 3

1. This section draws on personal interviews conducted for Peter Cappelli, Harbir Singh, Jitendra Singh, and Michael Useem, *The India Way: How India's Top Business Leaders Are Revolutionizing Management* (Boston: Harvard Business Press, 2010) and on author interviews and observations.

2. This section draws on personal interviews completed with Lenovo executives and directors by one of us and a colleague, Neng Liang (professor of management and Associate Dean for Faculty at the China Europe International Business School, Shanghai), reported in Michael Useem and Neng Liang, "Globalizing the Company Board: Lessons from China's Lenovo," in *Leading Corporate Boardrooms: The New Realities, the New Rules*, ed. Jay Conger (San Francisco: Jossey-Bass/Wiley, 2009); also see Neng Liang and Michael Useem, "China," in *The Handbook of International Corporate Governance* (London: Institute of Directors, 2009): 167–175.

3. Ling Zhijun, *The Lenovo Affair: The Growth of China's Computer Giant and Its Takeover of IBM-PC*, trans. Martha Avery (Singapore: Wiley, 2006); C. Z.

Liu, "Lenovo: An Example of Globalization of Chinese Enterprises," *Journal of International Business Studies* 38 (2007): 573–577.

4. Ling, *The Lenovo Affair*; Liu, "Lenovo."

5. "Newsmaker Q&A: Lenovo's 'Unique Opportunity,' CFO Mary Ma Says After the IBM PC Deal," *Businessweek*, December 8, 2004, http://www.businessweek.com/technology/content/dec2004/tc2004128_5989_tc121.htm.

6. International Data Corporation, PC Shipments Worldwide, by Vendor, 2004 and 2005, www.eMarketer.com.

7. Lee Chyen Yee and Huang Yuntao, "Lenovo Beats Q3 Net Forecasts by Raising Market Share," *Reuters*, February 9, 2012, http://www.reuters.com/article/2012/02/09/us-lenovo-idUSTRE8180HR20120209; Loretta Chao, "Lenovo Reaches Beyond PCs," *Wall Street Journal*, May 7, 2012, http://online.wsj.com/article/SB10001424052702303630404577387911080451538.html.

8. Board decisions and actions are drawn from personal interviews that we conducted with those in management and the boardroom.

9. Ibid.

10. One of us worked with Delphi to recruit the new board's directors, and one of us worked with the directors and chief executive on company strategy and leadership during this period.

Chapter 4

1. Korn/Ferry Institute, *What Makes an Exceptional Independent Non-Executive Director* (Los Angeles: Korn/Ferry International, 2012).

2. See appendix A.

3. Korn/Ferry Institute, *Cultivating Greatness in the Boardroom: What Makes an Exceptional Non-Executive Director in Australasia?* (Melbourne and Sydney: Korn/Ferry International, Australia, 2012).

Chapter 5

1. Cadbury Commission, *Report of the Committee on the Financial Aspects of Corporate Governance, 1992*, http://www.ecgi.org/codes/documents/cadbury.pdf.

2. Korn/Ferry International, *The Korn/Ferry Market Cap 100: New Directors and New Directions at America's Most Valuable Public Companies, 2011*, http://www.kornferryinstitute.com/reports-insights/kornferry-market-cap-100-board-leadership-america%E2%80%99s-most-valuable-public-companies; see Jason D. Schloetzer, Matteo Tonello, and Melissa Aguilar, *CEO Succession Practices, 2012 Edition* (New York: The Conference Board Report, 2012).

3. New York Stock Exchange, "Final NYSE Corporate Governance Rules," 2003, http://www.nyse.com/pdfs/finalcorpgovrules.pdf.

4. See appendix A.

5. Spencer Stuart, *Spencer Stuart Board Index 2012* (New York: Spencer Stuart, 2012).

6. This account is drawn from James Bandler with Doris Burke, "How Hewlett-Packard Lost Its Way," *Fortune*, May 8, 2012, http://tech.fortune .cnn.com/2012/05/08/500-hp-apotheker; Steve Lohr, "Even a Giant Can Learn to Run," *New York Times*, December 31, 2011, http://www.nytimes .com/2012/01/01/business/how-samuel-palmisano-of-ibm-stayed-a-step -ahead-unboxed.html?pagewanted=all; Quentin Hardy, "Meg Whitman's Toughest Campaign: Retooling H.P.," *New York Times*, September 30, 2012, http://www.nytimes.com/2012/09/30/technology/meg-whitmans-toughest -campaign-retooling-hewlett-packard.html?pagewanted=all; "How HP's Meg Whitman Is Passing the Buck," *CNNMoney*, November 30, 2012, http:// management.fortune.cnn.com/2012/11/30/hp-meg-whitman-autonomy -2; Quentin Hardy and Michael J. de la Merced, "Hewlett's Loss: A Folly Unfolds, by the Numbers," *New York Times*, November 20, 2012, http://dealbook .nytimes.com/2012/11/20/h-p-takes-big-hit-on-accounting-improprieties -at-autonomy/; James B. Stewart, "From H.P., a Blunder That Seems to Beat All," *New York Times*, November 30, 2012, http://www.nytimes.com/2012/ 12/01/business/hps-autonomy-blunder-might-be-one-for-the-record-books .html?pagewanted=all; and James B. Stewart, "The Case of H.P.'s Obstinate Director," *New York Times*, April 19, 2013.

7. Serena Ng and Joann S. Lubin, "Harvey Golub Resigns as AIG Chairman," *Wall Street Journal*, July 15, 2010, http://online.wsj.com/article/SB10001 4240527487047468045753367524244002534.html.

8. Korn/Ferry International, *The Korn/Ferry Market Cap 100*.

9. Michael J. de la Merced and Chris V. Nicholson, "Kraft to Acquire Cadbury in Deal Worth $19 Billion," *New York Times*, January 19, 2010, http:// www.nytimes.com/2010/01/20/business/global/20kraft.html.

10. Bill George, *Authentic Leadership: Rediscovering the Secrets to Creating Lasting Value* (San Francisco: Jossey-Bass, 2004).

11. Emily Glazer, Ellen Byron, Dennis K. Berman, and Joann S. Lubin, "P&G's Stumbles Put CEO on Hot Seat for Turnaround," *Wall Street Journal*, September 27, 2012, http://online.wsj.com/article/SB1000087239639044481 3104578016191845779524.html.

12. Michael Useem, "Corporate Governance Is Directors Making Decisions: Reforming the Outward Foundations for Inside Decision Making," *Journal of Management and Governance* 7, no. 3 (2003): 241–253.

13. See appendix A.

14. Spencer Stuart, *Spencer Stuart Board Index 2012*; H. David Sherman, Dennis Carey, and Robert Brust, "The Audit Committee's New Agenda," *Harvard Business Review*, June 2009, 92–99.

15. Dennis Carey, John J. Keller, and Michael Patsalos-Fox, "How to Choose the Right Nonexecutive Director," *McKinsey Quarterly*, May 2010. The panel included:

Board Leader	Title	Company
James G. Cullen	Non-executive chairman; Lead director	Agilent Technologies; Johnson & Johnson
David W. Dorman	Non-executive chairman	Motorola
Bruce S. Gordon	Lead director	Tyco International
James F. Hardymon	Lead director	WABCO Holdings
Bonnie G. Hill	Lead director	Home Depot
Irvine O. Hockaday Jr.	Lead director	Ford Motor
Constance J. Horner	Lead director	Pfizer
John A. Krol	Non-executive chairman; Former lead director	Delphi; Tyco International
Linda Fayne Levinson	Lead director	NCR
Harold A. Wagner	Former lead director	United Technologies
Tony L. White	Former lead director	Ingersoll-Rand

Chapter 6

1. Harvey Seifter and Peter Economy, *Leadership Ensemble: Lessons in Collaborative Management from the World's Only Conductorless Orchestra* (New York: Times Books, 2001).

2. This section draws on personal interviews and observations, and Bryce G. Hoffman, *American Icon: Alan Mulally and the Fight to Save Ford Motor Company* (New York: Random House, 2012); John J. Keller and Dennis Carey, "When Finding the Right CEO Is Job #1," Briefings on Talent and Leadership (Los Angeles: The Korn/Ferry Institute, 2011); and Kate Linebaugh, "Designated Driver: Ford Taps Boeing Executive as CEO," *Wall Street Journal*, September 6, 2006.

3. J. P. Donlon, "CEO of the Year Alan Mulally: The Road Ahead," *Chief Executive*, June 27, 2011.

4. Board decisions and actions are drawn from personal interviews that we conducted with those in management and/or the boardroom.

5. Ibid.

6. This section draws on Dennis Carey, Daniel Phelan, and Michael Useem, "Picking the Right Insider for CEO Succession," *Harvard Business Review*, January 2009, 24, 26.

7. GlaxoSmithKline, "Answering the Questions That Matter, Annual Review 2007," March 6, 2013, http://www.saadry-dunkel.com/publications/accounting-2/answering-the-questions-that-matter-gsk-annual-report-2007.

8. Board decisions and actions are drawn from personal interviews that we conducted with those in management and/or the boardroom.

9. Chris Rauber, "Humana Nabs McKesson's Bruce Broussard as CEO-in-Waiting," *San Francisco Business Times*, November 7, 2011, http://www.bizjournals.com/sanfrancisco/news/2011/11/07/humana-nabs-mckessons-bruce-broussard.html; Anna Wilde Mathews and Joann S. Lublin, "Humana Goes Outside for New CEO," *Wall Street Journal*, November 7, 2011, http://online.wsj.com/article/SB10001424052970203716204577018251085230234.html.

10. Dennis Carey, Melanie Kusin, and Jane Stevenson, "How Companies Can Avoid CEO Hiring Failure," *Fortune*, May 10, 2012, http://management.fortune.cnn.com/2012/05/10/how-companies-can-avoid-ceo-hiring-failure.

11. "Third Point LLC, Schedule 13 D," Securities and Exchange Commission, February 14, 2012, http://www.sec.gov/Archives/edgar/data/1011006/000089914012000135/t7465280.htm.

12. Evelyn M. Rusli, "Activist Investor Charts Plan to Revitalize Yahoo," *New York Times*, March 8, 2012, http://dealbook.nytimes.com/2012/03/08/activist-investor-charts-plan-to-revitalize-yahoo; Daniel S. Loeb, Chief Executive Officer, Third Point LLC, letter to the Yahoo! Inc. Board of Directors, September 8, 2011, http://www.sec.gov/Archives/edgar/data/1011006/000089914011000474/a6970038b.htm; Third Point LLC, "Schedule 13 D."

13. Amir Efrati and Joann S. Lublin, "Thompson Resigns as CEO of Yahoo," *Wall Street Journal*, May 13, 2012, http://online.wsj.com/article/SB10001424052702304192704577402224129006022.html; Michael J. de la Merced and Evelyn M. Rusli, "Yahoo's Chief to Leave as Company Strikes Deal with Loeb," *New York Times*, May 13, 2012, http://dealbook.nytimes.com/2012/05/13/yahoo-fires-thompson-and-nears-deal-with-loeb; Amir Efrati and Joann S. Lublin, "Yahoo CEO's Downfall," *Wall Street Journal*, May 15, 2012, http://online.wsj.com/article/SB10001424052702304192704577404530999458956.html; Andrew Ross Sorkin and Evelyn M. Rusli, "A Yahoo Search Calls Up a Chief from Google," *New York Times*, July 16, 2012, http://dealbook.nytimes.com/2012/07/16/googles-marissa-mayer-tapped-as-yahoos-chief.

14. Jonathan D. Rockoff and Joann S. Lublin, "J&J CEO Weldon Out," *Wall Street Journal*, February 22, 2012, http://online.wsj.com/article/SB1000

142405297020490910457723764204166718O.html; Jonathan D. Rockoff and Joann S. Lublin, "New J&J Chief to Face Repair Jobs," *Wall Street Journal*, February 23, 2012, http://online.wsj.com/article/SB10001424052970204778604577239662760967628.html; Katie Thomas and Reed Abelson, "J.&J. Chief to Resign One Role," *New York Times*, February 21, 2012, http://www.nytimes.com/2012/02/22/business/j-j-chief-to-resign-one-role.html.

15. Carey, Kusin, and Stevenson, "How Companies Can Avoid CEO Hiring Failure."

Chapter 7

1. Quotations from directors and executives are drawn from author interviews and observations, 2010 to 2013, unless otherwise noted.

2. Louis V. Gerstner, Jr., *Who Says Elephants Can't Dance? Inside IBM's Historic Turnaround* (New York: HarperCollins, 2002).

3. Michael Useem, Aneesha Capur, and Dennis Carey, "WorldCom, Inc.: Recruiting a New Chief Executive in 2002," Case 18, Wharton School, University of Pennsylvania, 2008.

Chapter 8

1. This and the following two chapters draw on Ram Charan, "Why Boards Fail to Choose the Right CEO, *Fortune*, August 8, 2012, http://management.fortune.cnn.com/2012/08/08/why-boards-fail-to-choose-the-right-ceo.

2. Jim Collins, *Good to Great: Why Some Companies Make the Leap . . . and Others Don't* (New York: HarperBusiness, 2001); Jim Collins and Morten Hansen, *Great by Choice: Uncertainty, Chaos, and Luck—Why Some Thrive Despite Them All* (New York: Harper Business, 2011).

3. Christopher S. Tuggle, David G. Sirmon, Christopher R. Reutzel, and Leonard Bierman, "Commanding Board of Director Attention: Investigating How Organizational Performance and CEO Duality Affect Board Members' Attention to Monitoring," *Strategic Management Journal* 31, no. 9 (2010): 946–968.

4. Board decisions and actions are drawn from personal interviews that we conducted with those in management and/or the boardroom.

5. The first author has written elsewhere about the challenges of execution: Larry Bossidy and Ram Charan, *Execution: The Discipline of Getting Things Done* (New York: Crown Business/Random House, 2002).

6. Bert A. Cannella, Jr., Sydney Finkelstein, and Donald C. Hambrick, *Strategic Leadership: Theory and Research on Executives, Top Management Teams, and Boards* (New York: Oxford University Press, 2008); Ruth Wageman, Debra A. Nunes,

James A. Burruss, and J. Richard Hackman, *Senior Leadership Teams: What It Takes to Make Them Great* (Boston: Harvard Business School Press, 2008).

7. Board decisions and actions are drawn from personal interviews that we conducted with those in management and/or the boardroom.

8. Ibid.

9. Ibid.

10. James B. Stewart, "Rewarding C.E.O.'s Who Fail," *New York Times*, September 30, 2011, http://www.nytimes.com/2011/10/01/business/lets-stop-rewarding-failed-ceos-common-sense.html?pagewanted=all; Betsy Morris and Patricia Sellers, "What Really Happened at Coke," *Fortune*, January 10, 2000, http://money.cnn.com/magazines/fortune/fortune_archive/2000/01/10/271736/index.htm.

11. Warren Boeker, "Power and Managerial Dismissal: Scapegoating at the Top," *Administrative Science Quarterly* 37, no. 3 (1992): 400–421; Albert A. Cannella and Michael Lubatkin, "Succession as a Sociopolitical Process: Internal Impediments to Outsider Selection," *Academy of Management Journal* 36, no. 4 (1993): 763–793; W. Glenn. Rowe, Albert A. Cannella, Debra Rankin, and Doug Gorman, "Leader Succession and Organizational Performance: Integrating the Common-Sense, Ritual Scapegoating, and Vicious-Circle Succession Theories," *Leadership Quarterly* 16, no. 2 (2005): 197–219.

12. Shayndi Raice, Spencer E. Ante, and Emily Glazer, "In Facebook Deal, Board Was All But Out of the Picture," *Wall Street Journal*, April 18, 2012, http://online.wsj.com/article/SB10001424052702304818404577350191931921290.html.

13. Board decisions and actions are drawn from personal interviews that we conducted with those in management and/or the boardroom.

14. Bossidy and Charan, *Execution*.

15. Board decisions and actions are drawn from personal interviews that we conducted with those in management and/or the boardroom.

16. Cannella et al., *Strategic Leadership*.

17. Board decisions and actions are drawn from personal interviews that we conducted with those in management and/or the boardroom.

18. Ibid.

Chapter 9

1. Howard Kunreuther, Erwann Michel-Kerjan, and Michael Useem, research project on "Effective Leadership and Governance Practices in Catastrophe Risk Management," Wharton School, University of Pennsylvania, 2010–2012, http://www.wharton.upenn.edu/riskcenter/effectiveriskmgmt.cfm.

2. Board decisions and actions are drawn from personal interviews and observations that we conducted with executives and directors.

3. Beth Kowitt and Kim Thai, "25 Top Companies for Leaders," *Fortune*, November 19, 2011, http://money.cnn.com/2009/11/19/news/companies/top_leadership_companies.fortune.

4. Board decisions and actions are drawn from personal interviews and observations that we conducted with executives and directors; also see David Stowell, *An Introduction to Investment Banks, Hedge Funds & Private Equity* (London: Academic Press/Elsevier, 2010), chapter 4; Rosabeth Moss Kanter and Matthew Bird, "Procter & Gamble in the 21st Century (A): Becoming Truly Global," and "Procter & Gamble in the 21st Century (B): Welcoming Gillette," Cases 9–309-030 and 9–309-031 (Boston: Harvard Business School Publishing, 2009).

5. Emily Glazer, Ellen Byron, Dennis K. Berman, and Joann S. Lublin, "P&G's Stumbles Put CEO on Hot Seat for Turnaround," *Wall Street Journal*, September 27, 2012, http://online.wsj.com/article/SB1000087239639044481 3104578016191845779524.html; A.G. Lafley, "What Only the CEO Can Do," *Harvard Business Review*, May 2009, 54–62; Jack Neff, "Why P&G's $57 Billion Bet on Gillette Hasn't Paid Off Big—Yet," *Advertising Age*, February 15, 2012.

6. Board decisions and actions are drawn from personal interviews that we conducted with those in management and/or the boardroom.

7. Raj Gupta, "How I Did It: Rohm and Haas's Former CEO on Pulling Off a Sweet Deal in a Down Market," *Harvard Business Review*, November 2010, 49–54.

8. Mars Incorporated, "About Mars Global Leadership," http://www.mars.com/global/about-mars/global-leadership.aspx; also see David A. Caplan, "Exclusive: Inside Mars," *Fortune*, February 4, 2013, available online as "Mars Incorporated: A Pretty Sweet Place to Work," http://management.fortune.cnn.com/2013/01/17/best-companies-mars/?iid=bc_sp_lead.

9. Board decisions and actions are drawn from personal interviews that we conducted with those in management and/or the boardroom.

10. See, for instance, Robert S. Kaplan and Anette Mikes, "Managing Risks: A New Framework," *Harvard Business Review*, June 2012, 48–60; Laurence Barton, *Crisis Leadership Now: A Real-World Guide to Preparing for Threats, Disaster, Sabotage, and Scandal* (New York: McGraw Hill, 2008); Jim Collins and Morten T. Hansen, *Great by Choice: Uncertainty, Chaos, and Luck: Why Some Companies Thrive Despite Them All* (New York: HarperCollins, 2011); Erika Hayes James and Lynn Perry Wooten, *Leading Under Pressure: From Surviving to Thriving Before, During, and After a Crisis* (Oxford: Routledge 2010); Howard Kunreuther and Michael Useem, eds., *Learning from Catastrophes: Strategies for Reaction and Response*, prepared in collaboration with the World Economic Forum's Global Agenda Council on the Mitigation of Natural Disasters (Upper Saddle River, NJ: Pearson, 2010); Charles Perrow, *The Next Catastrophe: Re-*

ducing Our Vulnerabilities to Natural, Industrial, and Terrorist Disasters (Princeton, NJ: Princeton University Press, 2011); Irwin Redlener, *Americans at Risk: Why We Are Not Prepared for Megadisasters and What We Can Do About It* (New York: Knopf, 2006).

Chapter 10

1. Names and other identifiers have been disguised.

2. This section draws on Michael Useem, "How Well-Run Boards Make Decisions," *Harvard Business Review*, November 2006, 130–138.

3. This section draws on Michael Useem and Andy Zelleke, "Oversight and Delegation in Corporate Governance: Deciding What the Board Should Decide," *Corporate Governance: An International Review* 14, no. 1 (2006): 2–12.

4. The itemized divisions of responsibilities between the board leader and the chief executive officer for two companies are included in appendix C.

5. Ibid.

6. John J. Brennan, "Memo to the Board from Your Permanent Stockholders," *Directors & Boards*, 2010 Annual Report 34, no. 4 (2010): 6–10; John J. Brennan, "Improving Corporate Governance: A Memo to the Board," *Wall Street Journal*, May 10, 2010, http://online.wsj.com/article/SB10001424052748 7043426045752224705051346441.html.

7. Board decisions and actions are drawn from personal interviews that we conducted with those in management and/or the boardroom.

Chapter 11

1. We draw on several sources, including Liam Pleven and Amir Efrati, "Documents Show AIG Knew of Problems with Valuations," *Wall Street Journal*, October 11, 2008; Ben Levisohn, "AIG's CDS Hoard: The Great Unraveling," *Businessweek Online*, April 6, 2009; Carrick Mollenkamp, Serena Ng, Liam Pleven, and Randall Smith, "Behind AIG's Fall, Risk Models Failed to Pass Real-World Test," *Wall Street Journal*, October 31, 2008; Gretchen Morgenson, "Behind Biggest Insurer's Crisis, Blind Eye to a Web of Risk," *New York Times*, September 28, 2008; Steve Lohr, "In Modeling Risk, the Human Factor Was Left Out," *New York Times*, November 4, 2008; Eric Dickinson, "Credit Default Swaps: So Dear to Us, So Dangerous," Fordham Law School, November 20, 2008 (available at SSRN: http://ssrn.com/abstract=1315535 or http://dx.doi.org/10.2139/ssrn.1315535); Donald L. Kohn, "Statement to the U.S. Senate Committee on Banking, Housing, and Urban Affairs," March 5, 2009; Eric Dinallo, "Testimony to the U.S. Senate Committee on Banking, Housing and Urban Affairs," March 5, 2009; Nell Minow, "Testimony

to the U.S. House of Representatives Committee on Oversight and Government Reform," October 7, 2008; Scott M. Polakoff, "Statement to the U.S. Senate Committee on Banking, House and Urban Affairs," March 5, 2009; William K. Sjostrom, Jr., "The AIG Bailout," *Washington and Lee Law Review* 66 (2009): 943; and American International Group, Inc., *2008 Annual Report*, http://www.aigcorporate.com/investors/annualreports_proxy.html.

2. Morgenson, "Behind Biggest Insurer's Crisis."

3. Polakoff, "Statement to the U.S. Senate Committee on Banking."

4. Board decisions and actions are drawn from personal interviews that we conducted with those in management and/or the boardroom; this section also draws on Michael Useem, "How Well-Run Boards Make Decisions," *Harvard Business Review*, November 2006, 130–138; and see Eric M. Pillmore, "How We're Fixing Up Tyco," *Harvard Business Review*, December 2003, 96–103; Rakesh Khurana and James Weber, "Tyco International: Corporate Governance," Case 9–408-059 (Boston: Harvard Business School, 2008).

5. Pillmore, "How We're Fixing Up Tyco."

6. One of us had worked to recruit John A. Krol to serve as lead director and Edward D. Breen to serve as chief executive officer.

7. This account draws on personal interviews with John Krol for Michael Useem, *The Go Point: When It Is Time to Decide* (New York: Random House, 2006); also see Michael Useem, "How Well-Run Boards Make Decisions."

8. Useem, "How Well-Run Boards Make Decisions"; see also Michael Useem and Andy Zelleke, "Oversight and Delegation in Corporate Governance: Deciding What the Board Should Decide," *Corporate Governance: An International Review* 14, no. 1 (2006): 2–12; other studies have similarly reported that directors bring substantial understanding of strategic issues into boardroom decisions. See, for instance, P. J. Bezemer, G. F. Maassen, F. A. J. Van den Bosch, and H. W. Volberda, "Investigating the Development of the Internal and External Service Tasks of Non-Executive Directors: The Case of the Netherlands (1997–2005)," *Corporate Governance: An International Review* 15, no. 6 (2007): 1119–1129; Terry McNulty and Andrew Pettigrew, "Strategists on the Board," *Organizational Studies* 20, no. 1 (1999): 47–74; C. Sundaramurthy and M. Lewis, "Control and Collaboration: Paradoxes of Governance," *Academy of Management Review* 28, no. 3 (2003): 397–415; Colin B. Carter and Jay W. Lorsch, *Back to the Drawing Board: Designing Corporate Boards for a Complex World* (Boston: Harvard Business School Press, 2004); Ram Charan, *Boards That Deliver: Advancing Corporate Governance from Compliance to Competitive Advantage* (San Francisco: Jossey-Bass, 2005); Richard Leblanc and James Gillies, *Inside the Boardroom: How Boards Really Work and the Coming Revolution in Corporate Governance* (Mississauga, ON: Wiley, 2005); David A. Nadler, Beverly A. Behan, and Mark B. Nadler, *Building Better Boards: A Blueprint for Effective Governance* (San Francisco: Jossey-Bass/Wiley, 2006).

Chapter 12

1. Business Roundtable, *Principles of Corporate Governance* (New York: Business Roundtable, 2012); see other definitions of governance at http://definitions.uslegal.com/b/board-of-directors; http://www.businessdictionary.com/definition/board-of-directors.html; and http://www.merriam-webster.com/dictionary/governing.

2. This section is adapted from Michael Useem and Jerry Useem, "The Board That Conquered Everest," *Fortune*, October 27, 2003, http://money.cnn.com/magazines/fortune/fortune_archive/2003/10/27/351638/index.htm; also see Maurice Isserman and Stewart Weaver, *Fallen Giants: A History of Himalayan Mountaineering from the Age of Empire to the Age of Extremes* (New Haven, CT: Yale University Press, 2008).

The Complete Director's Checklists

1. For how a checklist can serve well as a guide to action, see Atul Gawande, *The Checklist Manifesto: How to Get Things Right* (New York: Henry Holt, 2009).

Appendix A

1. Carolyn Kay Brancato and Stephan Rabimov, *The 2007 Institutional Investor Report*, (New York: The Conference Board, 2007).

2. Michael Useem, "Corporate Leadership in a Globalizing Equity Market," *Academy of Management Executive* 12, no. 4 (1998): 43–59; Michael Useem, "The Ascent of Shareholder Monitoring and Strategic Partnering: The Dual Functions of the Corporate Board," in *The Sage Handbook on Corporate Governance*, ed. Thomas Clarke and Doug Branson (Los Angeles: Sage Publications, 2012); 136–158; see also Gerald F. Davis, *Managed by the Markets: How Finance Re-Shaped America* (New York: Oxford University Press, 2009); Justin Fox and Jay W. Lorsch, "What Good Are Shareholders?" *Harvard Business Review*, July–August 2012, 48–57; Joe Nocera, "Down with Shareholder Value," *New York Times*, August 11, 2012, http://www.nytimes.com/2012/08/11/opinion/nocera-down-with-shareholder-value.html.

3. Spencer Stuart, *Board Index*, various years (New York: Spencer Stuart, 1998–2012).

4. Paul Gompers, Joy Ishii, and Andrew Metrick, "Corporate Governance and Equity Prices," *Quarterly Journal of Economics* 118 (2003): 107–156.

5. See, for example, Paul R. Kleindorfer, "Reflections on Decision Making Under Uncertainty," INSEAD Working Paper No. 2008/73/TOM/ISIC, 2008, http://ssrn.com/abstract=1310239; Gökçe Sargut and Rita Gunther Mc-

Grath, "Learning to Live with Complexity," *Harvard Business Review*, September 2011, 68–76.

6. For 2010 data, see http://www.prnewswire.com/news-releases/foreign-sales-by-us-companies-tick-down-in-2010–463-of-all-sales-were-derived-outside-of-the-states-125804878.html; for 2011, http://www.standardandpoors.com/servlet/BlobServer?blobheadername3=MDT-Type&blobcol=urldata&blobtable=MungoBlobs&blobheadervalue2=inline%3B+filename%3D20120809–500-global-sales-pr.pdf&blobheadername2=Content-Disposition&blobheadervalue1=application%2Fpdf&blobkey=id&blobheadername1=content-type&blobwhere=1244153889822&blobheadervalue3=UTF-8.

7. Spencer Stuart, *Board Index*, 2011 and earlier years.

Appendix C

1. John A. Krol, board leader, Tyco International, personal communication, February 24, 2012.

2. Shelly Ibach, president and chief executive officer, personal communication, August 12, 2012.

INDEX

ACKNOWLEDGMENTS

The authors thank their colleagues and clients for many helpful discussions on leadership and governance, and a number of company directors and executives in the United States and other countries for their interviews. They also very much appreciate the special guidance and support of the following:

Vindi Banga, operating partner, Clayton Dubilier & Rice; former member, Unilever Executive Board

Douglas M. Branson, professor, Masters of Law Program, University of Melbourne, Australia

Edward Breen, chairman, Tyco International

Gregory Brown, chairman, president, and chief executive, Motorola Solutions, Inc.

Sir George Buckley, former chairman and chief executive officer, 3M Company

Gary Burnison, chief executive officer, Korn/Ferry International

Cynthia Burr, executive assistant for Ram Charan

Peter Cappelli, George W. Taylor Professor of Management and director, Center for Human Resources, Wharton School, University of Pennsylvania

Matt Carey, student, University of Southern California (and son of Dennis Carey)

Thomas Clarke, professor of management; director, Centre for Corporate Governance; and chair, Academic Board, University of Technology, Sydney, Australia

Martin Conyon, chair in Corporate Governance, University of Lancaster, UK; senior fellow and lecturer, Wharton School, University of Pennsylvania

James Cullen, non-executive chairman, Agilent Technologies Inc.; presiding director, Johnson & Johnson

Richard L. Crandall, founding partner, Arbor Partners; director of Diebold and RR Donnelley; and former chair, Novell

Carol Davis, executive assistant for Ram Charan

David W. Dorman, lead director, Motorola Solutions, Inc.; former chairman and chief executive, AT&T

Sean Donovan, author, Prium Proceedings

Charles Elson, Edgar S. Woolard, Jr., Chair; professor of law; and director of the John L. Weinberg Center for Corporate Governance, University of Delaware

Abe M. Friedman, managing partner, CamberView Partners

Christopher Galvin, former CEO, Motorola, Inc.; cofounder, Harrison Street Real Estate Capital

Thomas Gerrity, Joseph J. Aresty Professor of Management and former dean, Wharton School, University of Pennsylvania

Donna Gregor, chief of staff for Dennis Carey

Mauro Guillen, Felix Zandman Professor of International Management and director, Lauder Institute, Wharton School, University of Pennsylvania

Raj Gupta, former chairman and chief executive officer, Rohm and Haas Company; lead director, Hewlett-Packard

Mark Hanna, independent researcher

Robert Hallagan, vice chairman, Korn/Ferry International

Bonnie Hill, lead director, The Home Depot

Irvine O. Hockaday, Jr., former chief executive officer, Hallmark Cards, Inc.

Shelly Ibach, CEO, Select Comfort Corporation

William Judge, E. V. Williams Chair of Strategic Leadership, College of Business & Public Administration, Old Dominion University

John J. Keller, vice chairman and Global Head of TMT Practice, CTPartners

Roger Kenny, president, Boardroom Consultants

Patricia Klarner, assistant professor of strategic management, Ludwig-Maximilians-University Munich, Institute of Strategic Management, Munich

James Kristie, editor and associate publisher, *Directors & Boards*

P.M. Kumar, business chairman, Institution Building and Governance, GMR Group

Howard Kunreuther, James G. Dinan Professor; professor of decision sciences and business and public policy; and codirector, Risk Management and Decision Processes Center, Wharton School, University of Pennsylvania

A. G. Lafley, chairman and chief executive officer, Procter & Gamble

Herman B. Leonard, George F. Baker, Jr. Professor of Public Sector Management, John F. Kennedy School of Government; Eliot I.

Snider and Family Professor of Business Administration, Harvard Business School, Harvard University

Neng Liang, professor of management and associate dean for faculty, China Europe International Business School, Shanghai

Jay Lorsch, Louis Kirstein Professor of Human Relations, Harvard Business School

Alex Mandl, executive chairman, Gemalto

Jane McAloon, group company secretary, BHP Billiton Plc

William McDonald, director of Humana Inc.

Howard Means, independent editor and writer

Nathan Means, independent editor and writer

Eduardo Melzer, CEO, Grupo RBS

Melinda Merino, executive editor, Harvard Business Review Press

Victor Meyer, director, Corporate Security and Business Continuity, Deutsche Bank

Erwann Michel-Kerjan, managing director, Risk Management and Decision Processes Center; adjunct associate professor, Operations and Information Management Department, Wharton School, University of Pennsylvania

Jacques Nasser, chairman, BHP Billiton Limited and BHP Billiton Plc

James E. Nevels, founder and chairman, The Swarthmore Group

Alexander (Sandy) Ogg, operating partner, Private Equity Group, Blackstone Group

Mukul Pandya, executive director/editor-in-chief, Knowledge@ Wharton

Michael Patsalos-Fox, director, McKinsey & Company

Daniel Phelan, adviser and former chief of staff for the chief executive officer, GlaxoSmithKline

Gilbert Probst, professor of organization and management, University of Geneva; managing director and dean, Leadership Office and Academic Affairs, World Economic Forum

G.M. Rao, group chairman, GMR Group

Raphael Sagalyn, founder, Sagalyn Literary Agency

Ivan Seidenberg, former chairman and chief executive officer, Verizon Communications Inc.

Kevin Sharer, former chairman and CEO, Amgen

Robbie W. Shell, managing director, Knowledge@Wharton

Harbir Singh, Mack Professor of Management; vice dean, Global Initiatives; and codirector, Mack Center for Technological Innovation, Wharton School, University of Pennsylvania

Jitendra Singh, Saul P. Steinberg Professor of Management, Wharton School, University of Pennsylvania

Nelson Pacheco Sirotsky, chairman, Grupo RBS

Geri Willigan, independent editor and content developer

Edgar S. Woolard, Jr., former chairman and CEO, DuPont

Andy Zelleke, MBA Class of 1962 Senior Lecturer of Business Administration, Harvard Business School

Participants in the Lead Director Academy, New York, February 24, 2012

Adam Beshara, managing director, J.P. Morgan Securities Inc.

Les Brun, independent chairman, ADP

Sir George Buckley, former chairman and chief executive officer, 3M Company

Michael Campbell, lead director, MeadWestvaco; former chairman and chief executive, Arch Chemicals Inc.

Michael Chesser, chairman and chief executive, Great Plains Energy Inc.

Earnest W. Davenport, Jr., chairman, Regions Financial Corp.; former chairman and chief executive, Eastman Chemical Co.

Patrick K. Decker, chief executive, Harsco Corporation

Bruce Gordon, chairman, ADT

Grayson Hall, chief executive, Regions Financial Corp.

Ira Kay, managing partner, Pay Governance LLC

John Krol, chairman, Delphi Automotive; former chairman and chief executive, DuPont

Anthony Massaro, non-executive chairman, Commercial Metals Co.; former chairman and chief executive, Lincoln Electric Holdings Inc.

James Rogers, lead director, Owens & Minor

Maggie Wilderotter, chairman and chief executive, Frontier Communications

Robert Wright, president and chief executive, Matthew G. Norton Co.; lead director, Expeditor's International

Participants in the Lead Director Academy, New York, April 30, 2009

Dennis Carey, founder, Lead Director Academy

James Cullen, lead director, Johnson & Johnson

Julian Day, chairman and chief executive, RadioShack Corporation

David Dorman, non-executive chairman, Motorola Solutions, Inc.

Jacques Esculier, chief executive officer, WABCO Holdings Inc.

Bruce Gordon, lead director, Tyco International

James Hardymon, lead director, WABCO Holdings Inc.

Herbert Henkel, chairman and chief executive, Ingersoll Rand Company

Bonnie Hill, lead director, The Home Depot Inc.

Irvine Hockaday, lead director, Ford Motor Company

Connie Horner, lead director, Pfizer

John Krol, former lead director, Tyco International

Linda Fayne Levinson, lead director, NCR Corporation

Caroline Nahas, director, dineEquity

William Nuti, chairman and chief executive, NCR Corporation

Marvin "Skip" Schoenhals, chairman, WSFS Financial Corporation

Ronald Sugar, chairman and chief executive, Northrop Grumman Corporation

Kathryn Sullivan, director, American Electric Power

Harold (Hap) Wagner, former lead director, United Technologies

Tony White, lead director, Ingersoll Rand Company